ZEAL *for* GODLINESS

ZEAL *for* GODLINESS

Devotional Meditations
on Calvin's *Institutes*

Edited by

Derek W. H. Thomas and R. Carlton Wynne

PUBLISHING WITH A MISSION

EP BOOKS
Faverdale North
Darlington, DL3 0PH, England

e-mail: sales@epbooks.org
web: http://www.epbooks.org

133 North Hanover Street
Carlisle, PA 17013, USA

e-mail: usasales@epbooks.org
web: http://www.epbooks.us

First published 2011

British Library Cataloguing in Publication Data available

ISBN-13: 978-085234-758-4   ISBN-10: 0-85234-758-8

Printed and bound in the USA by Thomson-Shore Inc., Dexter, MI.

To Linley

Contents

Foreword

For many people, the very thought of John Calvin conjures up the image of a theologian for theologians — someone whose writings are beyond the reach of the average person. But if we were to suggest that to Calvin himself, he would have been horrified. When asked, 'Why did you become a theologian?', Calvin is reputed to have answered, 'To become a better pastor!'

What is certainly clear from the life and work of the great French Reformer was that all his labours were devoted ultimately to the glory of God and for the good of ordinary people. The fact that he spent more time in the pulpit each week than many preachers do in a month and that so much of his practical work was geared towards helping the poor and disadvantaged speaks for itself. His heart's desire was to see the community in Geneva transformed by the grace of God in salvation.

In one sense there was nothing new or unique about Calvin's vision for God's work. It can easily be traced back to its roots in Paul's letters where again and again the Apostle speaks about the way that God is in the business of changing lives through the gospel. Being a Christian in biblical terms is never merely a nominal profession of faith, it is always something that can be seen in a person's life. More than that, it is never something static, but rather, from the moment of its beginning in conversion it becomes that lifelong process of renewal through which the believer is continually being transformed from one degree of glory into another until he or she, in totality, is made perfect in holiness when Jesus returns.

That same vision, recaptured by Calvin and his fellow Reformers, is the hallmark of authentic Christianity. It was the vision that inspired and energized the Puritans. Their conviction was that all truth leads to godliness. For them, as for Calvin, the message of salvation in Scripture is not merely about a person's private and personal experience of God, it is a whole world and life view. It sees God in all his unique and triune glory and it sees the entire cosmos as coming ultimately under his renovating lordship. So too this has been the conviction that has left an enduring mark on Christians and churches and, indeed, entire communities and nations through the ages.

It is the same vision that lies very much behind this book of readings and reflections from Calvin's *Institutes of the Christian Religion*, hence its title: *Zeal for Godliness*. It could just as easily have been entitled *Calvin for the Common Man*, because it very much reflects how Calvin viewed himself throughout his life and ministry.

It has been my privilege to personally know almost all the contributors to this volume and each of them have one thing in common: in their own lives and ministries they have sought to walk in the footsteps of Calvin and the Puritans as they have pursued godliness, knowing that it leads to the greatest gain. And their ministries have been moulded by that vision as they have sought to open up the Word of God for others.

For those who have perhaps been daunted by the thought of delving into the *Institutes*, as much because of their density as because of their length, here is a book that will more than dispel their fears and whet their appetite to take up the challenge to read them in their entirety. For all who work their way through it, it will do more than just enrich your appreciation for Calvin; it will deepen your longing for God.

Mark G. Johnston
Proclamation Presbyterian Church
Bryn Mawr, Pennsylvania
September 2011

Preface

Zeal for godliness is nothing less than zeal for the glory of God. It is the burning desire to please the Lord at all times, in all things, at all cost. It is the single-minded, soul-consuming pursuit of the heavenly prize of our salvation (Phil. 3:13-14). Zeal is a central goal of our redemption in Christ Jesus (Titus 2:14) and a sign of true repentance (2 Cor. 7:11). While such zeal has marked Christians of every age, it especially coursed through the veins of the Geneva Reformer, John Calvin (1509-1564).

Unfortunately, biblical zeal, like Calvin himself, is often misunderstood and maligned today. In our tolerance-exalting age, almost any focused zeal is discounted as fanatical, and that applies with special force when the zeal is for God or when the name of John Calvin is invoked. Zealousness alone, of course, can destroy churches and sear relationships, and much of the same has occurred in the name of Calvinism. But true zeal among followers of Christ — zeal that is channelled by the Word and Spirit of God, zeal that is, as Paul put it, 'according to knowledge' (Rom. 10:2) — is a blessing to the world. It unmasks the intellectual lethargy of today's tolerance and revives a dying culture with the light of the gospel of grace. It is no wonder, then, that true zeal lay at the heart of John Calvin's purposes for his majestic work known as the *Institutes of the Christian Religion*.

The original edition of the *Institutes* (1536) was only a six-chaptered manual on the Christian faith bearing the ambitious title, *Basic instruction [institutio] in the Christian religion, embracing almost the whole sum of piety, and all that needs to be known in the doctrine of salvation; a work very well worth reading by everyone zealous for godliness*. The book you are holding takes its title from Calvin's reference to godly zeal, but explores the much larger (by seventy-four chapters!) and definitive 1559 edition.

The one-page readings that follow are adapted from the 2009 'Blogging through the *Institutes*' project hosted by reformation21.org, the online magazine of the Alliance of Confessing Evangelicals. They are written by pastors, scholars and churchmen in order to explain and apply Calvin's *magnum opus* to the contemporary church and Christian. Each reading features the contributor's text, a reference to the portion of the *Institutes* under discussion (e.g., '1.1.1-1.2.1'), and the contributor's name. The content is divided into four sections that mirror the four-fold structure of the *Institutes* (Books 1 - 4). We hope this will enable you to use this book as a travelling companion as you journey through the *Institutes* yourself or as a self-contained, in-flight manual for those preferring a bird's-eye view of Calvin's theological landscape.

Following Calvin's intent with the *Institutes*, which sought to follow the character of Scripture itself, this book aims to display the coherence, trustworthiness and glory of biblical truth for all ages. We hope these readings will awaken you to the relevance of Calvin's theology, humble you by the depth of Calvin's insights, and stimulate your growth in the Christian life. Most of all, we hope this work helps you follow Calvin as he followed Christ into a deeper, Bible-saturated zeal for the triune God.

R. Carlton Wynne
September 2011

BOOK ONE

'The Knowledge
of God the Creator'

Introduction

Each of the four 'Books' of John Calvin's Institutes of the Christian Religion *bears a title that stands like a marble archway marking entry to vistas of Christian theology. Each title also bears witness to a specific dimension of those vistas, guiding the reader according to a kind of 'gospel order'. They point first to God (Book One), then to Christ (Book Two), next to the Holy Spirit (Book Three), and finally to the church (Book Four). This division supports how works on Calvin (including this one) refer to portions of the* Institutes. *The typical reference is by book, chapter and section (e.g., 1.3.5 = Book 1, Chapter 3, Section 5).*

As Book One's title ('The Knowledge of God the Creator') indicates, Calvin begins the Institutes *by focusing on God as he reveals himself as Creator. Knowing the Creator-God, says Calvin, is both inevitable for every human being and entails that we know ourselves as created by him (Chapters 1 - 4). Prior to Adam's fall into sin, every corner of the cosmos instilled this knowledge of God and knowledge of self such that, apart from the Fall, every human being would forever rejoice in belonging to him and would desire to worship him accordingly (Chapter 5). The tragedy of Adam's sin has not effaced that knowledge, says Calvin, but it has decimated humankind's response to it. As children of Adam, we are struck blind in the 'dazzling theatre' (1.5.8) of God's glory as we suppress our knowledge of him in unrighteousness (Rom. 1:18ff).*

In the context of this reality, Calvin continues Book One with a discussion on the necessity of Scripture and the Holy Spirit to give us new eyes (Chapters 6 - 9) in order that we might know how to worship our triune God aright (Chapters 10 - 14). We are responsible creatures who live and move in the atmosphere of a sovereign God (Chapters 15 - 18). To fallen sinners, this is a horrifying existence from which they must rebel. To saints redeemed by Christ, as Book Two will announce, this is a soul-satisfying residence sustained by a generous Father.

1.1.1 - 1.2.1

Calvin's *Institutes* opens with a strikingly important sentence. The line was first crafted by a young Calvin in his mid-twenties and only fine-tuned between its first appearance in 1536 and its final expression a few years before his death in 1564. Wisdom — the knowledge coupled with practical understanding and the piety that is the underlying concern of the entire project — involves knowing God and knowing ourselves. To know ourselves truly we need to know God; come to know God and at last we see ourselves in our true context.

The thought, as commentators on the *Institutes* point out, is not entirely original. But its roots (as they do not always note) go way beyond the Augustinian tradition of theology, to the opening chapter of the Bible. God made man as his image (Gen. 1:26). Our creation, our very being, is defined by that relationship to him. Living makes sense and gives joy only when we live out that relationship before him. So the question 'What is man?' must be answered by a sentence that has a reference to God in it.

When, in the pursuit of the project of the self, we exclude the person of God, we not only cut ourselves off from knowing him, but also from knowing ourselves. The project ends in frustration. A fulfilled life requires that we know God in Jesus Christ (John 17:3). By implication, if we exclude him then we lose all sense of proportion. For when we measure ourselves by ourselves we turn out to be the ideal height! But when we are persuaded that God is the fountain of every good, and we seek and find him (or are found by him), then, says Calvin, we begin to taste 'complete happiness' (1.2.1).

Only then will we gladly give ourselves to the Lord. Isn't that the truth!

SINCLAIR FERGUSON

1.2.2 - 1.3.3

If my first question about God is 'What is he?' then I am already mistaken. The really important question is 'Who is he?'

'Who is God?' The biblical answer is that he is the fountain of all good and reveals himself as such in creation. Yes, he is a Judge. The naïve reader would expect Calvin to stress that! But even his justice manifests his goodness. We need to understand that God in himself is so very good that 'even if there were no hell' (1.2.2), Christian believers would shudder to offend him. Yes, he is that good!

Of course, all men know there is a God (paradoxically, idolatry is one of the clearest proofs of this fact). For a certain knowledge of him, though it alone yields neither covenant fellowship nor saving knowledge, is inescapable. Where does this knowledge come from?

For one thing, we are his image. A sense of dependence on him and duty to him is engraved in us and can never be effaced, even though we repress and stifle it. The echoes of our destiny and calling to live as God's image can never be silenced, never finally repressed, no matter how hard we try.

Moreover, since the entire created cosmos is the theatre of his revealed glory, there is no 'where' we can go without being confronted by his handiwork. His autograph is everywhere. There is no 'where' to hide. Take the wings of the morning, travel faster than the speed of light to the uttermost parts of the earth — and his revelation awaits us the moment we land! It is not just in Brooklyn that there is No Last Exit!

But why would we ever want to escape from the God who is the fountain of all good?

That is the question.

SINCLAIR FERGUSON

1.4.1 - 1.5.1

The implanted knowledge of God in man, his image, is universal. Yes, it is perverted and fragmented by the Fall, but it is still real. It gives rise to the seed of religion, notes Calvin. An instinct to praise and worship is inbuilt in all men. Testimony to this is seen in true worship as well as in distorted form in idolatry (whether devotion to possessions or to the Philadelphia 76rs!). For if we will not worship the Creator we must worship something — the creature (Rom. 1:25). As Milton imaginatively expresses it in *Paradise Lost*, having refused to bow to the Lord and his Word, as Eve turns from the tree to the fruit she has stolen, 'she low obeisance made'. She who refused to worship the Creator (as C. S. Lewis pointed out in his *Preface to Paradise Lost*) now worships a vegetable!

In one way or another, as Calvin notes, recognition of God cannot finally be repressed and, at times, will be forced out of the mouths of even the reprobate. They cannot consistently maintain their denials of him.

At the memorial service for the 'atheist' British novelist Sir Kingsley Amis, his son Martin related how his father had been asked by the Russian author Yevgeni Yevtushenko if it were true he believed there was no God. Sir Kingsley tellingly replied: 'Yes. But it is more than that. You see, *I hate him!*'

If indeed we are both surrounded and invaded by the revelation of God, the unbeliever's denial of God's existence will eventually show itself for what it really is — a refusal of him.

We should always be on the lookout for that loose thread in the tapestry of the unbeliever's life and speech. It may require patience, but it may prove to be vital.

SINCLAIR FERGUSON

1.5.2 - 1.5.5

The heavens declare God's glory, and so the astronomer is also a theologian who explores the Book of Nature in which God has inscribed his name. But 'What is man that you are mindful of him?' (Ps. 8:4) means that the anatomist who explores the intricate, even microscopic, details of the human body also studies the revelation of God. Both above and within man God shows that he is our creating Father. This is Calvin's heartbeat! For, he notes, 'no one gives himself freely and willingly to God's service unless, having tasted his fatherly love, he is drawn to worship and love him in return' (1.5.3).

As God's image, we have within ourselves a veritable divine 'workshop' (1.5.4) — eyes, ears and toenails! Yet instead of praising him men swell with pride and find reasons for rejecting the revelation God has given to them. Instead of acknowledging the true and living God, men 'substitute nature for God' (1.5.4).

We have all seen or heard it on our television screens. A secular naturalist engages in the activities Calvin here describes — whether by exploring the heavens or investigating things on earth. Insects and animals with the most limited mental capacity are said to engage in all kinds of detailed logical thinking as they develop coping mechanisms in a hostile environment. And as the programme ends, the naturalist comments: 'And so again we find ourselves saying, "Isn't Mother Nature wonderful?"'

But who, one might ask, is Mother Nature? Why is her name always capitalized? On what logic has our agnostic or atheist presenter smuggled in his or her appeal to the transcendent? How profoundly true are Paul's words that men exchange the truth about God for the lie.

Mother Nature? Or Father God?

SINCLAIR FERGUSON

1.5.6 - 1.5.11

God has revealed himself *above and below* man, in the cosmos; he has also revealed himself *in* man, since he is God's image. But we might also say that God reveals himself *around* man in his providential governing of the universe.

As God directs and superintends the flow of history, two things become clear. First, he is extraordinarily kind in his protection of and provision for his people. Second, he engages in solemn judgement on sin and evil. Meanwhile, we are like cinema-goers watching an Imax screen, listening to 'surround sound', yet neither seeing nor hearing anything clearly.

The knowledge of God revealed in the created order does not require a profound intellect capacious enough to follow intricate philosophical arguments for the existence of God. It should be enough to see that his tender mercy is over all his works (Ps. 145:9).

Now if God's revelation in creation should lead us to worship, his revelation in providence should lead us to think of the future life — for this life here and now is marked by hints of the world to come and the judgement that awaits us. Calvin and his Puritan successors followed Augustine's insight at this point: God does not judge all sin now because there is to be a final judgement; but he does judge sin in some measure now, lest we mistakenly think he does not govern the world.

Alas, we are so often like the elderly who say, 'Speak up, young man; you are not speaking loudly enough!' but will not admit the problem lies in their hearing. True, we construct different gods for ourselves, but at the end of the day we suffer from the same spiritual diseases.

'Lord, make me more sensitive to your providences, that I may be weaned from my this-worldly deafness and short-sightedness and begin to live in the light of eternity.'

SINCLAIR FERGUSON

1.5.12 - 1.6.1

Whether or not Calvin patterns the *Institutes* after the Letter to the Romans, it is pretty clear that at this point he has Romans 1 - 2 in mind. God manifests his nature, his power and goodness to all men and women through the creation. Its regularity and power, beauty and order, as well as its bountiful goodness, unmistakably testify to God as Creator. But humanity, self-deceived through sin, generates idols, and 'casts out all awareness of God' (1.5.12).

Calvin's case for this verdict seems to be made in two phases. There is empirical evidence, from the confused notions of the pagans, Stoics, Epicureans, from the rough as well as the smooth. Even though not all are as bad as each other, no one jumps the hurdle. Though men and women know God (through the creation), they do not glorify him as God (Rom. 1:21). But since the knowledge of God is clear, they are without excuse. Though we should build on what we know, we fabricate idols.

Hence the need for Scripture, which acts like a pair of glasses, enabling its readers to focus. But focus on what? Not — at least not yet — on the God of gracious redemption, but on God the Creator. Calvin speaks here of Scripture's theology of nature. Only that? Are there within that testimony facts that may provide arguments for God? Is that the significance of Calvin's reference to 'common proofs' (1.6.1) at this point? However that may be, for Calvin grace builds on nature, God's hand in nature is revealed by direct testimony. But, especially, due to our sin, nature's Author and nature's purpose are revealed through Scripture. There God has opened 'his own most hallowed lips' (1.6.1).

PAUL HELM

1.6.2 - 1.7.2

What is the knowledge of God that Scripture makes plain? Calvin insists that, before it reveals the knowledge of God the Redeemer, Scripture presses home the true knowledge of God our Creator and Sustainer.

This Word of God originated with the patriarchs. It conveyed to them the knowledge of the one true God, kept them from idolatry, from forgetfulness and error, and prompted in them the hope of final redemption. Now written down and preserved, handed down to us in the form of sixty-six books, the Word of God to the patriarchs, prophets and apostles may do the same for us as it did for them.

The place of Scripture in giving us the knowledge of the God of nature and redemption leads Calvin to begin to think of the authority of Scripture and how that authority is recognized. First, Scripture is authoritative because it is the written Word of the living God. Faith does not make Scripture God's Word. But, second, neither is faith a leap into the dark. Faith, God-given faith, recognizes the evidence conveyed on the pages of the written Word that it is breathed-out by Almighty God. Trust in Scripture's witness to itself is, for Calvin, the paradigmatic and controlling act of faith. In at least two places (1.6.1 and 1.7.3), he notes that to separate the recognition of Scripture's authority from the life of faith is artificial and unnatural, anticipating the long discussion of faith that will occur in Book 3.

Calvin insists that this recognition is personal and immediate, though not necessarily all-at-once. It does not and cannot come via the say-so of the church or of any other intermediate authority, but by the Holy Spirit. Word and Spirit together — one great cry of the Reformation.

PAUL HELM

1.7.3 - 1.8.1

The Christian church is subordinate to the Word of God. She does not grant the Bible its authority. Divine authority exercised through Scripture comes before the church (since it forms the church); the church does not establish it.

Calvin therefore begins to develop a contrast between the certainty conveyed by the Holy Spirit and 'mere opinion' (1.7.3), a discussion that continues at least to the end of Book 1, Chapter 9. Certainty comes by the operation of the Spirit on our minds as we attend to Scripture. The Spirit begins to clear our ignorance and unbelief, making it apparent to us 'that the teaching of Scripture is from heaven' (1.7.4). The Spirit graciously compels this response in those hearts in which he works. How? By illuminating the content of Scripture, its saving message, its heavenly doctrine. The matter of Scripture is intrinsic to the manner of its reception.

How necessary is Scripture, then? Whoever remains ignorant of it cannot expect to have its divine authority conveyed to his soul; hence, the urgent need for Bible translation and for faithful preaching and teaching. The certainty that the Spirit conveys that the living God speaks in Scripture is stronger than mere opinion, which is as high as the authority of the church, or of human argument, can reach.

This is Calvin's famous and distinctive teaching on the self-authentication of Scripture. By the Spirit, Scripture bears testimony to itself. The doctrine is here stated briefly, forcefully and eloquently. 'By this power we are drawn and inflamed, knowingly and willingly, to obey him, yet also more vitally and more effectively than by mere human willing or knowing!' (1.7.5). What Calvin says here is not to be missed, for it is foundational for Christian living and for the entire theological project that is to follow.

PAUL HELM

1.8.2 - 1.8.9

Calvin noted earlier the distinction between certainty and opinion. The Holy Spirit brings about the *certain conviction* that Scripture is the Word of God, whereas the testimony of the church can only help us to form the *opinion* that it is God's Word. It is therefore somewhat surprising to find that in Chapter 8 he devotes two or three times more space to the place of reason in recognizing biblical authority than he does in Chapter 7 to the self-authenticating character of Scripture. Why is this?

Calvin's procedure certainly shows that he has some confidence in the use of reason, despite the fallenness of our natures. This also underlines the fact that Calvin is not a 'fideist' (i.e., one who exercises faith without reasons). If a label is needed, he is an 'evidentialist'. In Book 1, Chapter 7, the evidence that Scripture is the Word of God is made convincing by the Holy Spirit's powerful illumination of the text of Holy Scripture, arousing faith in the truth of its promises of mercy and grace through Jesus Christ. In Chapter 8, the authority of Scripture is vindicated at the level of opinion by the powers of human reason dwelling not so much on the distinctive evangelical content of Scripture as on its more formal properties — its antiquity, the presence of miracles, fulfilled prophecy, the coherence of its teaching, and so on. Neither strategy is fideist. First, the internal evidence, and then, in Chapter 8, the external evidence are highlighted.

But what is the use of such evidence, apprehended by reason, if the internal testimony of the Holy Spirit is already at work granting certainty? Part of the answer, at least, is that Calvin sees a role for reason in so-called 'negative apologetics', ensuring that Scripture is 'vindicated against the wiles of its disparagers' (1.8.13).

PAUL HELM

1.8.10 - 1.9.2

Calvin skilfully weaves themes together like strands of thread. Faith appears in connection with the self-authentication of Scripture, then disappears from view, only to return in Book 3. Word and Spirit come together, and then come together again. This style is partly due to his care to safeguard his teaching against misunderstanding. He qualifies what he says, and then qualifies the qualification.

At this point he can see a danger — that his emphasis on the Holy Spirit might be misunderstood as favouring the 'left wing' of the Reformation. The Anabaptists and Libertines, with their emphasis on the Spirit as against the Word, misused Paul's teaching on the Spirit and the letter. So the final chapter of Calvin's treatment of Scripture, on the character of divine revelation, is designed to head off this misunderstanding. Does his appeal to the Spirit mean that he also is among the Libertines? No, certainly not! The internal testimony of the Holy Spirit is neither fanatical nor frenzied. Why not? Because it is a case of Spirit *and* Word, not Spirit *against* Word.

The Spirit not only illumines and authenticates the Word, his authenticating is also tested by the Word. In his theological thought, Calvin is quite fond of the idea of two things being linked by a 'bond' — the knowledge of God and of ourselves, for example, and justification and sanctification. Here it is Word and Spirit. 'For by a kind of mutual bond the Lord has joined together the certainty of his Word and of his Spirit so that the perfect religion of the Word may abide in our minds when the Spirit, who causes us to contemplate God's face, shines' (1.9.3).

What God has joined together, no man may put asunder.

PAUL HELM

1.9.3 - 1.11.1

It is characteristic of Calvin's theology in general and of his *Institutes* in particular to give strong affirmation to the person and work of the Holy Spirit. Generally speaking, Calvin does not do this by treating the third person of the Trinity as a separate topic of doctrine, but by highlighting the Spirit's work in connection with every other subject that he addresses.

Calvin makes such a connection here, in his teaching about the Word of God. Because of their strong emphasis on the unique and indispensable authority of Scripture, the Reformers were sometimes accused of placing too much emphasis on the Bible, and thus of failing to heed Paul's warning that 'the letter kills', whereas 'the Spirit gives life' (2 Cor. 3:6).

Yet Calvin rightly understood that the best way to let the Spirit do his life-giving work is to teach more Scripture, not less. Remember that the Spirit gave us the Word to begin with, and that he is present in power whenever the Word is truly and faithfully preached. The way to experience the Spirit's work, therefore, is not through some experience apart from Scripture, but by hearing his voice in the reading and preaching of the Spirit's very own Word.

Also characteristic of Calvin's theology — from the very first sentence of the *Institutes* — is instruction in the knowledge of God, not as a matter of theological speculation, but as a living experience. Beginning in Chapter 10, Calvin moves beyond general revelation (what God has revealed of his character in creation) to special revelation (what God has revealed about himself through his Word). He does this so that we can know God 'as he is toward us' (1.10.2) — our Creator and Redeemer.

PHILIP RYKEN

1.11.2 - 1.11.6

The *Institutes* is a positive presentation of Christian faith and doctrine. But they are also something more: a polemical response to the Roman Catholic Church in which Calvin defends the theology and practice of the Reformation.

In Chapter 11, we find the Geneva Reformer arguing against the idolatrous practice of using images for God in public worship. To be more specific, Calvin is objecting to the crucifixes, icons and other visible representations of the divine being that became common in the Medieval church. Calvin's main argument against the use of such images is that they are unworthy of the majesty of God. God is an invisible, omnipotent and infinite being. To represent him in any physical form, therefore, is to reduce him. This is the problem with idolatry: it sullies the dignity of God by making him out to be something less than he is. Every idol, says Calvin, is an absurd and unworthy fiction.

While Calvin acknowledges that God has given us some visible signs of his invisible glory, he also points out that these visible signs — like the clouds and smoke on Mount Sinai, for example — always point in some way to God's mystery and inaccessibility.

The Roman Catholic Church often defended the use of images in worship as a practical necessity for people who are illiterate ('images are the books of the uneducated' [1.6.5], they claimed). Calvin responds by arguing that whatever people learn from images is false, and also by pointing to the example of the biblical prophets, who never viewed idols as anything except a distraction from the Word. God has not given us an image of himself to see and worship; he has spoken to us with a voice to hear, believe and obey.

PHILIP RYKEN

1.11.7 - 1.11.12

This section of the *Institutes* includes one of the most helpful comments that Calvin ever made about the Christian life. 'Man's nature', he said, 'is a perpetual factory of idols' (1.11.8).

In context, Calvin is referring to idols in their most technical sense as physical objects used as a substitute for the worship of God. But the principle behind his statement has a much wider application. Calvin teaches us to see the human heart as a locus for the manufacture of other gods.

We are always busy making ourselves new things to worship. Some of these idols may well be physical representations of deities, such as the Canaanite gods that the Israelites were tempted to worship, or the ones many Hindus and Buddhists worship today. Then again, some of our idols may be pleasures of the body (like sex), or objects in the world around us (like money), or attitudes of the heart (like the power to control other people). In any case, the problem is that we are idol producers; we carry the means for the production of false worship in our own souls.

Calvin's theology of idolatry is polemical as well as pastoral. In addition to exposing the idols of every human heart, he also attacks what he sees as the idolatry of the Roman Catholic Church. Although Catholic theologians tried to draw a distinction between the honour or service that they offered to various images and the worship they offered to God, Calvin argues that this was a distinction without a difference. To serve is to worship, and to honour God in any way through any image is to deface his deity.

PHILIP RYKEN

1.11.13 - 1.12.2

Calvin continues to make his case against the use of images (icons, crucifixes and the like) in Christian worship, which he believes to be nothing less than an idolatrous violation of the Second Commandment.

One of Calvin's arguments is *historical*: in the first five hundred years of the Christian church, there were no images in the church and pure doctrine flourished. The implication is that images have a corrupting effect on Christian theology.

Another argument is *practical*: when images are introduced to Christian worship, the power of the sacraments (baptism and the Lord's Supper) is diminished. As visible symbols of the Word, they now have to compete with other visual images, and thus they lose some of their unique and divinely intended force.

Yet another argument is *exegetical*: Calvin reviews many of the arguments in favour of images — such as those used at the Second Council of Nicaea (AD 787) — and judges them so inept as to be absurd.

But perhaps Calvin's most powerful argument is *theological*. When God is worshipped by way of idols and images, his powers and perfections are parcelled out to lesser gods and goddesses. Instead of seeing God as the locus of all majesty and grace, people look to other things in life to provide security, hope, protection, pleasure and satisfaction.

Earlier Calvin described the human heart as an idol factory. Here he says, in effect, that the human heart is also a distribution centre. The sinful nature takes the prerogatives that properly belong to God alone and divides them among many deities. This is an important insight about idolatry: our temptation is not simply to worship some false god, but also to worship less and less of the true God by taking away his glory a little at a time.

PHILIP RYKEN

1.12.3 - 1.13.3

After concluding his arguments against idolatry, proving that any use of images in worship is a sacrilege, Calvin turns to a consideration of Scripture's teaching on the Trinity.

In addition to providing a basic definition of the doctrine — there is one and *only* one God in three distinct persons — Calvin introduces some important principles to consider when practising biblical and systematic theology.

One is the principle of accommodation. In speaking of the mystery of God's infinite being, and of the impossibility of measuring him by our own physical senses, Calvin explains why the Bible nevertheless ascribes to him a mouth, ears, eyes, hands and feet. Of course God does not have a physical body. But, by using this familiar imagery to describe himself — 'lisping', as Calvin calls it in 1.13.1 — God is accommodating himself to our limited understanding.

The other principle Calvin introduces concerns the use of theological vocabulary. The orthodox definition of the Trinity uses the term 'person' to distinguish the Father, the Son and the Holy Spirit within the one Godhead. But some critics object to this term on the grounds that it is not biblical, but a word of human invention. Here Calvin defends the appropriate use of terms like 'person' (or 'Trinity', for that matter) as legitimate labels for biblical truths. Even if they do not come directly from Scripture, theological words can help to clarify the complex doctrines of Scripture. Such is the case here, where traditional terminology for the being of God can help us to grasp a fundamental truth of the faith: though united in one perfect and undivided essence, the Father, the Son and the Holy Spirit exist eternally as three persons.

PHILIP RYKEN

1.13.4 - 1.13.7

Having defended the use of technical theological language as an aid to our understanding of scriptural doctrines like the Trinity, Calvin argues that accurate theological terminology helps us to 'unmask false teachers' (1.13.4). Precise terminology nails us down as to what we believe is the truth, with the effect that false teachers are unable to 'evade it by their shifts' (*ibid.*). In characteristically colourful language, Calvin points out 'these slippery snakes glide away unless they are boldly pursued, caught, and crushed' (*ibid.*).

This section could hardly be more timely, since false teachers today hate nothing more than the confessional theology of the church. Why? Because it requires them to state their teachings plainly, affirming or denying clear propositions. Despite the complaints that such an approach enshrines human formulas over God's Word, the reality is that only by means of clear confessional theology is the church able to defend the truth of Scripture.

Calvin then cautions against becoming overly devoted to mere words when it is the truth of the ideas that really matters. Terminology must be a servant of truth, never the master. Thus, Calvin relates how numerous orthodox theologians of the early church wrestled with one another in their varied approach to terminology, but were able to come to eventual accord because of the orthodoxy of their ideas. What a wealth of wisdom Calvin offers to anyone who engages in theological dispute!

Calvin then specifies his own terminology in treating the Trinity, informing us that, for him, the three distinct 'subsistences' (persons) share the same 'essence' (being). Thus the word 'God' applies equally to all three persons of the Godhead, each distinctively and uniquely revealed as Father, Son, or Holy Spirit. Scripture, of course, grounds all. For example, he affirms the eternal deity of the Son by turning to John's description of God the Son as 'the Word' (John 1:1-3) and God's speech in Genesis 1. Calvin is practising the very procedure he earlier applauded: sorting carefully through the scriptural data so as to properly affirm truth.

RICHARD PHILLIPS

1.13.8 - 1.13.12

In these pages, Calvin proves the deity of Christ over against those who would deny it. The argument here provides a good example of the care Calvin exercises when proof-texting, a practice commonly frowned upon today. But Calvin's approach employs verses from Scripture that truly do demand the doctrine at hand, proving that a kind of proof-texting is not only wholesome but also necessary. It is with proof-texts like these that Calvin answers heretics like the Spaniard Michael Servetus (mentioned here in the *Institutes* for the first time).

Calvin's arguments for Christ's deity are both robust and edifying. Scripture presents the eternality of the Son by revealing him as the Word who was with God in the beginning (John 1:1-2). Calvin follows this argument with a survey of texts from both testaments, focusing on how Christ takes on divine titles from the Old Testament and, as Messiah, fulfilled prophecies that pertain directly to God. A Christian could powerfully demonstrate from Scripture the deity of Jesus by remembering these verses alone.

Calvin then shows how the apostles in the New Testament specifically identify Jesus as God and cite him as fulfilling prophecies about God. Moreover, the New Testament sees Jesus' works as the very works of God, especially as he forgives sins, a prerogative that even the Pharisees recognize exists essentially in God alone.

I particularly enjoy Calvin's argument for the deity of Christ from the use of the phrase 'Angel of the Lord' in the Old Testament (1.13.10). Most scholars today speak tentatively when identifying the Angel of the Lord as the second person of the Trinity. Calvin has no such reservations at all and persuasively argues that these verses point to the eternal Son.

RICHARD PHILLIPS

1.13.13 - 1.13.17

Calvin concludes his defence of Christ's deity with a discussion of his miracles, which he takes as self-evident displays of divinity. The bulk of this section is devoted to responding to anticipated quibbles and objections. For instance, one might point out that the prophets and apostles also did miracles, but they are not divine. The difference, Calvin argues, is that the apostles' miracle-working power is specifically ascribed to Christ's having dispensed to them those gifts (Matt. 10:8; cf. Mark 3:15; 6:7). Calvin's entire defence of Christ's deity shows our immense debt to heresy: orthodox theologians typically do their best work by most deeply mining the Scriptures in order to respond to false teaching.

Calvin turns next to the deity of the Spirit. It is not for nothing that he is known as 'the theologian of the Holy Spirit'. Mirroring his approach to Christ, Calvin begins at creation and argues that the Spirit's role 'in transfusing into all things his energy, and breathing into them essence, life, and movement, he is indeed plainly divine' (1.13.14). To this he adds an overwhelming array of texts that ascribe divinity to the Spirit and display the full scope of his activity in creation and redemption. As ever, Calvin's grasp of Scripture here is stunning.

Having proved the deity of the Son and of the Spirit, Calvin returns to the Trinity to reaffirm the unity of the Godhead in three persons. For this, Calvin appeals to Christ's institution of the sacrament of baptism, where believers are to be baptized into the name of the one God revealed in the Father, Son and Holy Spirit. The fact that there is but one faith (Eph. 4:5) proves that there is but one God. And this one God is known in three persons, each uniquely distinguished among the three.

Quoting Gregory of Nazianzus (one of the early church theologians whose writings brought consensus on the doctrine of the Trinity), Calvin asserts that we thus should always think of the one God whenever we think of the three persons, and of the three persons whenever we think of the one God. Our calling is to ascribe to each of the three persons of the Godhead actions appropriate to his role, while realizing that in all instances it is the one God who acts. Such is the glorious mystery we find in Scripture.

RICHARD PHILLIPS

1.13.18 - 1.13.22

These sections on the Trinity are especially valuable to Christians because they teach us to think of God and salvation in explicitly Trinitarian terms. In this way Calvin helps us avoid the charge that, as the liberals are said to worship only God the Father (the loving and accepting Father of all mankind, etc.) and the Charismatics worship only God the Spirit, evangelicals worship only God the Son.

Calvin begins by hesitating to borrow 'comparisons from human affairs' (1.13.18) to express the distinctions among the members of the Trinity. One sometimes hears about analogies of the Trinity, but Calvin is right in reminding us that the mystery of God as three-in-one transcends all analogy. However, Calvin does see a kind of order warranted by Scripture — Father, then Son, followed by Spirit.

Next Calvin turns to the issue that divided the East and West churches: the so-called 'processions', or intra-divine properties, of the persons of the Trinity. Calvin takes the Western side defending the formula that as the Son is begotten of the Father, the Spirit proceeds from the Father *and the Son* (these three words being the point of East-West contention). But what do we mean by 'begotten' and 'proceeds'? This is a classic instance of theology needing terms for topics in Scripture, deficient though they may be. Do not be distressed if you find all this hard to grasp; you might need to read Chapter 13, Section 19, slowly and carefully. Section 20 provides a very helpful summary that should help you to get your feet on the ground. Studying this will encourage you to think clearly and biblically about God.

When Calvin begins his refutation of Trinity heresies, I immediately thought, 'This is going to take a while.' This is in large part because of the number and severity of 'all the calumnies of the wicked' (1.13.21) in this area. Calvin approaches them all with his own guiding rule: 'let us use great caution that neither our thoughts nor our speech go beyond the limits to which the Word of God itself extends' (*ibid.*). It was his dogged adherence to this wisdom that made Calvin a truly great theologian and pastor.

RICHARD PHILLIPS

1.13.23 - 1.13.25

Let me begin my comments on this section of the *Institutes* with a general 'plug' for thinking about God in a Trinitarian way. We rightly talk about having a 'personal relationship with God', but we need to realize that our relationship is with the one God who is also *three persons*. As a Christian, I have a Father who loves me, provides for me, and disciplines me; I have a Shepherd-Saviour whom I follow and serve; and I have a living and divine Spirit powerfully moving within me to do God's will. These are vitally important and precious truths that ought to colour our Christian lives.

Calvin continues his discussion of the Trinity by tackling the heretical teaching that the Son is something less than fully divine since, in the Bible, 'God' typically refers to the Father. Calvin responds by noting that though this is often the case, the word 'God' may also refer to the Trinity as a whole, or to the Son, or the Spirit. Calvin gets a little prickly here, wondering whether his opponents think Jesus is not good when he says that only God is good (Matt. 19:17). 'If they deny it,' he writes, 'their impiety stands sufficiently convicted; by admitting it, they cut their own throats' (1.13.24). Clearly Calvin is not messing around when it comes to Christ's deity!

In the last paragraph of Chapter 13, Section 25, Calvin makes one of the more important points about the inner-relations of the Trinity. Some people do not understand how the Son, who is begotten of the Father, can thus be fully divine and eternal. In response, Calvin reproduces the great argument from the Nicene era that either God has always been the Father, in which the Son also has always been, or else God is eternally something other than Father, in which case he has not really revealed himself to us in his Word. Think about that.

Finally, I am reminded of a story Sinclair Ferguson told us in seminary about a conversation about the Trinity with his then-middle-school aged son. Before long, his son said, 'Daddy, this makes my head hurt.' Sinclair replied, 'Exactly. You are doing well.' So if you are struggling with this key truth, don't be shocked — you only have a human mind! But I hope you see the value of all this heavy sledding in Calvin. Remember, we are saved to know God (John 17:3), and the God whom we are to know is triune.

RICHARD PHILLIPS

1.13.26 - 1.13.29

In the final sections of Book 1, Chapter 13, Calvin considers two more arguments against the Trinity. *Theologically*, the anti-Trinitarians argued that Christ's subordination to the Father was counterevidence to the Trinity. *Historically*, they appealed to the Church Fathers against the Trinity.

The anti-Trinitarians argued that since the Father is greater than the Son (*cf.* John 14:28), the Son is thereby inferior to the Father and hence not equally divine with him. But Calvin shows from Scripture that while the Father and Son differ 'by reason of order' (1.13.26), they are still of the same 'essence'. Their roles in our salvation are distinct but they still share the same nature. So Jesus' office of Mediator to the Father does not overturn his deity.

The anti-Trinitarians' appeals to the Church Fathers are equally problematic. Yes, the second-century theologian Irenaeus did claim in *Against Heresies* that the Father of Jesus Christ is the sole and eternal God of Israel. But Calvin notes that the Bishop of Lyons: (1) used this language to refute denials that the Father of Christ was the same person throughout the Bible; and (2) elsewhere explicitly argued for Christ's eternal divinity and oneness with the Father.

Similarly, Tertullian of Carthage was 'sometimes rough and thorny in his mode of speech' (1.13.28), but Calvin shows that his meaning and intention is still fully Trinitarian.

The same orthodoxy is found in the writings of Justin Martyr, Hilary of Poitiers, Ignatius of Antioch, and Augustine, 'toward whom these rascals are most hostile' (1.13.29).

The doctrine of the Trinity, says Calvin, is biblical and finds abundant support in the early church against all objectors. His concluding paragraph issues a reminder to all who engage in the task of theology: strive to exposit Scripture faithfully and edify the church without falling prey to worthless curiosity and speculation (*cf.* Deut. 29:29).

JUSTIN TAYLOR

1.14.1 - 1.14.5

We now move into Chapter 14, on the creation of the world and mankind (Sections 1-2), the role of angels (Sections 3-12) and demons (Sections 13-19), and the relevant lessons we should learn (Sections 20-22).

In the first and fourth sections especially, Calvin continues to hammer home his case against speculation, calling it unhelpful, unfruitful, unprofitable, wicked, hurtful, empty and foolish. Instead, we must stick with the simplicity of Scripture and 'willingly remain enclosed within these bounds to which God has willed to confine us' (1.14.1).

For Calvin, to submit to Scripture means, at least, to know what it teaches. So he offers two reasons for why we should study the oft-neglected topic of angels: (1) 'If we desire to recognize God from his works, we ought by no means to overlook such an illustrious and noble example' (1.14.3); (2) 'This part of doctrine is very necessary to refute many errors' (*ibid.*). We may think Calvin's second reason is irrelevant today until we remember that, like the early heretics did with angels, sinners always strive to elevate created things above God (Rom. 1:25).

Calvin draws upon the scriptural witness and defines angels as 'celestial spirits whose ministry and service God uses to carry out all things he has decreed' (1.14.5). They adorn God's majesty and, particularly in the Old Testament era, manifest his will to men. As Calvin looks at the various designations of angels in Scripture — hosts, principalities, thrones, etc. — he touches upon one label that can be confusing both theologically and apologetically: 'gods' (e.g., Ps. 138:1). He explains that these ministers of God 'as in a mirror ... in some respect exhibit his divinity to us' (1.14.5). Hence, for Calvin, these created beings are 'gods' in whom the brightness of the glory of the only God shines.

What a wonder that God commissions these creatures to serve Christians, the heirs of salvation (Heb. 1:14)!

JUSTIN TAYLOR

Do we each have a guardian angel? Calvin admits: 'I dare not affirm with confidence' (1.14.7). Instead, Scripture teaches that the protection of an individual is not the task of one angel only, but 'all with one consent watch over our salvation' (*ibid.*). Many people find comfort in the thought that they are assigned a guardian angel; how much more so to think that we are protected by the heavenly host!

Scripture, Calvin teaches, only hints at the hierarchy, number and form of angels. We can be sure that they are spirits who have a real existence (1.14.9); but beyond this, Calvin urges patience until the final day of revelation. His general rule of thumb is: don't 'probe too curiously or talk too confidently' (1.14.8).

In Section 10, Calvin corrects the idea — still common in popular culture today — that angels minister and dispense *all* good things to us such that no honour from men is to be withheld from them. But, as the moon reflects the sun's brilliance, angels shine with a glory that finds its source in God alone, to whom alone praise is due.

One might ask why God sometimes chooses to use angels to declare his power, provide for the safety of believers, and communicate his goodness to them. Wouldn't we avoid much of the superstition surrounding angels if God did all of this *directly* rather than by angelic mediation? Calvin offers a creative answer: God does not need the angels, but employs them as a way to comfort us. God's promise that he is our Protector should be sufficient to calm our fears, but he accommodates our weakness by dispatching innumerable guardians to keep and defend us.

Are you filled with fear, surrounded by enemies, or confronted with danger? As Elisha told his servant, 'Do not be afraid, for those who are with us are more than those who are with them' (2 Kings 6:16).

JUSTIN TAYLOR

1.14.12 - 1.14.18

Whatever we may believe about angels, says Calvin, we are deceived in our thinking about them if by it we are not led to place our hope firmly in God alone. Specifically, the angels are given to lift our eyes to 'the one Mediator, Christ, that we may wholly depend upon him, lean upon him, be brought to him, and rest in him' (1.14.12).

If the worship of God is the purpose of angelology (the study of angels), how should we think about and respond to Satan and his fallen angels? Calvin's reply is to the point: if we care about God's glory or Christ's kingdom or our salvation at all, we will fight with all our strength against these armies of the empire of wickedness. All that we learn about demons in Scripture is designed to: (1) arouse us to take precaution against the enemy's methods; and (2) equip us with the weapons to vanquish our foes. 'Since this military service ends in death, let us urge ourselves to perseverance' (1.14.13).

That we may further know our demonic enemies, Calvin explains that 'they were when first created angels of God, but by degeneration they ruined themselves, and became the instruments of ruin for others' (1.14.16). Thankfully, they are not omnipotent. As displayed in the life of Job, Satan can do nothing but what God wills and permits. Why doesn't Scripture tell us more? Because the Holy Spirit did not see fit 'to feed our curiosity with empty histories to no effect' (*ibid.*).

Take courage from the simple fact that while Satan and his minions can attack us, they can never vanquish, crush, overwhelm, or conquer us. As we fight the good fight, let us call upon God for help, since only he 'can supply us with counsel and strength, courage and armour' (1.14.13). We may be distressed, but we will recover. We may receive blows, but we will rise. We may be wounded, but we will live. Be ready, Calvin says, since this toil will continue throughout our lives until at last we obtain the victory.

JUSTIN TAYLOR

1.14.19 - 1.14.22

Calvin wraps up his discussion of demons by emphasizing that they are not impulses or inspirations that God arouses in our minds, but are quite real.

These creatures present a gruesome contrast to Calvin's next topic, God's manifold creation. Calvin encourages Christians to take 'pious delight' in the works of God's 'most beautiful theatre' and 'spacious house' (1.14.20). The world around us, he says, ought to stir in us a 'pious meditation' upon the end for which God created all things (*ibid.*) — the manifestation of his glorious power, wisdom and goodness. If only we will ponder God's exquisite works, we will soon know what it means that he is our Creator.

When we recite the *Apostles' Creed*, we confess our belief that God is 'Maker of heaven and earth'. But how do we know whether we have apprehended with true faith what this statement means? Calvin offers a two-fold rule.

First, we should not pass over creation too quickly with a mere 'fleeting glance' (1.14.21), but thoughtfully and gratefully meditate upon 'those conspicuous powers which God shows forth in his creatures' (*ibid.*).

Second, we ought to consider our own lives — feeling his power and grace and goodness in ourselves (1.14.22). As a result, we will learn to:

1. Wait — for the fulness of all good things from him alone.
2. Trust him — that we will never lack what we need for salvation.
3. Ask him — for whatever we desire.
4. Thank him — for every benefit that comes our way.

Calvin concludes: 'So, invited by the great sweetness of his beneficence and goodness, let us study to love and serve him with all our heart' (*ibid.*). Amen!

JUSTIN TAYLOR

1.15.1 - 1.15.3

Calvin now turns to the creation of mankind, and he does so with a view to further elaborate his assertion that we cannot have a clear and complete knowledge of God without a corresponding knowledge of ourselves. Calvin does not have in view here some sort of introspective, therapeutic journey of self-discovery. He means that we must know ourselves as both created and fallen. We cannot properly appreciate man as created without understanding man as fallen, and we need to understand man as fallen in light of what he was when originally created.

One reason this is important is because we have a tendency to blame God for our own evil — excusing our sin with 'I'm only human' or 'To err is human'. But this is to place our sin at God's feet. 'Since, then,' Calvin says, 'we see the flesh panting for every subterfuge by which it thinks that the blame for its own evils may in any way be diverted from itself to another ... we must so deal with the calamity of mankind that we may cut off every shift, and may vindicate God's justice from every accusation' (1.15.1).

But what is man *per se*? In Chapter 15, Section 2, Calvin flatly asserts the obvious point that people are made up of both body and soul (theologians call this view of humanity 'dichotomy' as opposed to 'trichotomy', which differentiates human beings into 'body, soul *and spirit*'). He then proceeds to argue at length for the immortality of the soul by pointing to: (1) our conscience's perception of right and wrong, our dread of guilt, and our fear of punishment for doing evil; (2) the 'many pre-eminent gifts' (1.15.2) of the human mind, far superior to those of animals; (3) our ability to conceive of God and the supernatural, and to discern what is just and honourable; (4) our mental activity when we are asleep (would you have thought of this?), as we sometimes conceive of things that have never happened, or that will happen in the future; (5) copious arguments from specific texts of Scripture; and, above all, (6) the creation of men and women in the image of God.

To those who would put human beings on a par with trees and animals, Calvin declares that 'the likeness of God extends to the whole excellence by which man's nature towers over all kinds of living creatures' (1.15.3).

LIGON DUNCAN

1.15.4 - 1.15.7

Calvin introduced the subject of our creation in the image of God in 1.15.3. Now he argues that we learn what the image of God entails not only by studying man as originally created (Genesis 1 - 2), but also by studying what Scripture says about the image of God as it is renewed in Christ. A 'full definition of "image"', he says, '...can be nowhere better recognized than from the restoration of his corrupted nature' (1.15.4).

It should be noted that Calvin uses the terms 'regeneration' and 'renewal' here a little more broadly than do modern Reformed textbooks on systematics. The *Shorter Catechism*, however, perfectly mirrors Calvin's statements in 1.15.4 on the image (Question 10: *How did God create man?* Answer: God created man male and female, after his own image, in knowledge, righteousness and holiness, with dominion over the creatures). In the Fall, this image was severely marred, so that it is now 'confused, mutilated, and disease-ridden' (*ibid.*). But since 'Christ is the most perfect image of God; if we are conformed to it we are so restored that with true piety, righteousness, purity, and intelligence we bear God's image' (*ibid.*) in all its beauty.

Calvin continues by striking a blow at Andreas Osiander (1.15.4), a German Lutheran theologian who was also criticized by Calvin's Lutheran friend Philip Melanchthon. Calvin also rejects Augustine's speculation that the soul reflects the Trinity, then takes aim at the Manichaeans (their idea that the soul is derived from God's substance), Servetus (his resurrection of the old Manichaean error), and 'the philosophers' (1.15.5) (praising only Plato) in their views on the powers and faculties of the soul. While conceding that the philosophers may indeed say some true and helpful things about the soul, the main thing that Calvin wants to assert is that 'the human soul consists of two faculties, understanding and will' (1.15.7). The relationship between these two faculties — for him, the former governs the latter — becomes key for his later treatment of sin and free will.

LIGON DUNCAN

1.15.8 - 1.16.3

The section at hand is a 'rock your world' important passage in the *Institutes*. In it, Calvin explains a fundamental source of confusion in the quest for 'free will'. 'The philosophers', says Calvin, by discussing the question of free will apart from understanding the consequences of the Fall, 'were seeking in a ruin for a building, and in scattered fragments for a well-knit structure' (1.15.8). Christians who follow the philosophers in failing to take into account the gravity of the Fall when discussing human free choice are 'playing the fool' (*ibid.*). This section shows how crucial the doctrine of the Fall is to Calvin's understanding of humanity.

Those interested in Calvin's apologetic views will be fascinated by two comments in 1.16.1: 'the minds of the impious too are compelled by merely looking upon earth and heaven to rise up to the Creator...' and 'the wisdom, power, and goodness' of God revealed in creation 'are self-evident, and even force themselves upon the unwilling'. But the main thing Calvin wants to assert in this section is that creation and providence are inseparably connected, and that by his providence God 'sustains, nourishes, and cares for, everything he has made' (1.16.2). Consequently, there is no such thing as luck, fortune or chance.

Asserting again God's universal providence in 1.16.3, Calvin puts the truth to pastoral use immediately: those who praise God's power 'may safely rest in the protection of him to whose will are subject all the harmful things which, whatever their source, we may fear; whose authority curbs Satan with all his furies and his whole equipage; and upon whose nod depends whatever opposes our welfare' (*ibid.*).

LIGON DUNCAN

1.16.4 - 1.16.8

For Calvin, providence means God governs, not merely watches, his creation. Calvin is emphasizing that providence entails more than 'bare foreknowledge' (1.16.4). It involves God's will and his acts. Nor is it merely a general control, but a specific direction. Indeed, Calvin asserts that God 'directs everything by his incomprehensible wisdom and disposes it to his own end' (*ibid.*).

In 1.16.5, Calvin adduces biblical evidence for God's general providence. He says that 'not one drop of rain falls without God's sure command'. In 1.16.6, Calvin considers God's more particular governance over mankind. Again he compiles biblical testimony to show that 'Scripture, to express more plainly that nothing at all in the world is undertaken without his determination, shows that things seemingly most fortuitous are subject to him.' In 1.16.7, he considers what might be called God's providence over 'natural' occurrences (things that seem to be part of the normal course of events — the wind blowing, women having babies, etc.) and even here Calvin says that 'particular events are generally testimonies of the character of God's singular providence' (1.16.7).

In 1.16.8, Calvin both rejects the accusation that his doctrine of providence is a Stoic doctrine of fate (determinism or fatalism), and he likewise repudiates the ideas of fortune and chance (approving Basil the Great's [AD 330-379, one of the Cappadocian Fathers] strictures against and Augustine's retractions of his earlier use of this terminology). From hurricanes to hiccups, 'God so attends to the regulation of individual events, and they all so proceed from his set plan, that nothing takes place by chance' (1.16.4).

LIGON DUNCAN

1.16.9 - 1.17.2

Calvin reminds us that though all things are ordained by God's plan, yet the events of our lives and world often look to us as if they are random and fortuitous. As Calvin says, 'the order, reason, end, and necessity of those things which happen for the most part lie hidden in God's purpose' (1.16.9). This is a hugely important pastoral point. The believer must realize that events will happen in this life that are simultaneously seemingly senseless and fortuitous and yet also part of God's perfect plan. Thus, in our hearts, we must be fixed on the truth that nothing happens that the Lord has not decreed and foreseen.

Calvin now begins a sustained application of this truth in 1.17.1. He first announces four things (though he says he's going to give three!) that we need to remember when we are considering God's providence: 'Three things, indeed, are to be noted. First, God's providence must be considered with regard to the future as well as the past. Secondly, it is the determinative principle of all things in such a way that sometimes it works through an intermediary, sometimes without an intermediary, sometimes contrary to every intermediary. Finally, it strives to the end that God may reveal his concern for the whole human race, but especially his vigilance in ruling the church, which he deigns to watch more closely. Now this, also, ought to be added, [fourthly!] that although either fatherly favour and beneficence or severity of judgement often shine forth in the whole course of providence, nevertheless sometimes the causes of the events are hidden.' The echoes of this in the *Westminster Confession*, Chapter 5, are not difficult to hear.

Consequently, no mature believer will weigh the matter of God's providence without assuming a posture of reverence, awe and humility. This is important, Calvin says, because 'it happens that today so many dogs assail this doctrine with their venomous bitings, or at least with barking: for they wish nothing to be lawful for God beyond what their own reason prescribes for themselves' (1.17.2).

LIGON DUNCAN

1.17.3 - 1.17.7

In this section, Calvin mentions individuals who draw unwarranted inferences from the providence of God. One false inference is that means do not matter. One might say, 'If God has unchangeably set the time of my death, then what does it matter if I eat well, exercise, and see the doctor?' Calvin replies that the decree of God does not lay a hindrance before our decision making. On the contrary, 'God's providence does not always meet us in its naked form, but God in a sense clothes it with the means employed' (1.17.4).

Another false inference that some draw from the doctrine of providence is that there is no difference between virtue and vice. Again, one might say, 'If all things happen because of God's will, then how can one blame an adulterer for his adultery or a murderer for her murder? Aren't they just doing God's will?' Calvin answers: 'I deny that they are serving God's will … [rather] we must in our deeds search out God's will which he declares through his Word' (1.17.5). Doesn't, then, the existence of moral evil implicate the character of God in wrongdoing? No, says Calvin, borrowing an analogy from Augustine: a corpse decays under the heat of the sun, but no one says that 'the rays stink' (*ibid.*).

Properly understood, providence is the stay and support of the believer. God takes particular and 'special care' (1.17.6) not only of all humanity but also of the church. For Christians, God's 'singular providence' means that God 'will not suffer anything to happen but what may turn out to [our] good and salvation' (*ibid.*). How comforting it is to know that even the malice of our enemies and of the devil himself are under God's power!

How should we respond to the Bible's teaching about providence? Calvin points to three lines of response that are worth committing to memory: 'gratitude of mind for the favourable outcome of things, patience in adversity, and also incredible freedom from worry about the future' (1.17.7).

GUY WATERS

1.17.8 - 1.17.11

For Calvin, the biblical doctrine of providence is not a matter for idle speculation. On the contrary, 'ignorance of providence is the ultimate of all miseries; the highest blessedness lies in the knowledge of it' (1.17.11).

In this section, Calvin develops three practical observations concerning the doctrine of providence. First, the doctrine helps us to face adversity properly. When we realize that the hostilities and setbacks we experience do not come ultimately from the hand of man but from the hand of God, we are able to check the 'anger and impatience' (1.17.8) which tempt us in those situations.

Second, the doctrine of providence teaches us how to use means. If somebody helps us, it is appropriate to express appreciation for that person, even as we recognize that that help has come through that person from God. If we hurt ourselves through 'negligence or imprudence', we rightly accept blame for our carelessness, even as we recognize that the matter has come to pass because of the 'Lord's will' (1.17.9). As we face an uncertain future, we take up all proper means with energy and zeal, even as we 'entrust and submit' ourselves 'to God's wisdom', and entrust the outcome to God's hand (*ibid.*).

Third, without the doctrine of providence life would be terrifying. Danger, disease and death face every person every moment of the day. Neither unbeliever nor believer is exempt from the 'innumerable evils that beset human life' (1.17.10). Should the believer respond to these uncertainties with anxiety, fear and care, Calvin asks? No! 'His solace, I say, is to know that his Heavenly Father so holds all things in his power, so rules by his authority and will, so governs by his wisdom, that nothing can befall except he determine it' (1.17.11). We not only affirm that 'the Lord is everywhere at work', but we 'trust that his work will be for [believers'] welfare' (*ibid.*). To have a fixed and settled knowledge of this truth is 'highest blessedness' (*ibid.*) indeed.

GUY WATERS

1.17.12 - 1.18.2

In this section, Calvin responds to an objection to and clears up a misconception about the biblical doctrine of providence.

There are some who say 'that the plan of God does not stand firm and sure, but is subject to change in response to the disposition of things below' (1.17.12). They offer two reasons in support. First, they cite passages that speak of God's 'repentance' (e.g. Gen. 6:6; 1 Sam. 15:11; Jer. 18:8). Calvin, however, astutely observes from 1 Samuel that immediately after the Scripture speaks of God repenting (1 Sam. 15:11), it says that God does not repent (1 Sam. 15:29). He concludes from these passages that 'the mode of accommodation is for [God] to represent himself to us not as he is in himself, but as he seems to us' (1.17.13). 'Repentance', applied to God, means only the 'change of action' (*ibid.*) that, in the world of human beings, often springs from human repentance. Because God's eternal and unchangeable decree, as it unfolds in time, appears to human eyes to be a sequence of 'change with respect to his actions', Scripture therefore speaks on occasion of God's 'repentance' (*ibid.*).

The second reason is that 'the destruction which had once been pronounced upon the Ninevites [through Jonah] was remitted' (1.17.14). But, Calvin observes: 'It is to be understood from the outcome' of the Ninevites' repentance that there was 'a tacit condition' in the prophet's threat of judgement upon them (*ibid.*). 'It pleased the Lord by such threats to arouse to repentance those whom he was terrifying, that they might escape the judgement they deserved for their sins' (*ibid.*).

One misconception about providence is that evil happens by the 'bare permission', but not by the will, of God. This presents God as seated 'in a watchtower awaiting chance events, and his judgements dependent upon human will' (1.18.1). God is no such spectator. He decrees and commands the execution of all things: the calamities that befell Job; the lying spirit that entered Ahab's court prophets; the judgements of Israel and Judah by Assyria and Babylon; and crucifixion of Christ (*ibid.*). God's will is the ultimate 'cause' even of the 'hardening' of sinners (1.18.2). In summary, 'since God's will is said to be the cause of all things, I have made his providence the determinative principle for all human plans and works, not only in order to display its force in the elect, who are ruled by the Holy Spirit, but also to compel the reprobate to obedience' (*ibid.*).

GUY WATERS

1.18.3 - 1.18.4

Calvin takes up two further objections to the biblical doctrine of providence. First, 'if nothing happens apart from God's will', does it not follow that 'there are in him two contrary wills because by his secret plan he decrees what he has openly forbidden by his law' (1.18.3)?

It is true that God wills all things, Calvin observes (Job 1:21; 1 Sam. 2:25; Ps. 115:3; Isa. 45:7; Amos 3:6; Deut. 19:5; Acts 4:28). However, it is not true that there are two contrary wills of God. The divine will is 'one and simple', but 'it appears manifold to us because, on account of our mental incapacity, we do not grasp how in diverse ways it wills and does not will something to take place' (1.18.3). The doctrine of providence, therefore, is not inherently contradictory. It does, however, remind us that our minds are incapable of comprehending fully the divine will.

Second, if God wills the 'work, plans, and intentions' of the ungodly, then aren't 'men undeservedly damned if they carry out what God has decreed because they obey his will'? (1.18.4). The objection, Calvin replies, 'confuses' God's 'will' with his 'precept': 'while God accomplishes through the wicked what he has decreed by his secret judgement, they are not excusable, as if they had obeyed his precept which out of their own lust they deliberately break' (*ibid.*). Quoting Augustine, Calvin observes that, while both the Father and Judas delivered up Jesus, 'in the one thing they have done, the cause of their doing it is not one' (*ibid.*). Judas, therefore, deserves blame and not praise for delivering up Jesus to the authorities.

Calvin closes the chapter with the reminder that God has revealed these difficult matters to us because he has judged them 'useful for men to know' (*ibid.*). Our proper response, therefore, is not to 'scoff' but to 'embrace with humble teachableness ... whatever is taught in Sacred Scripture' (*ibid.*).

GUY WATERS

BOOK TWO

'The Knowledge of God
the Redeemer in Christ'

Introduction

The full title of Book Two — 'The Knowledge of God the Redeemer in Christ, First Disclosed to the Fathers Under the Law, and Then to Us in the Gospel' — broadly describes its content. Calvin explains that we have neither an excuse before God nor any ability to remedy our condition as fallen creatures. We are so permeated with corruption and so justly condemned for our guilt that our only hope is to be redeemed by Jesus Christ (Chapters 1 - 4). Calvin helpfully bridges from Book One to Book Two when he writes that '...the whole knowledge of God the Creator that we have discussed [in Book One] would be useless unless faith also followed, setting forth for us God our Father in Christ' (2.6.1).

Apart from salvation through the Son of God incarnate, we face only God's curse and, sooner or later, know only despair. But when the gospel is proclaimed to our ears and the Spirit elicits faith, the freely responsible but spiritually dead are brought to life in Christ (Chapters 5 - 6). The saints of the Old Testament grasped Christ's mediation through types and shadows such as the sacrificial system under Moses (Chapter 7) and apprehended true obedience from the requirements of the law (Chapter 8). New covenant Christians trust in the same Christ but now do so in light of his fulfilment of every earlier promise and demand of God (Chapters 9 - 11; cf. 2 Cor. 1:20).

Calvin finishes Book Two with a soaring description of Christ's person and work. Let your heart be stirred and your mind enlightened as you read about the eternal Son of God who was pleased to come down to rescue helpless creatures of dust (Chapters 12 - 14). He did so by taking our humanity to himself and by accepting divine judgement for our sake (Chapters 15 - 17). This crucified, risen and exalted Saviour has merited grace and salvation for us. This is the glorious message of Book Two.

2.1.1 - 2.1.4

Calvin proceeds from 'The Knowledge of God the Creator' in Book 1 to 'The Knowledge of God the Redeemer in Christ...' in Book 2. Here he begins with a meditation on self-knowledge (2.1.1-3). Why begin an exposition of 'the knowledge of God the Redeemer in Christ' in this way? Recall that Calvin established at the outset of Book 1 that the knowledge of God and self-knowledge are inseparable (1.1.1-3). Consequently, if we are to appreciate biblical teaching on the work of Christ, we must also understand our sin. To understand sin properly requires self-understanding.

Right self-understanding, Calvin argues, yields two conclusions. First, all that we are as creatures comes by the favour and provision of God. We should, therefore, respond to God with humility and a sense of dependence upon him. Second, 'our condition after Adam's fall' is a 'miserable' one (2.1.1). Thus we should be 'humbled' and 'overwhelmed with shame' (*ibid.*). One tragic consequence of sin, however, is that our natural gifts become the occasion of self-flattery and self-sufficiency (2.1.2). To be sure, sin has effaced neither our natural 'gifts' nor our divinely appointed 'purpose' as human beings (2.1.3). What sin has done is made us 'completely estranged' (*ibid.*) from that purpose.

Calvin begins his formal consideration of sin in Book 2 with a study of Adam's first sin in the Garden of Eden. What was the nature of that 'detestable crime' (2.1.4)? Calvin supplements Augustine's statement that 'pride was the beginning of all evils' with the observation that 'unfaithfulness ... was the root of the Fall' (*ibid.*). Ambition, pride and ingratitude closely followed in Adam's 'vile reproaches against God' (*ibid.*).

What are we to learn from Adam's sin in the Garden? Calvin draws out two practical observations. First, unbelief in God's Word results in our putting off 'all reverence' (*ibid.*) for God and the purity of his worship. Second, to deter sin we should always remember 'that nothing is better than to practise righteousness by obeying God's commandments; then, that the ultimate goal of the happy life is to be loved by him' (*ibid.*). May it be so for us.

GUY WATERS

2.1.5 - 2.1.8

Calvin self-consciously draws on Augustine as he explores further the meaning and effects of Adam's sin. Estrangement from his Maker, he says, was the death of Adam's soul (2.1.5). To make matters worse, he introduced the filth of sin and its rotten fruits not only to himself, but 'also entangled and immersed his offspring in the same miseries' (*ibid*.). When he sinned in the Garden, Adam lost the precious gifts which originally had been granted to the whole race. Says Calvin, 'when he was infected with sin, contagion crept into human nature' (2.1.7).

The Bible's diagnosis of every human being is devastating: from the point of our origin, we are polluted by sin. Calvin defines original sin as 'a hereditary depravity and corruption of our nature, diffused into all parts of the soul, which first makes us liable to God's wrath, then also brings forth in us those works which Scripture calls "works of the flesh"' (2.1.8). From the outset, therefore, we are corrupted in every part of our nature and stand justly condemned before God; and, from the outset, that corruption constantly bears 'new fruits' (*ibid*.). Original sin is more than a lack or deprivation of good. We are full of evil. To put it briefly, explains Calvin, 'the whole of man is of himself nothing but concupiscence' (*ibid*.).

The gurus of modern self-help peddle the view that man's basic problem is outside of himself, and that the solution lies within, in man's inner resources and hidden strength. That is not Calvin's position, because it is not the position of the Bible. For Calvin, man's problem lies squarely within his own constitution, and the solution therefore must come from outside of him. He summarizes it exactly in this way: 'guilt is of nature, but sanctification of supernatural grace' (2.1.7).

IAIN CAMPBELL

2.1.9 - 2.2.3

The so-called 'Five Points of Calvinism' were formulated by Calvin's followers. But were Calvin to explain the first of the five, he would likely say that the 'total' in 'total depravity' means that 'the whole man is overwhelmed — as by a deluge — from head to foot, so that no part is immune from sin and all that proceeds from him is to be imputed to sin' (2.1.9). The sin that is ours from the beginning of our existence invades and pervades every aspect of our being.

This is not to say that sin is any part of the definition of our divinely created humanness. We dare not, Calvin says, search out God's handiwork in our own pollution (2.1.10). It is in our fallen condition that our nature is deranged and degenerate. But the wound was not there from the beginning. It was inflicted, but it was inflicted by our own sin. Man, consequently, is 'corrupted through natural vitiation, but a vitiation that did not flow from nature' (2.1.11). Hence, God may not be blamed for our sin (*cf.* Eccles. 7:28).

Calvin's distinction between our original versus fallen states is necessary to maintain the true meaning of, for example, Paul's claim that we are all 'by nature children of wrath' (Eph. 2:3). This does not mean that the nature with which our Maker endowed us at the outset was objectionable to himself, or that our sin reflects some flaw in his original design. But it does mean that sin is now our natural condition, and it exists through no fault but our own.

Next Calvin will illustrate the 'total'-ness of this corruption with reference to man's loss of free will. Care is needed to explore this issue lest, on the one hand, we provide an excuse for ourselves by emphasizing our lack of power, and, on the other hand, rob God of his glory by crediting ourselves with too much. We have nothing of which to boast. The poverty of our fallen condition ought to leave us seeking the glory of the God whose grace alone is equal to our need.

IAIN CAMPBELL

2.2.4 - 2.2.7

What is free will?

Some theologians, according to Calvin, have come too close to philosophers who credit the will with too much. There is always a perennial temptation to try to make theology agree with the prevailing philosophy, and Calvin accuses some of the Church Fathers of following trends too far in this direction by teaching either that man's sensual appetites were corrupted but his will was not, or else teaching that man remains partially alive to spiritual things, despite having lost certain supernatural endowments.

Confusion over this issue remains because 'few have defined what free will is' (2.2.4). Definitions of free will among the Church Fathers have varied, but Calvin credits Augustine for at least highlighting the necessity of grace: man's will chooses what is good when empowered by divine grace, but chooses evil when grace is absent. In developing this idea, some taught that man's will was free in things not pertaining to God, but in need of grace in order to choose that which pleases God.

But is this really the case? Can man, on his own, ever choose what is good? To get round the difficulties inherent in these questions, some have suggested that God's grace prompts us to choose the good, and then co-operates with us in doing it. Calvin still sees this as giving too much latitude to man's own power of choice.

The reality is that man is a slave to sin, and as long as man's will remains under the corrupting power of sin, he will choose to do that which is contrary to the will of God. He rejects God necessarily, but does so willingly.

So, you may ask: is man's will free? By his own corrupt desires, says Calvin, the natural man is free only to sin every time. The sinner's freedom is a horrible one. No wonder Calvin asks: 'What purpose is served by labelling with a proud name such a slight thing?' (2.2.7).

IAIN CAMPBELL

2.2.8 - 2.2.11

Calvin's debt to Augustine is seen most clearly as in the discussion on free will. Of all the theologians who have gone before him, he finds Augustine's statements on the will to be biblical and pastorally significant.

Augustine's doctrine of fallen man turns upon the comprehensive nature of the captivity and bondage of the will. Not that man's bondage can excuse his sin. Quite the contrary — man's self-ruin by sin is the greatest evidence of his culpability. Consequently, what grace has not freed remains enslaved for ever, and man remains guilty for ever. The will, under the power of sin, freely and necessarily chooses what is contrary to the will of God. Only under the power of grace can the will, freely and necessarily, yield to God.

Man's knowledge of himself includes the knowledge of his enslavement and bondage to sin. Indeed, it is part of the purpose of Scripture so to denude us and to rob us of any ground of self-boasting and of self-confidence. It is said of God that he gives strength to the weak; and the operation of his grace brings that weakness home to us. Any notion of our own power or strength robs God of his honour, while God is most honoured when grace robs us of our boasting.

There is a lesson for the Christian here: it is equally foolish for sin-enslaved people to speak of the freedom of their wills, as it is for grace-liberated people to speak of their own strength of choice.

There is only one fitting response, says Calvin, when we have gazed into the mirror of Scripture and seen our true reflection: humility, humility, humility!

IAIN CAMPBELL

2.2.12 - 2.2.17

Grace restores what it did not take away. The restoration, therefore, of love to God and neighbour, or zeal for holiness and righteousness, implies the loss of them by original sin. These supernatural gifts were lost in the Fall. But our natural endowments were also compromised, so that they are not focused on the honour of God as they ought to be.

Our reason, for example, is a natural endowment, and cannot be taken from us. Human beings are rational creatures. We are not brute beasts. This is one arena in which our nobility in the created realm glitters, but it is shrouded in darkness. Man searches out his environment with a longing for truth; yet his mind stumbles on in darkness, unwilling to embrace or recognize truth. This is what left Solomon's search for wisdom, divorced from God, to be 'vanity of vanities' (Eccles. 1:2).

It is not that man is entirely without ability. Calvin mentions 'government, household management, mechanical skills and all liberal arts' (2.2.13) as tasks in which man has achieved much — even in the darkness. There are exceptions, of course, but, generally speaking, man is able to find his way around God's world, as one might find one's way round a darkened room.

What accounts for man's natural ability in the arts and science but 'the peculiar grace of God' (2.2.14)? Human competence in these areas is to be attributed specifically to the workings of God's *Spirit*. The Holy Spirit dwells in believers alone as Sanctifier; but, says Calvin, he 'fills, moves and quickens' (2.2.16) unbelievers to develop genius in the arts and in sciences, and we ought to respect them for it. The difference is that God is not glorified in the pursuit of these natural gifts. Depravity does not mean that we can do nothing; but it does mean that what we can do is liable to be done without any deference to the honour of the Creator.

Whether we call this 'the general grace of God' or God's special grace 'in common nature', it is evident that the natural endowments of fallen man evidence 'some remaining traces of the image of God' (2.2.17). Slaves we may be, but we are noble ones. Image bearers we certainly are; but we are in bondage to sin.

IAIN CAMPBELL

2.2.18 - 2.2.21

Having considered the knowledge of 'earthly matters' that reason can attain by God's common grace (2.2.13-16), Calvin argues that knowledge about 'heavenly matters' consists in three things: knowing God; knowing his fatherly favour on our behalf; and knowing how to frame our lives according to his law (2.2.18). Spiritual insight into these matters does not come through reason alone or even reason coupled with God's general grace. Rather, this knowledge becomes possible only when our minds have been made new by the illumination of the Holy Spirit (2.2.20).

With his emphasis upon the work of the Spirit, it is easy to see why Calvin has long been called 'the theologian of the Holy Spirit'. A generation later, John Owen was called the same. And yet few of our theologians and ministers today would bear that title. We often talk about God either in terms of the whole Godhead, God the Father, or, especially, Jesus; we recognize that our justification and sanctification come by grace. Yet we fail to recognize that it is God the Holy Spirit whose 'wonderful and singular power forms our ears to hear and our minds to understand' (2.2.20) and our wills to act.

How often do we pray for the Holy Spirit to accompany his Word to change people's hearts as it is read and preached? How often do we pray for the Spirit to dispel the darkness in the hearts of our loved ones, neighbours and friends? Do we really believe that 'wherever the Spirit does not cast his light, all is darkness' (2.2.21)?

SEAN LUCAS

2.2.22 - 2.2.27

Humans want to carve out some place for their own natural abilities when it comes to doings works that conform to God's law. Ethicists will sometimes talk about 'natural law', an inbred standard of right and wrong that is common to all people everywhere. Calvin knows the category of natural law, but defines it a bit differently: 'natural law is that apprehension of the conscience which distinguishes sufficiently between just and unjust, and which deprives men of the excuse of ignorance, while it proves them guilty by their own testimony' (2.2.22).

The first part of Calvin's definition is generally accepted: natural law is that part of human conscience that distinguishes right from wrong. But Calvin then moves in a more radical direction — natural law is not simply a standard to which one might attain for ethical life; rather, it leaves all humans everywhere guilty before God. Even if human beings could outwardly conform by nature to the two tables of the Ten Commandments, 'they take no account of the evil desires that gently tickle the mind' (2.2.24).

The problem is not the standard; rather, the problem is lodged in the human heart. Our mind refuses to heed warnings; self-interest excuses our worst sins; our reason is corrupted and subject to vanity.

It is this self-knowledge — the awareness of the depths of our blindness and darkness of heart — that should cause us to cry out to God in humility for his mercy. It should also cause us to recognize that anything good in us or our world is God's own work; and 'nothing is ours but sin' (2.2.27).

SEAN LUCAS

2.3.1 - 2.3.5

One key Reformation teaching which both Lutherans and Reformed held in common was the pervasive and inherited corruption of human nature. In this, Calvin was no different. He notes that the Bible 'painted a picture of human nature that showed us corrupt and perverted in every part' (2.3.1); 'the whole race of Adam's children' is characterized by 'the unvarying corruption of our nature' (2.3.2); and 'because of the bondage of sin by which the will is held bound, it cannot move toward good' (2.3.5).

Calvin affirmed this view of human beings not because he was a gloomy pessimist, but because he wanted to highlight the amazing graciousness of God and his powerful love for his chosen ones. In the midst of his descriptions of human sinfulness, there are notes of hopefulness and pointers toward the remedy: 'the grace of Christ is the sole remedy to free us from that blindness and from the evils consequent upon it' (2.3.1); the Bible teaches that 'only God's mercy can deliver' sinners from the 'unavoidable calamity' of sin that overwhelms them; and that 'the beginning of conversion to God' is 'ascribed entirely to God's grace' (2.3.5).

One lesson to take from this is that, only as the church has a thorough and experienced sense of human depravity will she preach the fulness and exclusivity of God's grace. Returning again to 'total depravity' will cause us to long for God's mercy and enliven our praise of God's steadfast love.

SEAN LUCAS

2.3.6 - 2.3.9

In this section, Calvin unpacks this statement: 'God begins his good work in us, therefore, by arousing love and desire and zeal for righteousness in our hearts; or, to speak more correctly, by bending, forming, and directing, our hearts to righteousness. He completes his work, moreover, by confirming us in righteousness' (2.3.6).

In the light of the thoroughness of human depravity, our only hope is God's grace coming to us from the outside and moving in. God must begin this renewing work and he must continue it in us. He must give us a new heart (Ezek. 36:26-27), a new will, good works, and a longing for righteousness. All our spiritual good, therefore, comes not from ourselves but from him alone (2.3.8). But God not only begins this work and sustains this work; by his grace, he also brings it to completion at the end of our days (Phil. 1:6). The result is that God is 'the author of spiritual life from beginning to end' (2.3.6).

Are you willing to bid farewell to your own labours, sufficiency, powers, abilities and performance in order to rest completely on God's working in and through us? Have you come to the end of your own sufficiency in order to rest on the sufficiency of the triune God's work for, in and through you (2 Cor. 2:14 - 3:6)? Will you stop robbing God of his rightful glory by claiming anything for yourself in your spiritual choices or accomplishments? Will you sing the riches of God's grace?

SEAN LUCAS

2.3.10 - 2.3.14

What makes God's grace so gracious? For Calvin, behind all grace is God's own determination to act: 'The apostle does not teach that the grace of a good will is bestowed upon us if we accept it, but that he wills to work in us. This means nothing else than that the Lord by his Spirit directs, bends, and governs, our heart and reigns in it as in his own possession' (2.3.10).

Because God is the one who starts the work of grace in our hearts, he is also the one who will bring it to conclusion. As Calvin notes, perseverance must be accounted God's free gift (2.3.11) together with election, effectual calling, justification, sanctification and adoption. It is all of grace from beginning to end.

What is the 'end result' in ascribing all to God's grace? The glory of God, for one. But also remember that Calvin is trying to persuade us to embrace genuine piety — that reverence joined with love of God which the knowledge of his benefits induces (1.2.1). Only by correctly appraising his benefits offered freely and graciously to us may we truly live piously, reverencing and loving God with our entire beings.

So, the real question is whether we delight in and cherish the grace of God. Is our song, 'Grace, grace' from beginning to end? Do we magnify God's grace in our personal and corporate worship? With our children? In our world view? In the workplace? If every benefit we have comes from God's hand and choice, then we must be the most grateful people in the world.

SEAN LUCAS

2.4.1 - 2.4.6

How do we make sense of evil? And, more specifically, how do we make sense of the evil that human beings perpetrate against one another? Who is the responsible agent? If American comedian Red Skelton were here, or — for younger members of the audience — American TV's pious 'Churchlady', from *Saturday Night Live*, the answer would come back as Satan. Or is it ourselves? Or is it God?

In these first paragraphs of Chapter 4 Calvin takes up this difficult and knotty question. His answer might surprise us as he comes back with another alternative; that is, all of the above. God, Satan, and even we, are all active in events. Calvin uses a difficult example: the slaughter of Job's servants as they were guarding his camels (Job 1:17). God is behind this event. Then again, Satan is behind it, too. And, yet again, the Chaldeans are also behind it. But then Calvin quickly adds that all of the respective actions are quite different, springing from quite different motives. In the case at hand, God sought to sanctify Job; Satan wanted to persecute him; the Chaldeans planned to rob him. Calvin concludes: 'Therefore we see no inconsistency in assigning the same deed to God, Satan, and man; but the distinction in purpose and manner causes God's righteousness to shine forth blameless there, while the wickedness of Satan and of man betrays itself by its own disgrace' (2.4.2).

Calvin observes that many shrink back from addressing this hard issue, noting that even Augustine was a bit wary here (2.4.3). Calvin counters by bringing up biblical texts for a guide. God, various portions of Scripture tell us, blinds, hardens, turns, inclines and impels (2.4.3.) human hearts. In God's grand scheme, even the actions of hardened hearts are in his hands, and yet his righteousness shines forth in it all.

STEPHEN NICHOLS

2.4.7 - 2.5.3

'The king's heart is a stream of water in the hand of the LORD; he turns it wherever he will' (Prov. 21:1).

In this section, Calvin again raises the difficult question of human freedom. He begins by stressing God's dominion. 'If the king's will is bent by God's hand,' Calvin understands the Proverb to argue, 'our wills are not exempt from that condition' (2.4.7). Of course, not everyone quite agrees with Calvin, prompting him to address objections in Chapter 5. In the process, Calvin harks back to the debates between Augustine and Pelagius, which popped up again between Luther and Erasmus, and actually seem to reappear wherever theological conversations take place. The same objections are voiced today and are aptly answered by Calvin.

The first objection is a syllogism: if sin is a necessity, done automatically and not freely, it is not sin; if it is voluntary, and we are free to do it or not to do it, then sin may be avoided. That is the alleged argument in 2.5.1. The second objection holds that 'unless virtues and vices proceed from the free choice of the will, it is not consistent that man be either punished or rewarded' (2.5.2). Then, there is the third objection, that without free will, human beings must be either all bad or all good (2.5.3).

The first two are the most troubling. They have the net effect of asking: how can God hold us responsible, or reward us for that matter, if we are not free? This cannot be answered in a one-page reading, but here is a start: none of us really wants what we deserve. None of us actually wants the 'reward' for what we too often willingly do. Thankfully, God 'bestows undeserved grace' (2.5.2).

STEPHEN NICHOLS

2.5.4 - 2.5.8

The next argument for an unbiblical view of free will involves exhortations or commands. It asks the question: 'What good is any moral instruction if we are not free?'

In my reading of Pelagius this concern seems to drive him the most in his debates with Augustine. How can I hold people accountable? How can I expect anything of them if they are not free? These questions by Pelagius brought about Augustine's *On Rebuke and Grace* and *On the Spirit and the Letter.* These questions elicit from Calvin some rather helpful ideas on obedience, what we might call 'sanctification', or 'spiritual formation'.

First, Calvin points to our moral inability due to sin, which in turn points us to Christ. John 15:5 has it fairly direct: '...apart from me you can do nothing'. Paul chimes in too, at 1 Corinthians 3:3; 3:7; and 16:14; Romans 9:16; and also at Philippians 4:13 (see 2.5.4). No amount of exhorting, cajoling or demanding will make a person holy; God must move the heart.

Next, Calvin examines the nature and purpose of exhortations. They serve a confirming purpose on the reprobate, 'to press them with the witness of conscience' (2.5.5) and leave them without excuse before God. Contrarily, they serve a convicting and chastising purpose on the elect. In this latter case, we are drawn away from ourselves to God's graciousness and to Christ's work on the cross. Calvin again turns to the words of his friend Augustine: 'Faith achieves what the law commands' (2.5.7).

Do you say, by God's grace, 'Oh how I love your law!' (Ps. 119:97)?

STEPHEN NICHOLS

2.5.9 - 2.5.12

Long before Benjamin Franklin said that God helps those who help themselves, others had said it too. This becomes another argument in favour of free will that we, through our own obedience, contribute to our salvation. Calvin responds: 'It is pointless to require in us the capacity to fulfil the law, just because the Lord demands our obedience to it, when it is clear that for the fulfilment of all God's commands the grace of the Lawgiver is both necessary and is promised to us' (2.5.9).

Yet another objection comes in 2.5.10, that Scripture allegedly teaches that the realization of certain promises is contingent upon our choice and ability to obey. After all, hasn't God said, 'If you obey my voice...'? Calvin answers: 'The greater our desire for righteousness, the more fervent we become to seek God's grace' (2.5.11). When we hear God's commands, only the Spirit can 'direct us into the right path' (*ibid.*).

The next objection looks at the opposite of the previous one, God's reproach of people, so the argument goes, stems from their own fault through their own actions by their own free will. God would not hold people accountable who were in bondage to sin. Calvin retorts by simply pointing to the perversity of the will: 'Let them therefore answer whether they can deny that the cause of their obstinacy was their own perverse will' (2.5.11), which is to say that sinners are bound to sin by their own corruption.

In all three of these sections I find it interesting that Calvin finds a place for the word 'grace'. That, coupled with his concluding reference to the gospel in 2.5.12, shows us his priority in these debates. The view that we contribute to our salvation at the very least weakens — Calvin would say nullifies — God's grace. And that just isn't a good place to be, theologically or spiritually.

STEPHEN NICHOLS

2.5.13 - 2.5.17

Objections still remain to Calvin's view of free will. Such is the stubbornness of the human heart. The first is raised in 2.5.13: what about the biblical passages where God leaves us to our own devices, such as Hosea 5:15: 'I will return again to my place, until they acknowledge their guilt and seek my face'? Calvin points out that how we understand texts (like this one) that speak to the interaction between God and his people is crucial. It could very well be, Calvin explains, that God withdraws (in the case of Hosea 5, he points out that the withdrawal concerns the withholding of prophecy) in order 'to make us more humble' (*ibid.*). God may temporarily hide his face for a time not to bring out our ability, but our inability. So Calvin says, 'For he does it for no other purpose than to compel us to recognize our own nothingness' (2.5.13).

Another set of texts concerns the reference to 'our' works, as if they originate in us. Calvin steps in to say that they are 'ours' only insofar as they are God's gifts to us. These works are not of our doing, but are done 'out of [God's] lovingkindness' (2.5.15), at work in us. Calvin closes by adding, 'we are with good reason said to do those things the praise for which God rightly claims for himself' (2.5.15).

There has been a lot of raising and refuting of objections (and there is more to come in the next reading!). One could rightly ask why; what's all the fuss? Calvin seems to be pursuing one thing — an understanding of the human will and human ability that is faithful to Scripture and preserves the biggest room possible for God's grace. Not everyone will be convinced by Calvin's arguments for his view of free will. But, seeking a capacious place for grace in our theology strikes me as a worthwhile task for us all.

STEPHEN NICHOLS

2.5.18 - 2.6.2

Ready or not, more arguments against Calvin's view of free will emerge. One comes from Ecclesiasticus (note: not Ecclesiastes!) which Calvin, knowing it to be of dubious authority as an apocryphal document, nevertheless patiently answers, viewing this text as supportive of his point of view even if it is apocryphal. Even here, though, the Word of God remains central to his case.

The next one is Luke 10:30, contained in a parable in which thieves set a man down half-alive on the road. So, some conclude, we must be spiritually 'half-alive' (2.5.19). Calvin's comment is fascinating: first, he dismisses allegorical interpretation and adds that to base a doctrine on an allegory is entirely false as a rule for interpreting Scripture. But even if he conceded the allegory — that man still retains some vestiges of his created-ness (such as wisdom and honesty) — he sides with Augustine: 'the free goods upon which salvation depends were taken away from man after the Fall, while the natural endowments were corrupted and defiled' (*ibid*.).

So, if man's will is not free to choose salvation, what hope has he? Only in the provision of a Mediator, is Calvin's answer. We need cross-centred preaching. Through the foolishness of the preaching of the cross (1 Cor. 1:21) sinners unable to save themselves may find hope.

Nothing in my hands I bring,
Simply to Thy cross I cling.

The necessity of the cross is true whether we are talking about the Old Covenant or New Covenant. Here (at 2.6.2) is Calvin's genius as a covenant theologian: the same way of salvation operates in both testaments, since there is one covenant of grace operating in both periods of redemptive history: '...apart from the Mediator, God never showed favour toward the ancient people, nor ever gave hope of grace to them'; and 'since God cannot without the Mediator be propitious toward the human race, under the law Christ was always set forth before the holy fathers as the end to which they should direct their faith' (2.6.2). No place for 'Dispensationalism' here!

DEREK THOMAS

2.6.3 - 2.7.1

Here we have more Christ-centred hermeneutics from Calvin: in short, what is seen in the New Testament is promised in the Old; that by covenant (mentioned five times in 2.6.3 alone) God administers salvation by one means — 'the hope of all the godly has ever reposed in Christ alone' (2.6.3); 'apart from Christ the saving knowledge of God does not stand' (2.6.4); 'from the beginning of the world he ... set before the elect that they should look unto him and put their trust in him' (2.6.4); 'God is comprehended in Christ alone' (2.6.4). No matter how much we may talk about God, all talk of him outside of his revelation to us in Christ (as in Islam) is idolatry.

Calvin adds that Christ was particularly anticipated in the time of Moses. The addition of the law four hundred years after the death of Abraham (citing Gal. 3:17) did not annul the principle of grace operating under the Abrahamic covenant; rather 'it was as if [Moses] were sent to renew it' (2.7.1). However, there is no 'renewal of a covenant of works under a Mosaic covenant' for Calvin, but rather, a continuation of the *one* gracious administration of the covenant established with Abraham and fulfilled in Jesus Christ. Under Moses, the sacrifices served as 'types' (2.7.1), foreshadowing the coming Mediator.

It is also here that Calvin introduces us to one of his telltale signatures: God has 'accommodated himself to our little measure lest our minds be overwhelmed by the immensity of his glory' (2.6.4). What we know of God we know only in part, only to the extent to which he has revealed himself, and even *that* revelation is just so much 'baby-talk'. We must always remember that it is so.

In Christ alone... is Calvin's theme in these pages. We do well to heed his certainty.

DEREK THOMAS

2.7.2 - 2.7.7

Calvin reads the whole Bible together: the covenant with David stands in a line of continuity with Moses, and the entirety as a preparation for the coming of Christ. Dealing again with the law, Calvin walks between the (Lutheran) Scylla — that the sole purpose of the law is to instruct and convict us, and so lead us to Christ (what Calvin calls the *narrow sense*; 'Christ is the end of the law for righteousness to everyone who believes' [Rom. 10:4]) — and the Charybdis, where the law merely functions as a moral guide for the Christian life ('graced with the covenant of free adoption' [2.7.2]).

Taking the former sense, Calvin outdoes Luther: 'they [i.e., the curses of the broken law] hang over ... and pursue us with inexorable harshness, so that we discern in the law only the most immediate death' (2.7.3). And in language that sounds as though Calvin believed in the perpetuity of the covenant of works, he affirms that 'the reward of eternal salvation awaits complete obedience to the law' *(ibid.)*. Given that we cannot fulfil the law's demands, are the promises empty and insincere? Not at all — and here Calvin anticipates what he will later say of justification by faith — God provides One who obeys the law *on our behalf* and 'causes us to receive the benefit of the promises of the law as if we had fulfilled their condition' (2.7.4).

Elaborating further on the doctrinal function of the law, Calvin writes that the law 'shows God's righteousness' and 'condemns ... every man of his own unrighteousness' (2.7.6). Those who dare to deny their status as guilty are proud or insane. Just as mirrors show the spots on our face, the law functions as a mirror in which we contemplate our weakness. Here Calvin shows personal acquaintance with the deceptiveness of sin: 'There is no doubt that the more clearly the conscience is struck with awareness of its sin, the more the iniquity grows. For stubborn disobedience against the Lawgiver is then added to transgression' (2.7.7).

How Calvin knows my heart!

DEREK THOMAS

2.7.8 - 2.7.13

The pedagogic (and first) use of law is to 'shut our mouths' (*cf.* Rom. 3:19), not to lead us to utter despair, as is the case with the reprobate, but to lead us to Christ: 'But in Christ [God's] face shines, full of grace and gentleness, even upon us poor and unworthy sinners' (2.7.8). This is true not just for unbelievers as they first come to Christ but for believers too.

The second use of the law is as a civil code so that 'hindered by fright or shame, they dare neither execute what they have conceived in their minds, nor openly breathe forth the rage of their lust' (2.7.10). In this way, God's grants grace to entire societies.

The third ('principal', 'proper') use of law 'finds its place among believers in whose hearts the Spirit of God already lives and reigns' (2.7.12). Though we can never keep it as it demands, we should not be 'frightened away' (2.7.13). We must see this life of ours in Christ as 'a race' (1 Cor. 9:24-26); 'when its course has been run, the Lord will grant us to attain that goal to which our efforts now press forward from afar' (2.7.13). Thus, in the *Genevan Catechism*, Calvin asked: 'What is the rule of life which [God] has given us?' and replied, 'His law.' In this race, the law exhorts, encourages, and sometimes, even among believers, it functions as whip: 'The law is to the flesh like a whip to an idle and baulky ass, to arouse it to work. Even for a spiritual man not yet free of the weight of the flesh the law remains a constant sting that will not let him stand still' (2.7.12).

Calvin has only just begun to expound on the law's function in the Christian life, but already we sense the magnitude of what he is saying. He was to see detractors in his day as we see in our own. Nevertheless, may we say, with Paul, that the law is holy, righteous and good (Rom. 7:12).

DEREK THOMAS

2.7.14 - 2.8.1

The obligation to keep the law as believers seems to many too legalistic and contrary to the gospel. Antinomianism has ever been an issue; to confront it, Calvin notes Jesus' words that he did not come to 'abolish the Law ... but to fulfil [it]' (Matt. 5:17) and sets out to distinguish 'what in the law has been abrogated' and 'what still remains' (2.7.14).

First, says Calvin, the law no longer condemns believers, for condemn it would, apart from perfect obedience. But Christ has redeemed us from the curse of the law, taking the law's curse upon himself: Christ was made subject to the law that he might 'redeem those who were under the law' (Gal. 4:5). There is no more condemnation if we are hidden in him (Rom. 8:1).

Second, the ceremonial law has been abrogated 'not in effect but only in use' (2.7.16); meaning that the ceremonies still function as they did under the old covenant — in pointing to Christ who, by his death, 'sealed their force and effect' (*ibid.*).

Third, Calvin suggests that the 'written bond against us' (2.7.17) has been wiped clean. Calvin interprets the phrase in Colossians 2:13-14 — 'cancelling the record of debt that stood against us with its legal demands' — in this way: Paul understands that Jews under the Old Testament engaged in the ceremonies, not to receive forgiveness of sins through them, but merely as a testimony to their guilt. Forgiveness came through anticipation of the Mediator to which they pointed. Such ceremonies attested to the people's sins but could do nothing to blot them out (Heb. 10:4). Such legal bonds against us have now been abolished.

At this point Calvin moves to an exposition of that which endures, namely, the moral law of God. We ought to have known this from the law that is written on the hearts of all men, he says, but sin has so marred us that God has provided a 'written law to give us a clearer witness of what was too obscure in the natural law' (2.8.1).

His law teaches us how to live as redeemed children.

DEREK THOMAS

2.8.2 - 2.8.7

John Calvin is full of surprises.

As he comes to expound the Decalogue (the third longest chapter in the work, after his expositions of Prayer and the Lord's Supper), how will the master biblical theologian introduce the God of the law? Answer: as Creator who has the place of Father and Lord in our lives — as the One to whom, put simply, we owe everything. His law teaches us how to live in his will as the children we don't deserve to be. If only we understood things as clearly as that!

Is this Calvin gone soft? Far from it. He speaks into a situation of tragedy. Our ability to keep God's law is 'utterly nonexistent' (2.8.3). But the tragedy is not unmitigated. For our failure drives us to God's mercy. And Calvin's God — no, Moses' God, the God and Father of our Lord Jesus — stoops down low in kindness to help us. Therein lies the rationale for the promised rewards and threatened punishments that attend the law.

Calvin's references to God's 'great kindness' and his 'benevolence' in 2.8.4 remind us that the *Institutes* is written by a child of God for the children of God. But we are children of GOD — whose law reaches beyond outward action to heart-motivation. Calvin will not allow us to fall into the abyss of legalism, which always separates the law of God from the person of God. We do not understand the law or please God through it apart from personal (rather than formal) and relational (rather than abstract) obedience to the Father.

That is why — as Calvin everywhere shows — in the hands of our Lord Jesus the meaning of the law is restored to its original integrity.

SINCLAIR FERGUSON

2.8.8 - 2.8.14

There is more to obedience to God's commandments than meets the eye! Calvin's reason? The law is full of synecdoche.

Synecdoche? — that un-spellable figure of speech from high school English in which the whole of something is used to refer to a part, or a part is used to designate the whole. In other words (actually Calvin's): 'He who would confine his understanding of the law within the narrowness of the words deserves to be laughed at' (2.8.8). If it were not so sad, Calvin would have a good chortle to himself.

But Calvin never laughs with a lofty spirit. He wants to help us understand how to use the law. Here, then, are two simple Calvin-principles for reading the Decalogue:

1. Ask: What is the reason for this commandment?
2. Ask: What is the grace or pattern of obedience which stands in antithesis to the sin which is forbidden? Learn that it is this which pleases God

Unintentionally Calvin here gives us a clue as to why he was such a superb interpreter of Scripture. He asked the simple question: 'What is the point here?' Thus the point of 'Do not kill' is not merely to forbid the outward act of murder; the command carries in its bosom the responsibility to do all we can to help our neighbour.

Why then express the commandments this way? God emphasizes the worst expressions of a sin ('murder'), Calvin says, to warn us about the true nature of what may seem to us to be lesser expressions.

The Decalogue comes in two tables: Commandments One to Four deal with our relation to God; Commandments Five to Ten relate to man, his image. This is the gospel order: worship is the foundation for ethics, godliness is the foundation for righteousness. And to encourage his people to holiness, God 'attracts them with sweetness by declaring himself God of the Church' (2.8.14). He is not only Lawgiver. He is the Lord *our God*.

SINCLAIR FERGUSON

How misunderstood the Law of Moses has been! It begins with and is grounded in — grace. Always! For the exodus from Egypt was but the foreshadowing of the greater exodus of gospel deliverance in Christ. This is why, says Calvin, 'There is no one, I say, who ought not to be captivated to embrace the Lawgiver, in the observance of whose commandments he is taught to take especial delight' (2.8.15).

'Captivated'!

Thus the First Commandment calls us to adoration, trust, invocation, thanksgiving. It compels us 'to drive away all invented gods' (2.8.16). But it also provides us with a powerful motivation. God bids us to have no other gods 'before my face' any more than a woman would bring her adulterous lover before her husband's eyes.

The Second Commandment follows and calls us to purity in worship. Our hearts, Calvin has taught us, following Ezekiel, are a 'perpetual factory of idols' (1.11.8). God is a jealous husband, 'unable to bear any partner' (2.8.18) — and rightly so. We are called to spiritual chastity.

But how can the jealous husband be a righteous husband if he visits the sins of men on the third and fourth generations of their family? This, for Calvin, is not an arbitrary phenomenon. It is how life is, how God has constituted the blessing of family. Ungodly parents breathe their ungodliness into their children. Their children breathe the air in and follow their example, breathing their ungodliness into the next generation — unless God graciously intervenes.

Observation of the world teaches us that this is so. How strange, then, that parents do not learn the lesson from observation, never mind from biblical instruction. But — like some smokers who have become so accustomed to the atmosphere they enjoy — all such parents do is protest that God should have the audacity to find this atmosphere polluted and then, sometimes when family life disintegrates, they blame him for not doing something about it.

SINCLAIR FERGUSON

Ungodly people always take the higher ground when arguing with God and the lower ground when living their own lives. Is God unjust to visit iniquities on successive generations? On the contrary, Calvin argues, we are all responsible human beings and are punished for our own offences (Ezek. 18:20). Note how he states this plainly: 'They perish by their own iniquity, not by any unjust hatred on God's part ... Nor does it accord with God's justice for a righteous son to pay the penalty for a wicked father, and this is not implied in the present threat...' (2.8.20).

Note, too, the abundance of God's contrasting mercy: God remembers the faithful to a thousand generations! No wonder, then, that Calvin moves seamlessly on to the Third Commandment. In the light of such favour, who would treat God's name lightly? Rather we seek to honour it greatly.

This Third Commandment, Calvin reminds us, applies to our thoughts as well as our words, and summons us to three things:

1. To 'savour' (2.8.22) God's excellence. Enough said!
2. To honour God's Word and his ordinances.
3. To praise all his works.

How beautifully simple is the life that pleases God.

Does Jesus' exposition of this command prohibit oath-taking (as many of Calvin's Anabaptist contemporaries and Quaker forerunners insisted)? On the contrary, says Calvin — remember the intention of the command. What is forbidden is the vain use of God's Name through the hypocritical swearing by something other than God as an escape hatch. In Jesus' command not to 'take an oath at all' (Matt. 5:34), the 'not ... at all' refers to the forms of casual oaths, not to the God-sanctioned principle of calling him to witness one's integrity. Public oaths are usually safest, but in every case simplicity in Christ will not be led astray by 'wily sophistry' (2.8.26)!

SINCLAIR FERGUSON

Calvin's thoughts on the Sabbath are the 'Continental view'! 'The purpose of this commandment is that, being dead to our own inclinations and works, we should meditate on the Kingdom of God...' (2.8.28).

There are three facets for Calvin in 'the keeping of this commandment' (*ibid.*):

1. By spiritual rest. Believers ought to lay aside all their own works in order to allow God to work in them.
2. As a stated day for worship and meditation. It was given as a day for training in piety.
3. As a day to provide physical rest.

How, then, are we to receive this commandment in Jesus Christ? To begin with, Christ fulfils the Sabbath. What was foreshadowed in the Sabbath is now given in substance and reality to those who have come to him to find 'rest' (Matt. 11:28-30). 'This is not confined within a single day, but extends throughout the whole course of our life...' (2.8.31). Therefore, 'Christians ought ... to shun completely the superstitious observance of days' (2.8.31).

Yet, for Calvin, points 2 and 3 above remain. A Genevan Sunday was, therefore, rather different from that of many contemporary congregations that lay claim to 'the Continental view of the Sabbath'. In fact, Calvin was accused of nourishing people in Judaism (2.8.33)!

For Calvin, there is no twenty-four-hour time slot more inherently holy than any other; just as there is no place or space that is more inherently holy than another. In that respect 'holy space' and 'holy time' are fulfilled in Christ.

But a day for worship and meditation has not been reduced to a morning. Nor has the commandment been rescinded that calls us to do everything within our power to allow others to rest. So 'Why should we not obey the order laid upon us by God's will?' (2.8.32).

SINCLAIR FERGUSON

2.8.33 - 2.8.38

Calvin's understanding of the Fourth Commandment is notably restrained. Its present application has chiefly to do with the ordering of public worship at a set time, a time (or times) appropriately enough during the day of the Lord's resurrection. But we should remember that it must have a lenient or liberal tone, and not be superstitious. No day is more holy than any other, and so observance of the Lord's Day does not make that day more 'spiritual' than the others. If other churches make other arrangements, we ought not to fuss about it.

Calvin's treatment of this commandment, and of those that follow, reveals his general way of interpreting the law. None of them are to be interpreted in a restrictive way. We are not to keep the Lord's Day as if it alone is holy, but we should consecrate all our days to God. We are not to honour our father and mother as if they alone are worthy of honour, but we must include all those who are set over us in positions of authority. Honour to whom honour is due, fear to whom fear is due. 'By that subjection which is easiest to tolerate, the Lord therefore gradually accustoms us to all lawful subjection, since the reason of all is the same' — it is God who establishes 'the degrees of pre-eminence' in our relations (2.8.35). As with his treatment of the Sabbath day, Calvin blends the teaching of the Testaments. Obedience to those in authority is only to be 'in the Lord' (Eph. 6:1), though elsewhere he is notably cautious on the legitimacy of civil disobedience.

Regarding the promise attached to the Fifth Commandment and its implied threat, obedience to authority does not guarantee long life, despite the promise (*cf.* Eph. 6:2), but it entails divine blessing, which a long life may or may not express. Similarly, the implied threat does not ensure shortness of life, but a life 'bereft of blessing' (2.8.38). In either case, God's Word is sure.

PAUL HELM

2.8.39 - 2.8.46

The commands forbidding murder and adultery are, if anything, interpreted with a wide scope by Calvin. The command not to kill implies not merely a refraining from certain kinds of action, but carries the obligation to look out for a neighbour's welfare. The command also reaches inward, extending godly acting and refraining to the heart. Expressions of anger and feelings of hatred toward someone are intentions to do harm. Why are such attitudes evil? Because, Calvin says, 'man is both the image of God, and our flesh' (2.8.40).

Similarly, the command forbidding adultery also forbids all immodesty and impurity. Here Calvin displays a positive view of marriage beyond the purpose of procreation. Marriage is for the enjoyment of mutual help and companionship (2.8.41). Characteristically he advises that while the chastity of celibacy is a gift for some, it does not elevate such people to a class superior to those who marry. Celibacy is warranted only because it may provide greater opportunity for carrying out the Lord's work. Those to whom God withholds this gift must seek marriage as the 'sole remedy' (2.8.43) for resisting unchastity. The forbidding of fornication also includes the forbidding of what may promote or provoke it 'with wanton dress and obscene gestures and foul speech' (2.8.44).

Calvin's remarks on the forbidding of stealing are similarly wide in scope, and they reveal Calvin's rather stratified, rigid view of society in which every man's place and possessions come by the appointment of God. He is not an advocate of 'upward mobility', though he does not oppose gain, if it is honestly and lawfully obtained. In Christian ethics, whether in marriage or society at large, integrity and simplicity are what count.

PAUL HELM

2.8.47 - 2.8.52

Calvin's distinctive way of setting forth the true purpose of the law is now apparent. And so the Eighth Commandment ('You shall not bear false witness') goes beyond avoiding lies and includes having a general regard for truth and telling the truth, for God is truth. In our truth telling, we should aim to help others, to build them up, neither slandering them, nor speaking evil of them, nor deceiving them of what is lawfully theirs, including their good name. So — no jokes at another's expense if these have a tendency to drag him down, as they usually do.

Given his pattern thus far, Calvin strikes a different note regarding covetousness. He reckons that covetousness refers to the first workings of those desires that lead to the evil intentions to lie, to steal, to commit adultery, and all the rest. In this way the last commandment undergirds all the rest. Not only should we not act in accordance with our evil intentions, nor have such intentions, we should explicitly guard against the tendency we have to form them. This tendency is covetousness, the common denominator of all those sins forbidden in the Second Table. It is interesting that Calvin does not here mention the special place that the forbidding of covetousness has in Romans 7.

To sum up, keeping the law from the heart, embracing love to God and neighbour, has to do with the re-forming and the shining of the image of God in his people. One might even say that Calvin sees the law as an instrument for cultivating virtue toward God rather than a call to keep a set of rules. The fact that sometimes Scripture lays particular emphasis upon the Second Table should not lead us to think that the commandments of the First Table may be taken for granted.

PAUL HELM

Calvin's approach to the moral law is not moralistic but evangelical. Keeping the commands is to spring from the fear of God that the gospel engenders. For the Law and the Prophets give first place to faith towards God, but a faith that works itself out in love (Gal. 5:6).

In the remainder of this chapter, Calvin ties up some loose ends, though this does not mean that the ends are unimportant! The law has love for others, not the promotion of self-love, as its purpose (2.8.54); after all, we do not need any encouragement to promote ourselves. But who are these others? Certainly those near at hand, next to whom God has placed us. But also 'the whole human race without exception' (2.8.55).

Next Calvin deals with those who would shirk the law as mere counsel. We cannot opt out of the law, he says, nor do some people have a deeper obligation to keep the law than others, nor are some transgressions of the law less sinful than others, even though the social consequences of transgressing the law may differ. All sin is mortal, for all sin is a defiance of God whose law has been transgressed.

In these loose ends there is a common thread: Calvin is reluctant to leave any opportunity for partial or discriminatory ethical attitudes to arise; by thinking of ourselves before others, or some group (members of some school, or club, or class, or race, or church) before others, or some laws before others. To exercise such discretion, picking and choosing between this person or that, or this law or that, is to put in jeopardy that simplicity and integrity which is characteristic of a true love for God and his law.

PAUL HELM

2.9.1 - 2.9.5

Calvin now begins to emphasize what had become apparent in Chapter 8. There we saw that there is one law of God, as obligatory in the New Testament era as in the Mosaic era. So now he insists that there is one gospel of God's grace, anticipated in the Old Testament and clearly revealed in the New. Calvin's language emphasizes that the difference across the testaments is one of degree: in contrast to Moses, the gospel is now 'before our very eyes' and we can 'richly enjoy' it, since the 'light of the knowledge of the glory of God' has been manifested to us (2.9.1). We ought never to forget the privilege of hearing the gospel this side of the cross.

Yet even for those with such privileges, there is more to come. For it does not yet appear what they will be like (1 John 3:2). Even though the Messiah has now come, and his work of redemption has been accomplished, New Testament believers must live by faith and not by sight every bit as much as did the patriarchs.

This perspective enables us to treat carefully the contrast between the law and the gospel, lest we assign the law exclusively to the Old Testament and the gospel to the New. There is but one way of salvation that runs through the whole Bible.

Nevertheless, there is transition from Old to New as anticipation gives way to fulfilment. Between the law (here understood not as the moral law but as the preparatory, Mosaic regime) and the gospel (understood as the full manifestation of God's grace in Jesus Christ) stands John the Baptist, heralding the coming of the Messiah in language drawn from the law. But, Calvin explains, 'what John began the apostles carried forward to fulfilment, with greater freedom, only after Christ was received into heaven' (2.9.5).

These passages are an excellent example of Calvin's dialectical style, how he states and re-states theological themes, qualifying and refining them by masterly attention to the detail of Scripture.

PAUL HELM

2.10.1 - 2.10.7

John Calvin is a covenant theologian; that is to say, he comprehends the whole biblical teaching on salvation under the category of God's gracious covenant for the redemption of his people in Christ.

While Calvin recognizes differences between the Old and New Testaments, he emphasizes continuities in the administration of God's grace. In this section of the *Institutes*, he argues that the old and new covenants are fundamentally the same. Whether they lived before or after the coming of Christ, the people of God are all adopted into the same family, all bound by the same law, all saved by the same grace, and all promised the same everlasting inheritance.

To prove the continuity of the covenant, Calvin clarifies the teaching of the Bible from three common misperceptions about the operations of God's grace in the Old Testament.

First, the blessings that God promised to his Old Testament people were not merely physical and temporal (like the promised land, for example), but also, and more fundamentally, spiritual and eternal (like the promise of everlasting life).

Second, the basis for salvation in the Old Testament, no less than in the New, was the mercy of God. The Jews who were saved before the coming of Christ — like the Jews and Gentiles who were saved afterwards — were saved by the free grace of God and not by their own merits. Justification has always been by grace alone.

Third, the Old Testament believers were saved by their union with Jesus Christ, who is the one and only Mediator for the one and only covenant people of God.

PHILIP RYKEN

2.10.8 - 2.10.13

It is sometimes thought that whereas the blessings that God gave to his people in the Old Testament were earthly, the blessings that he promises to give his New Testament people in Christ are heavenly. Calvin disagreed with drawing such a sharp distinction between the old and the new covenants. There is only one way of salvation, he believed, which is one and the same in both testaments.

Already in the Old Testament, the people of God were looking beyond any earthly blessing to hope for everlasting life. Calvin proves this from the language of the covenant itself, in which God always promised to be his people's God (e.g. Lev. 26:12) — a spiritual rather than a material promise.

Calvin believed further that God's covenant promise is eternal. If this were not so, then when God styled himself 'the God of Abraham, the God of Isaac, and the God of Jacob' (e.g. Exod. 3:6), he was claiming to be 'the God of those who do not exist' (2.10.9), which would be a manifest absurdity.

The patriarchs themselves well understood and firmly believed that the promise of the covenant 'extended into eternity' (2.10.9). Calvin demonstrates this in a dramatic way by rehearsing many of the hardships that Abraham, Isaac and Jacob faced during their earthly pilgrimage — a litany of misery. If these men were living for earthly blessings, then God failed to deliver on the promises he made to them. But these men were not living for earthly blessings. By faith in God's covenant promise, they were looking for a life to come, just like the New Testament people of God.

Calvin knew that God's promise to be our God is the best of all promises. When he gives us himself, God gives us everything that we could ever need.

PHILIP RYKEN

2.10.14 - 2.10.20

Somehow the myth persists that the Old Testament has no clear doctrine of the afterlife. Apparently, the scholars who believe this have never read Calvin, because the *Institutes* make a clear and compelling case that the people of God have always believed in a life to come. This is part of Calvin's wider argument for the unity of the old and new covenants.

Having established that, to their dying breath, the patriarchs were still waiting for the salvation of their God, Calvin turns to the prophets. When David declared that his hope was in God (Ps. 39:7), or that 'the steadfast love of the LORD is from everlasting to everlasting' (Ps. 103:17), or that 'his righteousness endures for ever' (Ps. 112:9), he was expressing his confidence in an eternal salvation. Similarly, David's frequent appeals for God to judge evildoers looked beyond his present troubles to a Day of Judgement when God would set everything right for ever.

Job had the same hope. He believed that his living Redeemer would raise him up on the Last Day, when his own body would live again and his own eyes would see his Saviour and his God (Job 19:25-27).

Calvin believed that the biblical witness to eternal life shone increasingly brighter throughout the Old Testament, becoming radiant in the prophets who predicted the coming of a Saviour, until finally culminating in Christ himself — 'the sun of righteousness' (Mal. 4:2).

Thus there is progress in the revelation of redemption. Yet through it all, the entire Old Testament consistently points people to the blessedness of eternal life. Even where it promises temporal benefits, these blessings are intended 'to lift up the minds of the people above the earth ... to ponder the happiness of the spiritual life to come' (2.10.20).

PHILIP RYKEN

2.10.21 - 2.11.3

In this section, Calvin continues to prove the doctrine of eternal life from the Old Testament Scriptures, this time by pointing to Ezekiel's prophecy that dead, dry bones will live and rise again (Ezek. 37).

No one should think that the covenant promises God made to the Jews were merely carnal, which was the error of the Sadducees. On the contrary, everyone should know that 'the Old Testament or Covenant that the Lord had made with the Israelites had not been limited to earthly things, but contained a promise of spiritual and eternal life' (2.10.23).

As a final proof, Calvin points to the strange miracle of the saints who rose again at the resurrection of Jesus and were seen in the city of Jerusalem (Matt. 27:52-53). Whatever else we may learn from this marvel, it proves that God made good on the promise he had always made to his people — the promise of eternal life.

Having firmly established the unity of the old and the new covenant in the promise and purpose of God, Calvin begins in Chapter 11 to acknowledge some of the differences between the Old and New Testaments — differences that should not be allowed to detract from the more fundamental unity of all God's promises in Christ.

The first major difference is that whereas the Old Testament people of God tasted eternal benefits through earthly blessings, the New Testament people of God exercise their faith directly on heavenly things.

According to some theologians, the land of Canaan only typified a heavenly inheritance after the coming of Christ. But Calvin believed that even before the coming of Christ, the earthly possession of that promised land taught the people of God to look for the highest and ultimate blessedness prepared for them in heaven, where God himself would be their 'portion for ever' (Ps. 73:26).

PHILIP RYKEN

Although the unity of the old and new covenants is primary, the differences between the two covenants are also important.

The first of these differences, as we have seen, concerns the manner in which eternal benefits are experienced, whether first by tasting a related blessing on earth (the Old Testament), or simply by exercising faith in a future inheritance (the New Testament).

A second difference between the Old and New Testaments relates to the use of various figures that typify Christ. Whereas the Old Testament often uses shadows and images to portray the gospel, the New Testament 'reveals the very substance of truth as present' (2.11.4).

The book of the Bible that teaches this principle most clearly is Hebrews, where the priesthood of the Old Testament is connected to the priestly ministry of Jesus Christ. His priesthood is superior in every way: in its permanency, in the perfection of its sacrifice, and in the holiness it brings to sinners. By comparison, the Old Testament priesthood was merely a 'shadow of the good things to come' (Heb. 10:1).

A third difference between the Old and New Testaments is that whereas the former is literal, the doctrine of the latter is spiritual. Calvin finds this teaching its classic location: Jeremiah's promise of a new covenant that will be written on the hearts of God's people (Jer. 31:31-34). He also finds it in 2 Corinthians 3, where the apostle Paul distinguishes between the death that the law brings by revealing unrighteousness, and the life that the gospel offers by giving us the righteousness of Christ.

Then there is a fourth, closely related difference between the two testaments. The Old Testament, with its law, keeps sinners in bondage to fear, but the New Testament, with its gospel, offers sinners freedom in Christ.

PHILIP RYKEN

2.11.10 – 2.11.14

Martin Luther famously taught that everything in the Bible that is *commanded* falls under the heading of 'law' — what we must do — and everything in the Bible that is *promise* falls under the heading of 'gospel' — what God will do. Calvin is not in conflict with Luther here, but there is a difference. For Calvin, the gospel is also present in the Old Testament even as it comes to fruition in the New Testament.

The Old Testament saints, therefore, did not believe in atonement via animal blood but had access to the gospel. But it was through the typological significance of their sacrifices that they looked to Christ who was to come. The patriarchs and prophets lived under the old covenant with an eye to the new 'and thus embraced a real share in it' (2.11.10).

Another difference between the Old Testament and the New Testament, says Calvin, is the expansion of the gospel call. In the OT, God allowed 'all other nations to walk in vanity' (2.11.11), but in the NT he sends the gospel to all nations so that Jew and Gentile might be 'welded into one people' (*ibid.*). This was indeed foretold in the OT, but its realization marks the supremacy of the NT. Though Calvin did not possess the full-blown covenant theology of the Westminster Standards, the contours of a single 'covenant of grace' (2.11.11) clearly emerge in the *Institutes*.

One final question: do the differences between the OT and NT administrations undermine God's unchanging character? Calvin answers (2.11.13) that God should not be charged with inconsistency if, in his wisdom, he adapted his purposes to new situations. God has ever taught the same doctrines, Calvin insists, and demanded the same worship in both eras. The changes in outward administration merely reveal God's freedom to order all things according to his will. 'Who then, I pray, will say it is not meet that God should have in his own hand and will the free disposing of his graces, and should illuminate the nations as he wills?' (2.11.14).

RICHARD PHILLIPS

2.12.1 - 2.12.5

Chapter 12 introduces a new line of thought, concerning the reason for Christ's incarnation. Readers who have persevered through the *Institutes* to this point will be rewarded here with sacred eloquence of the first order as Calvin addresses the same concerns treated in Anselm of Canterbury's medieval classic, *Cur Deus Homo* (or *Why Did God Become Man?*), and rehearses much of Anselm's doctrine (though, strangely, without reference to Anselm).

Christ's becoming man was not *absolutely* necessary, says Calvin, since it was God's free decree of our salvation that accounts for the incarnation. However, given the decree, it then became necessary for Christ to take up our flesh, since no mere man could take up the calling of Mediator, all of Adam's children now being 'terrified at the sight of God' (2.12.1). Calvin therefore (following Anselm) points us to the genius of the incarnation: 'since neither as God alone could he feel death, nor as man alone could he overcome it, he coupled human nature with divine' (2.12.3) so that man could die and God could conquer, all in one mediatorial person.

The work of this Mediator, Calvin goes on to say, includes what many refer to as Christ's active obedience. As the Westminster Divines declared, the saving remedy must actually redress the failure: Christ as a man must obey where Adam rebelled. And so our justification rests in the whole of Christ's life, as much in his keeping of the law as in his atoning sacrifice for our sins.

As usual, Calvin turns from exposition to defence, putting false objections in his sights. The target is Lutheran Andreas Osiander's doctrine that Christ might well have become man even if Adam had not plunged our race into sin. Calvin's refutation manifests once again his exemplary submission to Scripture. We simply must not speculate beyond the Bible. Osiander's defence that Scripture does not specifically refute his doctrine receives Calvin's full and just scorn, as he points out that the most blasphemous and ludicrous doctrines might be defended in the same fashion.

RICHARD PHILLIPS

2.12.6 - 2.13.1

Calvin's diatribe against Osiander gains steam as he dismantles the notion of Christ's becoming man apart from the entrance of sin. Osiander had claimed that because God always intended to conform humankind to his Son, Christ needed to become man even apart from our redemption from sin. Calvin labours to argue that the mediation of Christ always had the purpose of advancing Adam's offspring 'out of ruin' (2.12.7) to the state of glory. This is Calvin's point in the varied arguments found here. We would do well to adopt Calvin's rejection of all extra-biblical speculation and his refusal to advance beyond or step outside of the text of Holy Scripture.

Calvin is quick to point out the absurdities to which Osiander ends up through his imprudence; the claim, for instance, that Christ would be inferior to angels were it not for his humanity. Readers who find it hard to follow Calvin's point-by-point refutation of Osiander receive a helpful object lesson in avoiding the kind of speculative theology to which Calvin finds it necessary to respond.

Blessedly, Calvin moves on to Chapter 13, where he argues the vital matter of Christ's true humanity. Here again we are treated to theological eloquence of a high order. There may be no other writer who has so clearly grasped how important this issue is, or who has done more to fix his followers upon this truth.

First, Calvin notes the ancient opposition to the full manhood of Jesus by two heretical groups known as the Manichees and Marcionites. He then responds with clear biblical testimonies to refute their errors. But Calvin is amiss, I believe, in using the title 'Son of Man' to argue Christ's humanity. Later scholarship has persuasively argued that 'Son of Man' does not refer strictly to Christ's humanity, but rather to the divine figure of Daniel 7 who, having accomplished God's will on earth, is received back into heaven and enthroned with glory and honour. Despite this brief problem, Calvin marshals a host of Scriptures to prove his point: Christ became truly and fully man in his incarnation. Because Christ is truly man, he is able to bestow on us what reward God has bestowed upon him in his mediatorial humanity.

RICHARD PHILLIPS

Calvin not only refutes the heresies and errors pertaining to Christ's humanity, he also discerns the causes behind these errors. The false teaching of the Marcionites and the Manichees relies on isolated texts without consideration of other Scriptures that speak to the matter. Worse, they are abstracted from their contexts in order to fit unbiblical philosophical systems. Through his response, Calvin warns us against imposing the wisdom of man upon Scripture. Heretics not only miss the teaching of Scripture but the wisdom of God.

In this section, Calvin responds to those who believe Christ only appeared to have a human body. Most impressive and successful is Calvin's appeal to the second chapter of Hebrews, with its many claims to the reality and necessity of Christ's true humanity. In the process, he shows that Christ receives a new and far greater glory in light of his self-abasement as God's Servant and our Saviour.

Next Calvin meets his opponents' objection that the titles 'seed of Abraham' and 'offspring of David' indicate that Christ's humanity was merely allegorical. Calvin points out that whatever else is meant by these titles, they both necessitate Christ's true humanity. The argument that women do not have 'seed' is refuted as absurd and ignorant, as is the accusation that 'son of David' makes a merely notional connection between Jesus and David, rather than a physical one.

Finally, in 2.13.4, Calvin rails against the last of the 'childish calumnies' levelled against Christ's true humanity. For example, some supposed that Christ's full humanity would entail a sinful nature, despite the clear teaching of the apostle Paul to the contrary (Rom. 5:12, 18; 8:3-4). The upshot of this is of real pastoral importance today, namely, that humanity is not wicked or worthless in and of itself, but was only made wicked by the fall into sin. Humanity was created with divinely wrought dignity and goodness. This alone dispels both the Gnostic loathing of all things material and today's nihilistic anti-humanism. Calvin concludes by returning us to the wonder that the God who fills the universe deigned to be born in a virgin's womb.

RICHARD PHILLIPS

2.14.1 - 2.14.4

Chapter 14 delves us deeper into Trinitarian theology and Christology by dealing with the two natures and one person of Christ. Calvin begins with an entirely lucid statement of the true doctrine: God the Son *became* man, not by coming into existence in the Bethlehem manger, but by taking our flesh upon himself. 'We affirm his divinity so joined and united with his humanity that each retains its distinctive nature unimpaired, and yet these two natures constitute one Christ' (2.14.1). This is Calvin's doctrine, and it is crucial.

I confess that I get nervous when it comes to analogies to help explain the incarnation, including Calvin's analogy of the human body and soul (modern science would not be very approving of him here either). Calvin's main point is that a man possesses both body and soul — two different 'natures' — while remaining only one person. On the surface, it illustrates his Christological teaching, but we ought not to take this illustration any further. The reality is that there are no true human analogies for the incarnation.

Still, we may ask, how do the two natures of Christ relate to one another? This is another question of great moment in antiquity. Here, Calvin explains that Scripture may reference Christ's deity in one place and his humanity in another without neglecting their union in his person. Sometimes Scripture rhetorically expresses this union by describing one nature in terms of the other. Thus Paul may rightly speak of God having blood (*cf.* Acts 20:28). How can this be? Because God the Son took up human nature and died. Hence, there is nothing wrong with saying that 'God died' on the cross, so long as in our minds the two natures of Christ are always distinguished and never mingled.

The key to relating the two natures of Christ, then, is the unity of the person of Christ. But Calvin takes this further and focuses on the one person of Christ *as our Mediator*. As man, the divine Christ has become Lord for the greater glory of God in our salvation.

We are reminded why Calvin is so valuable after so many years. Here, as elsewhere, he excels in sober exposition and in soaring sacred prose. Anyone considering these matters should consult Calvin first and often.

RICHARD PHILLIPS

2.14.5 - 2.14.8

In these sections, Calvin looks at some of the arguments of Michael Servetus (1511–1553), a famous Spanish theologian and physician who sought to refute the doctrine of the Trinity. (As readers undoubtedly know, Servetus ended up being burned at the stake in Geneva, where heresy was considered a capital crime. What is often overlooked in this event is its historical setting, as well as Calvin's pastoral concern for Servetus.)

Calvin explains Servetus' twin errors. First, he believed that Christ was a mixture of divine and human elements, rather than fully God and fully man, distinctly yet inseparably. Second, Servetus believed that to say Christ has always been a Son yet also became incarnate is to posit two sons of God. Calvin reaffirms that the one Son of God 'took human nature in a hypostatic union' and 'was manifested in the flesh' (2.14.5). In this way, his eternal sonship was more clearly displayed in the incarnation but was never replicated.

As usual with Calvin, the goal of this refutation is not to score theological points but to tear down false teaching that dishonours God, hurts God's people and undermines their hope. Pulling no punches against Servetus' theology, Calvin asserts that 'the crafty evasions of this foul dog' ultimately extinguishes 'the hope of salvation' (2.14.8).

'Only he can be our Redeemer who, begotten of the seed of Abraham and David, was truly made man according to the flesh' (*ibid.*). Christ is fully God and fully man, in one person. There is no salvation apart from him.

JUSTIN TAYLOR

2.15.1 - 2.15.4

Jesus the Christ bears the threefold office of prophet, priest and king. Calvin insists that we must not only know these names, but press through to see their purpose and use. In these sections, therefore, Calvin looks at what it means for Christ to be prophet and king.

As prophet, the anointed Messiah is the 'herald and witness of the Father's grace' (2.15.2) whose perfect doctrine puts an end to all prophecies. This means that 'all who by faith perceive what he is like have grasped the whole immensity of heavenly benefits' (*ibid*.). Because all doctrine is summed up in Christ, it is eminently personal.

Moving next to Christ's spiritual kingdom and kingship, Calvin shows that the 'eternal power' of Christ ensures 'the everlasting preservation of the church' (2.15.3). Believers can take comfort that 'the devil, with all the resources of the world, can never destroy the church, founded as it is on the eternal throne of Christ' (*ibid*.). Though the church is buffeted with trials, she awaits the full fruit of Christ's protection and defence in the age to come.

Only in eternity will we experience full and final happiness, so we must not think that life in this age is one of perfect peace or prosperity. Nevertheless, today we are enriched by Christ and enjoy all things necessary for eternal life, and we are fortified with courage to stand against our spiritual enemies. Our King, says Calvin, will never leave nor forsake us, but will provide for us until we reach our final triumph in him. By graciously giving to us what he has received from the Father, we are sustained with 'confidence to struggle fearlessly against the devil, sin, and Satan' (2.15.4) and bear much fruit to the glory of God.

May God continue to equip his church to be fearlessly faithful and fruitful for the fame of his name.

JUSTIN TAYLOR

2.15.5 - 2.16.2

Rather than summarizing each section in this reading, I want to draw our attention to 2.16.2, where Calvin shows the importance of regarding the wrath of God against all who have not fled to Christ on account of their individual sin and guilt. His point is that the clearer our doctrine of sin and wrath, the sweeter will be our understanding of grace, mercy and liberation. Consider how the forceful clarity of the bad news leads to increased joyful awareness of the good news.

'For example, suppose someone is told: "If God hated you while you were still a sinner, and cast you off, as you deserved, a terrible destruction would have awaited you. But because he kept you in grace voluntarily, and of his own free favour, and did not allow you to be estranged from him, he thus delivered you from that peril." This man then will surely experience and feel something of what he owes to God's mercy. On the other hand, suppose he learns, as Scripture teaches, that he was estranged from God through sin, is an heir of wrath, subject to the curse of eternal death, excluded from all hope of salvation, beyond every blessing of God, the slave of Satan, captive under the yoke of sin, destined finally for a dreadful destruction and already involved in it; and that at this point, Christ interceded as his advocate, took upon himself and suffered the punishment that, from God's righteous judgement, threatened all sinners; that he purged with his blood those evils which had rendered sinners hateful to God; that by this expiation he made satisfaction and sacrifice duly to God the Father; that as intercessor he has appeased God's wrath; that on this foundation rests the peace of God with men; that by this bond his benevolence is maintained toward them. Will the man not then be even more moved by all these things that so vividly portray the greatness of the calamity from which he has been rescued?' (2.16.2).

Calvin concludes that God has so mercifully saved us that we cannot 'seize upon life ardently enough or accept it with the gratefulness we owe, unless our minds are first struck and overwhelmed by fear of God's wrath and by dread of eternal death' (*ibid.*).

Apart from Christ we can do nothing. Apart from Christ we are objects of destruction. Praise be to God for his fatherly kindness in and through his Son.

JUSTIN TAYLOR

2.16.3 - 2.16.6

We have all heard that 'God loves you and has a wonderful plan for your life.' But Calvin draws our attention to another biblical teaching: 'All of us ... have in ourselves something deserving of God's hatred' (2.16.3). So why does God love us nonetheless? Because in his kindness and free grace he 'wills not to lose what is his in us' and 'still finds something to love' (*ibid.*). To borrow from Augustine, God loved us even when he hated us.

The Bible teaches that the righteous (i.e., God) cannot receive the unrighteous (i.e., us) apart from the expiatory work of Christ on the cross. Yet even here we must remember the primacy of divine love. So often we are tempted to think that Christ's work *causes* God to love us — but it is really the other way around. It is out of love that the Father sent his Son to be our sacrifice and substitute (John 3:16). So if we want assurance of God's grace and pleasure, 'we must fix our eyes and minds on Christ alone' (2.16.3).

How has Christ accomplished his reconciling work? Calvin answers that it was 'by the whole course of his obedience' (2.16.5). Though Scripture focuses peculiarly and properly on Christ's death as the culmination of his obedience, the price of redemption for liberation began in Bethlehem, not Gethsemane. His righteous life was offered up on the cross, where we find our acquittal: 'the guilt that held us liable for punishment has been transferred to the head of the Son of God' (*ibid.*). The Christian's enduring peace is found in this blessed exchange!

JUSTIN TAYLOR

2.16.7 - 2.16.11

Next Calvin turns to that confusing phrase in the *Apostles' Creed* that Christ 'descended into hell' — what he calls 'a matter of no small moment in bringing about our redemption' (2.16.8). He wants us to understand and not despise this mystery. If it was dropped from the *Creed*, he says, that would mean the loss of an important component of our redemption. Even though the words appear to have been inserted later, Calvin thinks they represent a 'common belief of all the godly' (*ibid.*), attested by the fact that all the Church Fathers reference it.

Some say that 'hell' here is redundant, a conceptual repetition of the *Creed's* statement on Christ's burial. But why would they choose such an obscure synonym or explanation, he asks, especially in a creed that is otherwise so careful and concise? He likewise dismisses the idea that Christ entered into the nether world to announce redemption to the souls of the imprisoned patriarchs.

Instead, Calvin offers his own interpretation, which he finds both biblical and wonderfully consoling: Christ not only experienced bodily death (which by itself would have been ineffectual for our salvation), but also suffered 'the armies of hell and the dread of everlasting death' (2.16.10). In other words, he was crushed by 'invisible and incomprehensible' (*ibid.*) judgement from God — 'the pangs of death' (Acts 2:24) — that we deserved.

As you read the following quote from Calvin, exult in Christ's sin-bearing, enemy-defeating, wrath-averting work that brings us to God and keeps us from hell:

'By his wrestling hand to hand with the devil's power, with the dread of death, with the pains of hell, he was victorious and triumphed over them, that in death we may not now fear those things which our Prince has swallowed up' (2.16.11).

JUSTIN TAYLOR

2.16.12 - 2.16.15

Calvin lingers over the sufferings of Christ to counter the 'foul evasion' of 'quibblers' that Jesus' dread of the cross prior to his death signalled a weakness unbecoming of the Saviour. Others have marched towards certain death with steely eyes and calm resolve, they claim; why the anguish of Gethsemane? Wasn't Jesus a *real* man? Calvin's answer explains what no painting of the crucifixion can capture: '[Christ] knew that he stood accused before God's judgement seat for our sake' (2.16.12).

Jesus experienced pure agony of soul as he fell under the shadow of the cross. To question the genuineness of his temptations, or diminish his human suffering as though he were somehow only pretending, reveals *our* lack of faith, not his. 'Yet this is our wisdom: duly to feel how much our salvation cost the Son of God' (*ibid.*). A profound awareness of the horror of sin, a selfless love for God's people, and a solemn resolve to do nothing but obey the Father to his final breath; this is precisely what makes Christ the most *real* man who will ever live.

Next Calvin directs us beyond Golgotha to the empty tomb, lest we miss the triumph of the resurrection; for here is where our faith attains to 'full strength' (2.16.13). It is Christ crucified *and raised* who comprises our salvation: 'through his death, sin was wiped out and death extinguished; through his resurrection, righteousness was restored and life raised up' (*ibid.*). Calvin then schools us in the grammar of redemption: there is a 'synecdoche' involved in the Son's death and resurrection; we cannot speak of the one event without considering the other with it, and vice versa. Hold them together, too, if you want to understand justification (see Rom. 4:25) and growth in holiness ('we must mortify our members ... [and] strive after newness of life' [2.16.13]).

Having opened this section vindicating Christ from sinful despair, Calvin concludes by guarding us against the same by magnifying Christ's ascension to the Father. Do you sometimes envy the disciples' enjoyment of the bodily presence of Christ on earth? If so, says Calvin, turn and rejoice that he now rules over you from heaven 'with a more immediate power' (2.16.14). His outpoured Spirit abiding in our hearts means that though we have to look with faith, 'we always have Christ according to the presence of his majesty' (*ibid.*). By his Spirit, he is nearer to us than the pre-Pentecost apostles could imagine.

CARLTON WYNNE

Calvin patiently and pastorally unpacks the benefits of Christ's ascension for believers. First, Jesus has 'opened the way into the Heavenly Kingdom' (2.16.16) to assure us that we will one day be with him bodily. In fact, our names are so written into his glorified flesh, says Calvin, that Paul can speak of our already sitting there with him (Eph. 2:6). Second, the ascended Christ 'appears before the Father's face as our constant advocate and intercessor' (*ibid.*). As the Father showers his exalted Son with love, the blessings of God's forgiveness and care cascade down onto those united to Christ. Third, Christ's position of power at the Father's right hand is for us a wellspring of strength and protection in this life until he comes again.

These benefits of the ascension, staggering though they are, do not compare to the glory that lies ahead. Christians live as undercover agents of a kingdom 'hidden in the earth, so to speak, under the lowness of the flesh' (2.16.17); but not for long. Our Saviour will soon appear in a display of such unfathomable power and splendour that no one will miss or misunderstand the event. Judgement Day casts its shadow — or beams its light, if you belong to Christ — back onto this life, beckoning us to be ready for the Judge. For those who are eagerly waiting for him (Heb. 9:28), there is no fear of shame, since 'we shall be brought before no other judgement seat than that of our Redeemer, to whom we must look for our salvation!' (2.16.18).

Calvin closes his survey of the *Apostles' Creed* by reminding us that we have been talking about Christ all along. Here he pens some of my favourite words in the *Institutes*:

'We see that our whole salvation and all its parts are comprehended in Christ. We should therefore take care not to derive the least portion of it from anywhere else ... If we seek strength, it lies in his dominion; if purity, in his conception; if gentleness, it appears in his birth ... if purification, in his blood; if reconciliation, in his descent into hell ... if newness of life, in his resurrection ... if protection, if security, if abundant supply of all blessings, in his Kingdom; if untroubled expectation of judgement, in the power given to him to judge. In short, since rich store of every kind of good abounds in him, let us drink our fill from this fountain, and from no other' (2.16.19).

CARLTON WYNNE

2.17.1 - 2.17.6

Over the years theologians have debated whether the word 'merit', even as it applies to the work of Christ, somehow obscures the grace of God in salvation. Strictly speaking, Calvin sides with those who oppose the term, since 'no worthiness will be found in man to deserve God's favour' (2.17.1). God, by definition, is never obligated to show goodness to any creature. Even Christ's merit, Calvin argues, should be understood within the structure of redemption established by 'God's ordinance, the first cause' (*ibid.*). In this way, divine grace and the Saviour's merit sweetly cohere, all to our benefit.

Just when you think this parsing of terms is getting a bit tedious, Calvin uses it to uncover a frequent misunderstanding among Christians of the Father-Son relationship, namely, that the penal substitutionary atonement of Christ was really an extreme attempt to appease a stubborn and angry Father; and that the Son now intercedes in heaven by begging a reluctant God to wring out just one more blessing on a distant people. Never! It was God the Father who freely gave his only Son 'that nothing might stand in the way of his love toward us' (2.17.2). How can this be, since God rightly burns against all sin (Ps. 7:11)? Here all words fall short, even for Calvin: 'in some ineffable way, God loved us and yet was angry towards us at the same time, until he became reconciled to us in Christ' (2.17.2). Mystery of mysteries, God freely provides on the cross that which satisfies the wrath that his own character demands.

No one can read 2.17.5 and miss Calvin's understanding of the meaning of the cross. Christ's death was 'the payment or compensation that absolves us of guilt' (2.17.5) and, therefore, paid 'the price to redeem us from the penalty of death' (*ibid.*). By faith 'the righteousness found in Christ alone is reckoned as ours' and 'by his grace the Father is now favourable to us' (*ibid.*). Calvin then adds something he thinks is 'worth noting', namely, that 'to devote himself completely to saving us, Christ in a way forgot himself' (2.17.6).

Just pause for a moment and consider that the atonement was initiated by the Father, accomplished by the Son, and applied to us by the Spirit (see the next reading) 'while we were still sinners' (Rom. 5:8). How can anyone be arrogant if they live near the cross?

CARLTON WYNNE

BOOK THREE

'The Way in Which We Receive the Grace of Christ'

Introduction

Calvin knew that spiritual — better yet, Spiritual (i.e., from the Holy Spirit) — vitality is not manufactured by man's self-esteem or will power, but flows to the believer from the resurrection life of Christ. Hence the title of Book Three: 'The Way in Which We Receive the Grace of Christ: What Benefits Come to Us from it, and What Effects Follow'. Having dealt in Book Two with the once-for-all work of Christ in history, Calvin now turns to the necessity of the Spirit's application of salvation ('the grace of Christ') to the believer as he or she is united to Christ by faith. This, as Calvin shows, is the 'way' or manner in which sinners appropriate Christ and all his 'benefits', with all their consequent holy 'effects'. We could say that while Books One and Two teach us about God the Creator and Christ the Redeemer, Book Three urges us to know Christ personally through union with him by faith. This is what it means to receive the incarnate Son 'as he is offered by the Father: namely, clothed with his gospel' (3.2.6).

Therefore, Book Three opens with the sovereign work of the Spirit to produce saving faith (Chapters 1 - 2). Significantly, Calvin deals with lifelong growth in holiness (what he calls 'regeneration' or 'repentance') (Chapters 3 - 5) and the biblical marks of the Christian life (Chapters 6 - 10) before he hammers home the Reformation's hallmark doctrine of justification by grace alone through faith alone (Chapters 11 - 14). This is an ingenious way to show how our good works are not the grounds of our standing before God, but neither are they inimical to that standing (Chapters 15 - 16). After all, the exalted Christ to whom we are bound is simultaneously righteous and holy, the Victor over sin and the Vindicated One. In him and by his Spirit, we exhibit the fruit of good works (Chapters 17 - 18) as slaves liberated to serve a new King (Chapter 19).

Finally, Calvin reminds us that any truly good thing we know in this life, whether in joy or sorrow, comes from the Father who answers the prayers (Chapter 20) of his chosen people (Chapters 21 - 24). And as our prayers rise to God, the awesome Day draws nearer when he will glorify our bodies (Chapter 25) and bring us to our heavenly home on earth. Then, says Calvin, we will know 'a happiness of whose excellence the minutest part would scarce be told if all were said that the tongues of men can say' (3.25.10).

3.1.1 - 3.1.4

Calvin opens Book 3 with a remark so stunning some of us will have to read it twice: 'As long as Christ remains outside of us, and we are separated from him, all that he has suffered and done for the salvation of the human race *remains useless and of no value for us*' (3.1.1; my emphasis). Did you get it? If gospel is for us only a series of historical events (however spectacular) or a world-wide announcement (however exhilarating) or even a divine revelation (however authoritative), but is not also an offer to be received — or better, a Person to be trusted — we are like those penniless on the street with our faces pressed against the window of a storehouse of riches. We may like what we see, but we will remain in rags until we enter in and make it ours.

So Calvin urges his readers to obtain Christ and all his benefits 'by faith' (*ibid.*). The necessary response is so clear, so simple to grasp — so why, to borrow from Isaac Watts, would anyone rather starve than come to the banquet hall? To answer this we must 'climb higher' and peer from a heavenly perch 'into the secret energy of the Spirit' (*ibid.*). 'The Holy Spirit', Calvin explains, 'is the bond by which Christ effectually unites us to himself' (*ibid.*). He secures the 'sacred wedlock' (3.1.3) through which we are made one with Christ; he is that 'inner teacher' who implants the promise of salvation in our hearts (3.1.4). We could even call him the 'key that unlocks for us the treasures of the Kingdom of Heaven' (*ibid.*). The point is clear: without the Spirit's application of redemption to us by faith, the person and work of Christ as Mediator would be worthless to us.

This chapter on the Holy Spirit is remarkably brief given its significance in the unfolding of Calvin's treatise. On the one hand, this is fitting, since the Spirit prefers to throw the spotlight on Christ rather than himself (John 15:26). On the other hand, the Spirit is present indirectly throughout the remainder of Book 3 as Calvin covers topics such as faith, repentance and justification, all of which the third person of the Trinity effects in the life of the believer.

Isn't that just how the Spirit works in your life? Often inconspicuously, always patiently, but vitally and with the quiet strength that brought Christ to you, communicates his benefits to you, and keeps you bonded to him with a seal that will never be broken.

CARLTON WYNNE

3.2.1 - 3.2.6

Here the Reformer turns to the chief work of the Spirit in the believer: faith. Calvin will spend a while exploring the true character of faith 'because many are dangerously deluded today in this respect' (3.2.1). In our age, when many self-proclaimed 'persons of faith' aimlessly engage in all manner of 'spiritual' activities, Calvin's words of clarity on Spirit-wrought faith could hardly be more timely.

First, says Calvin, saving faith finds its object in Christ alone. Until the confession 'I have faith in God' connotes: 'I know the invisible Father and perceive his glory in the face of Christ my Saviour', we have not yet attained to true faith.

Second, and related to the first, faith 'rests not on ignorance, but on knowledge' (3.2.2). Knowing God in Christ means much more than simply knowing about God, but it does not mean less. To place one's faith in a Christ abstracted from his biblically given purpose, self-witness and work in history is to trust in no Christ at all. This is why Calvin 'slam dunks' the medieval notion, promoted by the Roman Church, that people did not really have to understand anything about the Bible or doctrine to be saved, but only trust that the church experts knew what was right. As far as Calvin is concerned, such 'implicit' faith throws a cloak over Christ and leads the masses into a maze of confusion.

Certainly there will be times when we bump against divine mysteries or struggle to understand a difficult passage of Scripture; in such cases 'we can do nothing better than suspend judgement, and hearten ourselves to hold unity with the church' (3.2.3). But a humble submission to the historic faith of the church (as Calvin is encouraging) is dimensionally different from a blind allegiance to ecclesiastical authorities all the way to the 'very brink of ruin' (*ibid.*).

Judging from what is packed into the religion section at our local bookstores, many professing Christians would rather follow the latest church personality, prophecy maker, or prosperity hawker than imitate the Bereans (Acts 17:11) by testing everything by the light of Scripture. Instead, whatever other helps God may use to sanctify us, if we fix our minds and plant our hearts in Scripture, we will find the knowledge that faith requires. Better yet, we will know Christ 'as he is offered by the Father: namely, clothed with his gospel' (3.2.6).

CARLTON WYNNE

3.2.7 - 3.2.10

In this section, Calvin defines true faith over against false alternatives. It is, he says, 'a firm and certain knowledge of God's benevolence toward us, founded upon the truth of the freely given promise in Christ, both revealed to our minds and sealed upon our hearts through the Holy Spirit' (3.2.7).

A number of comments are in order. First, we see here the centrality of assurance in Christianity. This emphasis heavily contrasts with medieval Catholicism, where lack of assurance provided — and still provides — much of the ethical motivation for Catholicism. The perpetual uncertainty regarding one's membership in God's true family acted as a deterrent against wandering from the visible fold of the church and her teachings. This medieval paradigm even lingered in the thought of those often heralded as forerunners of the Reformers, such as John Wyclif and Jan Hus. Not until Martin Luther and his heirs did the Reformation emphasis on assurance emerge.

Second, Calvin's view of faith is thoroughly Trinitarian: a knowledge of God the Father's benevolence towards us, revealed in Christ and sealed to us by the Holy Spirit. Each person of the Trinity plays his part in the salvation of each individual. This is catholic theology in the best sense of the word.

Third, Calvin rejects the medieval distinction between so-called 'formed' and 'unformed' faith. Citing 1 Corinthians 13:2, Rome argued that faith had to be perfected (or 'formed') by love in order to be saving. For Calvin, this marked a misunderstanding of faith's essence. Mere knowledge of gospel facts does not true faith make, nor does mere assent to the truth of such facts. We must yield our lives to the gospel of Christ. Calvin's teaching here points toward what later Reformed thinkers would see as the three essential and inseparable elements of true faith: an accurate knowledge of the gospel, a conscious assent to its truth, and a wholehearted *trust* in Christ for salvation.

Protestants can — and indeed, should — rejoice that their faith holds out the promise of assurance. While true Christians may struggle with a lack of assurance at times, the Reformed Protestantism of Calvin draws from Scripture the joyous expectation that assurance of God's favour should be the normal experience of every believer.

CARL TRUEMAN

3.2.11 - 3.2.15

In these paragraphs, Calvin continues to address the many complexities that surround the relationship between true faith and its counterfeits. Both pastoral experience and accounts given in Scripture lead Calvin to believe that there is such a thing as false faith, and that this can, at least for a time, give every appearance of genuine faith, both to the watching world and to the individual who possesses it.

Even the reprobate, he acknowledges, can have a semblance of true faith, but, for all of its specious authenticity, it never rises to the level of the cry of 'Abba, Father!' (Rom. 8:15; Gal. 4:6), cited by Paul as the hallmark of the truly adopted children of God. Sure, the reprobate can understand something of divine benevolence, but this always terminates for them on transient, temporary things. They have no real understanding of the fact that God is good, whatever outward circumstances might seem to indicate. Such faith is scarcely the faith of Job, who knew that God was good, and remained good, despite his incredible suffering.

In this context, Calvin indicates his sensitivity to the different ways in which the term 'faith' is used in Scripture: sometimes it refers to the body of sound doctrine, sometimes to trust, sometimes to the power to perform miracles. Saving faith, though, includes a knowledge of the love of God in Christ. This is apprehensive knowledge: the human mind is finite and cannot ever fully comprehend God; but it can grasp what God has chosen to reveal of himself. He has spoken to us in ways we can understand, given himself to us in the finite flesh of Christ and the finite words of human speech. While these revelations do not exhaust who God is, they are yet true, reliable and grounds for certainty.

In our Western world today, the idea that God could be angry with us is implausible, and in this context assurance is little more than a sentimental belief in our own inherent goodness — exactly the kind of faith held by the reprobates. We hesitate to confess that God is good when there is so much suffering in the world. And there is now widespread belief that because we can never have exhaustive knowledge, and all our knowledge takes place in a context, we can never have certain knowledge at all. Yet both of these errors fail to understand the nature of God's revelation of himself, and ultimately cannot account for the certainty of faith that drips from every page of Paul's letters.

CARL TRUEMAN

3.2.16 - 3.2.21

Calvin's discussion of faith addresses the manner in which the believing individual lives in a fallen world. What is particularly significant here is the way in which Calvin moves seamlessly from theological exposition to pastoral concern.

Central to the believer's experience is the internalizing of God's promises. It is of the nature of faith that it does not merely assent to the truth but involves an existential commitment to that truth. The words of Kierkegaard come to mind: it is not necessary that something simply be true; it must be true *for me*. So with Calvin: the promises cannot remain outside of us, having the same relation to us as, say, a mathematical equation; instead, we must grasp them in a way that changes our very lives by giving us confidence, peace of conscience, and assurance of God's love.

Now Calvin is pastoral enough to know that, in the face of this ideal, each believer is divided, fighting an internal battle between the new nature in Christ and the remaining old in Adam. The life of David, particularly as expressed in the poetic wrestling featured in the Psalms, gives ample evidence that the life of faith is not one of unfettered joy and assurance. Sometimes God will seem distant, if not absent; at other times he might seem angry. Yet in all of these periods of darkness, true faith clings to his revelation, to Christ, and to his unshakeable promises in a way that prevents despair. Believers may be, as it were, divided against themselves, and faith may ebb and flow in terms of its strength, but even weak faith is true faith, and its strength is not intrinsic to itself but is derived from the Word of God.

For this reason, it is surely incumbent upon us to prioritize the reading and the hearing of God's Word. Too often, when times are tough and we feel that God is distant or even absent, our instinct is to respond by distancing — or even absenting — ourselves from the humble reading of and listening to God's Word. How many times have I listened to the woes of those who think God has forsaken them, when really it is they who have forsaken God's Word! The thirsty man who refuses to drink cannot complain that his throat remains parched. To neglect God's Word is lethal. Indeed, it cuts faith off from its very life source and is a recipe only for further mischief and disaster.

CARL TRUEMAN

Next Calvin turns to the relationship between faith and fear, taking his cue from Paul's reference to 'fear and trembling' in Philippians 2:12. Fear can, of course, be a very bad thing, antithetical to the kind of assurance which lies at the heart of a robust Christian faith. Such is servile fear, a fear of punishment, a fear which derives from a failure to grasp the mercy of God in Christ and offered in the promises of the gospel. Yet Paul teaches that there is a fear which is essential to the Christian's walk, given that God is holy, we are sinful, and only Christ can stand between as Mediator.

Godly fear, then, is a function of knowledge of God and knowledge of self (recall the two-fold definition of true wisdom in 1.1.1). Knowledge of our own sin, of our precarious existence, and of the holiness of God all drive us towards despair; knowledge of the love of God manifest in Christ raises our souls heavenward and imbues us with fear, but one that is reverent rather than servile. To support his point, Calvin does not 'just have his Bible' and thus doom himself to reinventing the faith; rather, he draws judiciously on the fruit of past exegetical, theological and pastoral reflection upon Scripture by the church.

For Calvin, fear of God is central to Christian piety. It combines love and reverence, adoption and servanthood, in a manner that shapes our entire relationship with God and thus our entire relationship with the world around. Only as we come to know who we are as sinners, and who God is as both holy and merciful, will we develop that sure knowledge of God which is the constant theme of Calvin's life and work as a theologian, churchman and pastor.

Ironically, we live at a time when fear is more pervasive than ever in society — fear of the government, of global warming, of terrorism, of our neighbours, of superbug diseases, etc. Yet it is also a time when fear of God is virtually non-existent, even in the church. In terms of wider society, this fear indicates what happens when we strike out on our own and lose sight of the one who sustains the world; within the church it speaks of a culture where the therapeutic obsessions of the world have become the pathologies of what now passes for our theology. Only a return to the Word of God as the measure of man, and not vice versa, will reverse this trend both in society and in church.

CARL TRUEMAN

3.2.28 - 3.2.31

As Calvin continues to discuss the nature of faith, he makes the point that the assurance of faith is not connected to any promises of worldly prosperity or comfort, but rather to the expectation of the life to come. In this world, we are pilgrims and sojourners, resident aliens, who find no real rest here but await the life to come. Calvin, of course, was himself an exile, a Frenchman living in Geneva, and so he was unusually well positioned to understand such things, and this is undoubtedly why he had such an affinity with many of the psalms, with their cries of lament and sense of geographical dislocation.

The believer's assurance is built not upon outward circumstances but upon the promises of God. Now, as Calvin acknowledges, God's Word contains more than just his promises; but the promises are the most basic and important aspect of that Word. Here, Calvin references some Catholic opponents who make the whole truth of God in general the object of saving faith. Such 'barking' of 'dogs' (those were the days when theologians called it as they saw it!) misses the mark (3.2.30). Sure, Calvin says, the whole of God's truth is to be believed, but faith is only firm when it grasps the freely given promise in Christ; and it only reconciles to God when it unites to Christ.

This leads to Calvin's final point in this section: faith is bound to God's Word. It has content. It is not some vague sentimental feeling; nor does it have as its object some human aspiration as to who or what God should be. Errors can be mixed with faith — as the examples of Sarah, Rebecca and Isaac indicate — but true faith, maintained by the Spirit, will ultimately have the upper hand. Nevertheless, the existence of such erroneous admixture serves as a warning to keep believers ever vigilant and in conscious dependence on the Word.

Calvin's words here are a salutary warning to the kinds of mindless notions of faith that pervade our society, where the term seems to mean little more than a nebulous confidence that everything will turn out all right in the end. But also in the church, faith, along with other notions such as calling and guidance, has become detached from the Word of God and now drifts along in a river of sentiment, whether of the psychobabble or Pollyanna variety. Life is messy. Only faith anchored in the Word can do justice to the world's complexity without being undermined or swept away.

CARL TRUEMAN

Having emphasized that faith rests on the promises of the covenant, Calvin stresses again that these promises are in Christ, the knowledge of whom IS the gospel. While sinful man enjoys God's bounty and goodness, the believer recognizes God's love for what it is, and also that it is in Christ that God loves sinners. Even the saints of the Old Testament — with the relatively small degree of spiritual light they enjoyed — trusted in the promises through Christ. For this reason, 'we should turn our eyes to [Christ] as often as any promise is offered to us' (3.2.32).

But for anyone to look to Christ, Calvin reminds us, requires the inward illumination of the Holy Spirit. Calvin proof-texts this doctrine by such passages as 1 Corinthians 2:14, with its statement that without the Spirit's work, the things of God remain foolish to us; and John 6:44, where the drawing of sinners to Christ by God is the necessary antecedent to the knowledge of God. He also refers to Luke 24, where Christ is seen opening both the Scriptures and the mind, which enables us to understand the Scriptures. Spurgeon comments in one place that in opening the Scriptures, Christ has many helpers; but in opening the understanding he stands alone.

Moreover, only the Holy Spirit sustains us in Christ; this, too, is the gift of God: 'the Spirit is not only the initiator of faith, but increases it by degrees until by it he leads us to the Kingdom of Heaven' (3.2.33).

Faith is the work of the Spirit of Christ, illuminating our minds as he unites us to our Lord. Such work is deep: it is of the heart in order that it might be in the mind, worked in the subconscious before it can become a genuine matter of the intellect. Such faith may often be assailed by doubt, but believers cannot finally be shaken out of their confidence in Christ.

IAIN CAMPBELL

3.2.38 - 3.2.42

Can we be certain of our salvation? Calvin was neither the first nor the last to tackle the issue of assurance of salvation, but with profound pastoral insight he wants to show how faith and hope co-exist.

He begins this section, however, by confronting the medieval scholastic view of faith and assurance, and in particular the idea that assurance can be enjoyed only in the light of moral purity and uprightness. Calvin will return to this error when he comes to discuss human merit; at this point he simply highlights the fact that no assurance is possible where it is grounded in merit: 'With what sort of confidence will we be armed ... if we reason that God is favourable to us provided our purity of life so merit it?' (3.2.38). This view turns the gospel on its head; in Calvin's words, 'these men devise a Christianity that does not require the Spirit of Christ' (3.3.39).

It is true that there is an introspective element to Christian experience — we are called to examine ourselves, after all. But unlike the scholasticism that called for self-merit, the believer knows that faith cannot be separated from the Spirit, and it is in the indwelling Spirit that the Christian rejoices.

In other words, there is a complementarity between the grace of the Spirit and the exercise of faith. The latter grows out of the former, and consciously rejoices in it. Faith is a receiving, non-contributory grace, which enables the believer to say, 'This is the LORD's doing' (Ps. 118:23).

The grace of God does not come to us with confidence for the present only. The certainty of faith, says Calvin, cannot be limited to a point of time (3.2.41), but is bound up with hope for the future. 'Hope', he says, 'is nothing else than the expectation of those things which faith has believed to have been truly promised by God' (3.2.42). Faith believes the promises; hope awaits their fulfilment. Faith is the foundation of hope, but hope, in turn, is the nourisher of faith. It also restrains faith, 'that it may not fall headlong from too much haste' (*ibid.*). Hope strengthens faith; it refreshes and invigorates faith.

Such hope is the necessary companion of faith, if for no other reason than that the Lord often delays fulfilling his promises to us. It is hope that enables faith to wait on the Lord.

IAIN CAMPBELL

Sometimes Scripture uses faith and hope as synonyms, joining them closely together. They have the same foundation and the same goal — to rest in the mercy of God, abandoning ourselves to him. But faith has another companion also; any discussion of faith, says Calvin, that neglected 'repentance and forgiveness of sins' would be 'barren and mutilated' (3.3.1). Calvin's introduction to this theme is worth quoting:

'It ought to be a fact beyond controversy that repentance not only constantly follows faith, but is also born of faith. For since pardon and forgiveness are offered through the preaching of the gospel in order that the sinner, freed from the tyranny of Satan, the yoke of sin, and the miserable bondage of vices, may cross over into the kingdom of God, surely no one can embrace the grace of the gospel without betaking himself from the errors of his past life into the right way, and applying his whole effort to the practice of repentance' (3.3.1).

It is not as though faith slowly gives rise to repentance, bringing it to birth after a long period of gestation. Those who are serious about God fear him, and those who fear him repent before him. True believers know that repentance before God is the work of a lifetime, precisely because it is faith's constant companion.

Calvin is aware of a definition of repentance which says it consists of mortification — the hatred of sin which makes one wish one were another man — and vivification, 'the consolation that arises out of faith' (3.3.3). Calvin is happy to distinguish between these elements of repentance, but not to separate them, and not to insist that one always follows after the other. The two acts of abhorrence of our sin and appreciation of God's grace are constantly working hand in hand.

He is also aware of the view that there are two kinds of repentance: evangelical and legal. Repentance of the law he understands as the wounding of the conscience by the law, with its consequent moral inability to find peace. Repentance of the gospel he understands as a similar wounding of conscience, with a subsequent laying hold of Christ 'as medicine for his wound' (3.3.4). Both Old and New Testament saints experienced this gospel repentance, since, by faith, they were brought to bitter weeping yet not to hopeless despair. They found grace as they turned to God.

IAIN CAMPBELL

What is repentance?

Both the Hebrew and the Greek vocabulary for repentance signify a turning, and this brings Calvin to his definition:

'It is the true turning of our life to God, a turning that arises from a pure and earnest fear of him; and it consists in the mortification of our flesh and of the old man, and in the vivification of the Spirit' (3.3.5).

Sometimes the idea of turning is present in the biblical text, such as when God says to Israel, 'If you return, O Israel ... to me you should return' (Jer. 4:1).

Repentance is, first, then, a transformation of the soul. It is not merely a change of behaviour, but a change in the source from which all our actions spring. Isaiah warned against religious ceremonies and duties which were made the basis of an appeal to God, yet in which there was no engagement of the heart.

Second, repentance springs from an earnest fear of God. The thought of judgement ought to take our breath away, and stir us to reflect on the kind of life that God will accept. Thus Jeremiah (in chapter 4) and Paul (in Acts 17, for example) preach God's ultimate judgement and make it the ground of an appeal for repentance.

In similar manner, God sometimes uses punishments already inflicted to stir people up to the correcting of the slothfulness of their flesh. Such is the depravity of our nature that God must sometimes use hard things in order to rouse us to our spiritual duties: '...it would be vain for him to allure those who are asleep' (3.3.7).

Third, repentance does consist in two parts: mortification and vivification. This is no more than the Psalmist calls for when he says, 'Turn away from evil and do good' (Ps. 37:27). Our sinful nature is so perverse that only a complete renewal will enable us to stand before God: it is 'as if God had declared that for us to be reckoned among his children our common nature must die' (3.3.8).

Although the new birth takes place only once, repentance is a continual cleansing of our guilt in a warfare that ends only with death. It is by running what Calvin calls 'the race of repentance' (3.3.9) that we grow in likeness to Christ. Sin may still deceive, but final victory is coming.

IAIN CAMPBELL

3.3.11 - 3.3.15

In believers, says Calvin, 'sin ceases only to reign; it does not also cease to dwell in them' (3.3.11). One of the reasons for this is to humble us before the grace of God, which has freed us from sin's guilt, and which we need daily in order to free us from sin's corruption. The Christian is one who at the same time cries out to God, and cries out against himself. Here Calvin points to Paul's experience as a believer in Romans 7; and we, like Paul, know that in the mercy of God there is a place where our sin can be dealt with (Rom. 7:24-25).

Although sin is natural to us, sin is no constituent part of our nature. It is the result of a vitiated and compromised nature. So Calvin can say that 'all human desires are evil' (3.3.12), not because they are human, but because they are polluted. The believer, therefore, is justified, yet sinful; forgiven, yet still enticed by sin. It is present with us, though it need not reign: 'So long as you live, sin must needs be in your members. At least let it be deprived of mastery' (3.3.13). We may be no longer in sin, but sin will always be in us, so long as we are in this world.

To recognize this is a recipe against both perfectionism and antinomianism. We are 'far removed from perfection' (3.3.14), but we must move closer and closer towards perfection. The Spirit of Christ is not the patron of sin: he is the author of our sanctification, and through him we battle with the sin that remains in us, and aim to conquer and to eradicate it. This can only be done through repentance, with its earnestness, eagerness, indignation, fear, longing, zeal and punishment (2 Cor. 7:11), the seven constituent elements of genuine repentance. Calvin closes with a quotation from Bernard of Clairvaux:

> Sorrow for sins is necessary if it be not unremitting. I beg you to turn your steps back sometimes from troubled and anxious remembering of your ways, and to go forth to the tableland of serene remembrance of God's benefits. Let us mingle honey with wormwood that its wholesome bitterness may bring health when it is drunk tempered with sweetness. If you take thought upon yourselves in your humility, take thought likewise upon the Lord in his goodness (3.3.15).

IAIN CAMPBELL

3.3.16 - 3.3.18

Having unpacked the nature of repentance as a lifelong process of mortification of the flesh and vivification of the Spirit, Calvin makes a distinction that was needed in his sixteenth-century world: one between the inward disposition and external actions of repentance.

Such a distinction was important because the centre of medieval Christendom was a penitential system in which annual confession produced actions of penance that would admit one to the Mass, which in turn conferred forgiveness of sin. Even fellow Reformers, such as Melanchthon and Bucer, had a high view of the external actions of penances to demonstrate genuine repentance.

In Calvin's view, these prevailing views 'depend too much on such exercises' (3.3.16) prescribed for penance. And this is because 'when we have to deal with God nothing is achieved unless we begin from the inner disposition of the heart' (*ibid.*). There might be occasions when external acts such as fasting and mourning would be appropriate — particularly when the church's pastors 'see ruin hanging over the necks of their people' (3.3.17). Yet even in these times, pastors must always urge their people 'with greater and more intent care and effort that they should "rend [their] hearts and not [their] garments" [Joel 2:13]' (*ibid.*).

How often do we deal with our own hearts before the Lord? When was the last time your heart was broken because of sins that offended the One who loved you and gave himself for you?

SEAN LUCAS

3.3.19 - 3.3.20

Calvin returns to the points with which he opened Chapter 3: how do repentance and forgiveness of sins relate? And how does repentance connect with faith? Behind these questions is his main point: against the claims of his Catholic opponents, justification and sanctification always come together for, and in, those who put their faith in Christ and are so united to him.

Calvin demonstrates this larger concern by opening with a rhetorical question:

> Now if it is true — a fact abundantly clear — that the whole of the gospel is contained under these two headings, repentance and forgiveness of sins, do we not see that the Lord freely justifies his own in order that he may at the same time restore them to true righteousness by sanctification of his Spirit? (3.3.19).

In order for a person to repent, he must know that he is a sinner and that 'the treasures of God's mercy' (*ibid.*) are available in Jesus. Having seen this mercy, the individual repents of his sins and trusts in Jesus for forgiveness. And yet, this repentance is continual throughout life: 'the life of a Christian man is a continual effort and exercise in the mortification of the flesh, till it is utterly slain, and God's Spirit reigns in us' (3.3.20). Hating our sins and hastening to God, dying and rising daily, is the contour of the Christian life.

Is that your experience? Do you come daily before God, decrying your sins, hating and despising them, and fleeing to God in Christ for mercy and cleansing?

SEAN LUCAS

3.3.21 - 3.3.25

Repentance is 'a singular gift of God' (3.3.21), Calvin notes. Such makes the problem of apostasy, sham repentance and continued hypocrisy explainable. Those who wander away from the faith, who despise the gospel, and resist the truth until their deaths, were those who never received the gift of repentance from God, even though they may have heard the gospel, known the 'common operations' (*Westminster Confession of Faith* 10.4) of the Spirit, and sojourned with the church for a time.

In the end, all those who reject the gospel knowingly and willingly are those who commit the 'unpardonable sin' (*cf.* Matt. 12:31-32). For Calvin, the unpardonable sin is when people 'with evil intention, resist God's truth, although by its brightness they are so touched that they cannot claim ignorance' (3.3.22). These people know God's Word, are convinced that it is in fact God's truth, and yet 'repudiate and impugn' it — this is what it means to 'blaspheme against the Spirit' (*ibid.*). By rejecting the gospel willingly, completely and knowingly throughout their lives, these men and women put themselves beyond any possibility of repentance.

Behind it all is the strange mystery of God's ways — choosing Jacob and not Esau, sparing David and not Ahab, listening to Nineveh but not Judah. Lest we think that we can muster up repentance, we must return again to God, begging him for his Spirit so that our 'sins might be blotted out, that times of refreshing may come from the presence of the Lord' (Acts 3:19-20).

SEAN LUCAS

3.4.1 - 3.4.3

After discussing what the biblical doctrine of repentance is, Calvin moves to show how medieval theologians failed to understand repentance correctly. He structures the section dealing with the medieval view of repentance into three parts: contrition (3.4.1-3), confession (3.4.4-24), and satisfaction (3.4.25 - 3.5.10). In each part he demonstrates the pastoral failure of the medieval approach.

The medieval approach to contrition was quite simple. Contrition for sin — weeping bitterly for sins to demonstrate one's displeasure and hatred toward them — had to be 'just and full' (3.4.2). The problem came in the fact that it was never determined 'when a man can have assurance that he has in just measure carried out his contrition' (*ibid.*). Further, if the bitterness of one's sorrow was to match the magnitude of the crime, how could one muster up appropriate levels of contrition: 'If they say that we must do what is in us, we are always brought back to the same point. For when will anyone dare assure himself that he has applied all of his powers to lament his sins?' (*ibid.*).

By believing that forgiveness is conditioned on how contrite one was for their sins, there was no pathway for a genuine assurance of pardon. Against this faulty pastoral approach, Calvin reminded his readers that 'we have taught that the sinner does not dwell upon his own compunction or tears, but fixes both eyes upon the Lord's mercy alone' (3.4.3). Jesus is the only resting place for the hearts of anxious sinners. Amen.

SEAN LUCAS

3.4.4 - 3.4.9

The second aspect of repentance for medieval theologians was confession. Calvin starts by dismantling the Roman practice of 'auricular confession', that is, the practice of annual confession of one's sins to his or her priest. Calvin demonstrates that the support for such practice is slender at best, resting on allegorical and inadequate exegesis of key Bible texts (3.4.4-6). He also points out that the practice was only established in 1215, was not practised in some parts of the Eastern church, and was not enjoined by Chrysostom (3.4.7-8).

Again, Calvin's concern here is pastoral: 'We maintain that Christ was not the author of this law which compels men to list their sins ... and so this tyranny was at length introduced when, after piety and doctrine were extinguished, mere ghosts of pastors had taken all licence, without distinction, upon themselves' (3.4.7). Because pastors were not familiar with the biblical doctrine of repentance, they developed external activities that bound consciences and damaged souls.

While there might be benefit in mutual confession of sins (3.4.6), biblical confession was straightforward: 'Since it is the Lord who forgives, forgets and wipes out sins, let us confess our sins to him in order to obtain pardon. He is the physician; therefore, let us lay bare our wounds to him ... He it is, finally, who calls sinners: let us not delay to come to God himself' (3.4.9). The only way we will confess our sins to God — meaningfully, deeply, truly — is when we believe that the Lord is the faithful one who beckons sinners to himself to find peace, comfort and healing. 'Trust in him at all times, O people; pour out your heart before him; God is a refuge for us' (Ps. 62:8).

SEAN LUCAS

3.4.10 - 3.4.15

Nothing to do with Calvin, just a note to say it is great to pick up where Sean left off. Back in seminary we used to finish each other's sentences in class discussions. It's good to see we are still at it. Now to Calvin.

Despite there being those who got public confession quite wrong, as was just covered, Calvin commends appropriate public confession of sin. It might be worthwhile to break from Calvin's criticism of Rome here and think about the possible benefits of public confession. To guide us, Calvin makes two key statements:

1. Public confession should come after secret or private confession to God.
2. Public confession should be used 'extraordinarily in a special way, whenever it happens that the people are guilty of some transgression in common' (3.4.10).

When might public confession occur? When pestilence, war, or barrenness, as Calvin lists out the calamities, happens to a people, it is cause for soul-searching, (maybe) repentance and fasting, and then the awaiting of forgiveness. A good case study can be seen in the New England Puritan practice of fast day sermons. Some call this retribution theology, as though God will mechanistically reward good deeds in this life and punish bad ones. Others think of it differently.

What strikes me the most about this practice is its 'otherness' to our experience. What an alien thought to believe that God speaks to us, prods us, convicts us, through the events around us. And what a further alien thought to think that we stand and fall — not in an ultimate sense, mind you — as a community before God.

Calvin again: 'For since in every sacred assembly we stand before the sight of God and the angels, what other beginning of our action will there be than the recognition of our own unworthiness?' (3.4.11).

STEPHEN NICHOLS

3.4.16 - 3.4.20

Throughout this chapter, Calvin keeps bumping into the notion of the 'power of the keys' — the earthly authority to admit entrance to God's kingdom — in the medieval practice of forgiveness and satisfaction for sin. His fundamental point is that the keys are connected to the Holy Spirit (3.4.20). Calvin asserts: 'I deny that anyone can use the keys unless the Holy Spirit has first come to teach him and tell him what to do' (*ibid.*). Without the Spirit, those 'priestlings' who profess to have the keys merely 'babble' (*ibid.*). But that is not the worst of it.

Those who confess to the priest, he argues, are then 'emboldened throughout the year to sin ... they never sigh unto God, they never return to their senses, but heap up sins upon sins until they vomit all of them up at once' (3.4.19). Once disgorged, they convince themselves that they 'have made God forgetful when they have made the priest their confidant' (*ibid.*). Then the cycle starts all over again at the next confession.

This malpractice creates a licence that leads only to self-destruction. At the end of his *Ninety-Five Theses*, Luther says, 'Away with the false prophets who say "Peace, peace," when there is no peace.'

Calvin's pastoral concerns here cannot be missed. I think what he is dealing with is not restricted to the medieval abuses of the confessional. Sadly, false prophets are still out there who soothe guilty consciences with lies and flattery.

STEPHEN NICHOLS

3.4.21 - 3.4.26

After an extended discussion on medieval repentance, now comes the 'payoff' as Calvin offers a summary of his critique (3.4.24). This medieval Roman Catholic practice of confession, he says, is nothing but a 'tyrannous law', adding that it is 'one promulgated in contempt of God' who alone 'binds consciences to his Word' (3.4.24). Against the medieval view Calvin simply puts the 'freely given remission of sins' (3.4.25) as taught plainly by Scripture.

I am (again) reminded here of the story of Luther. Luther once said, 'It is very hard for a man to believe that God is gracious to him. The human heart cannot grasp this.' The human heart likes the futile attempts at self-righteousness, at works, at merits. Luther tried his hand at all of it. Or, conversely, the human heart likes the licence of liberty and pure freedom (see the previous reading). There are plenty of examples around us to confirm that. But grace and forgiveness in and through Christ — that is a different matter. It speaks right to our inability to merit God's favour.

Calvin puts it this way: 'When Scripture says, "by the name of Christ", it means that we bring nothing, we claim nothing of our own, but rely solely upon the commendation of Christ' (3.4.25). It is either Christ or it is us. For those of us who say, 'It is Christ!' those are the very best words, for the good news of the gospel has come home. For others, those who say, 'It is I,' the words of the gospel are an offence and a stumbling block.

STEPHEN NICHOLS

3.4.27 - 3.4.31

Among the things I missed by not growing up as a Catholic would be the discussion of venial and mortal sins. Alas, all is lost on me. But one thing I do remember hearing while growing up is that sin is sin, that the heart is desperately wicked (Jer. 17:9), and that, well, sinners sin ... a lot. Calvin puts it this way: 'For not a day passes when the most righteous of men does not fall time and again' (3.4.28). Hence, no amount of time in the confessional will make amends.

The categorizing of sin, venial or mortal, and the development of sophisticated schemes of 'satisfaction', penance and absolution, merely serve to minimize sin and its heinousness by making it clinical, sterile, manageable — all of which sin is not. Scripture, Calvin tells us brilliantly, gives 'a stout battering ram' (3.4.40) to any such programme. Sin requires a complete payment, total satisfaction. And that satisfaction only comes through the sinless (venial and mortal sinlessness) life and atoning death of Christ.

STEPHEN NICHOLS

3.4.32 - 3.4.35

Here Calvin turns to a subject that is not easy to talk about, let alone experience. He distinguishes between God's chastisement of his children as opposed to the divine vengeance and punishment reserved for his enemies. A couple of things may be worth emphasizing.

First, Calvin sets God's chastisement in the context of God as Father. Calvin lands on the metaphor with both feet. Fathers want to see their children flourish under their care, and they recognize that certain behavioural patterns in their beloved ones will either encourage or hinder this worthy aim. Similarly, Calvin emphasizes, our heavenly Father will confront our sinful behaviour, swiftly if necessary. But all is done in perfect love. Wise fathers also want to be quick to be merciful, quick to restore, and will discipline with the care of their children as the goal. Hence, 'Although the Lord teaches that chastisements serve to cleanse his people, he adds that he tempers those chastisements so as not to wear down his people unduly' (3.4.32).

One other point is this: 'In the bitterness of afflictions, the believer must be fortified by these thoughts' (3.4.34). How? Calvin tells us that 'he who in the end profits by God's scourges is the man who considers God angry at his vices, but merciful and kindly toward himself' (3.4.34). Calvin is right: We are 'more helped by God's fatherly chastisements than oppressed by them' (3.4.34). Do you believe this? God, our Father, always knows what is best for us, seeks what is best, and brings what is best. God is for us, *Deus pro nobis*, as the theologians say. Whatever your experiences of fatherhood, God as Father beautifully transcends them in every way.

STEPHEN NICHOLS

Divine chastisement ought to elicit obedience, but never as payment to God. Hence, there are more attacks here on man's perennial problem of a works-righteousness mentality, this time by the medieval Catholic insistence that 'love covers a multitude of sins' — that is, *with God*. Calvin corrects misinterpretations of Scriptures which suggest that works of pity, love and kindness on the part of those wishing to be received back into communion in the church following some grievous act 'satisfy' for sin in God's sight. Calvin's opponents claim the support of Church Fathers — a suggestion that is like a red rag to a bull for the Reformer who variously describes this shoddy scholarship as 'twisted' and the work of 'unwashed hands' (3.4.38-9).

From this arises (in 3.5.1) the 'mad' Catholic doctrine of 'indulgences' — 'the distribution of the merits of Christ and the martyrs, which the pope distributes by his bulls', according to which salvation could be bought at the price of 'a few coins ... which were filthily spent on whores, pimps and drunken revelries'. Calvin's language reaches new heights of expressive anger and disgust: traffickers in 'the treasury of the church' engage in 'tricks, deceit, thefts, greediness', and are 'a profanation of the blood of Christ, a Satanic mockery' (3.5.2).

Why the vitriolic language? Because, for Calvin, the practice of indulgences denies what is at the heart of the gospel: that sin is forgiven by the shed blood of Christ alone and made effectual in us by faith alone. 'The blood of Jesus his Son cleanses us from all sin' (1 John 1:7).

Salvation, Calvin insists, is by Christ *alone*, without any other mediating agent. The doctrine and practice of indulgences is unbiblical, a gross violation of the principle that salvation belongs to God alone and not to some cooperative agency of angels, saints or virgin.

DEREK THOMAS

3.5.3 - 3.5.8

We now have more on the error of indulgences, 'this impious dogma', and 'more astounding blasphemy' which, by suggesting the worth of 'the heavenly treasury', turns Christ into a mere 'saintlet' (3.5.3). He accuses the Roman Church of twisting Paul's words in Colossians 1:24 — that in his own body he makes up what is lacking in Christ's sufferings — and adds the weight of Augustine for his understanding that those in union with Christ will suffer as he did, but not in a way so as to make their sufferings of any atoning worth.

Next, Calvin turns to the doctrine of purgatory, a belief forged upon men's minds by 'Satan's craft' (3.5.6). Since it teaches that expiation can be attained elsewhere than the blood of Christ, 'We must cry out with the shouting not only of our voices but of our throats and lungs that purgatory is a deadly fiction of Satan, which nullifies the cross of Christ, inflicts unbearable contempt upon God's mercy, and overturns and destroys our faith' (*ibid.*). There is no equivocation, then, on Calvin's part here!

As for so-called scriptural proofs of purgatory, the attempts are puerile; and as for alleged citations from 2 Maccabees, despite erroneous claims to the Church Fathers, Calvin deems them 'unworthy of reply, lest I seem to include that work in the canon of the sacred books' (3.5.8).

The notion of a purgatory after death, which turns sinners into saints, is a lying invention of man and is nowhere taught in Scripture. It is yet another example of the 'damnable plus' that fatally mars medieval soteriology.

DEREK THOMAS

3.5.9 - 3.5.10

Calvin continues with still more on purgatory. He really does not like this absurd doctrine and takes up another passage, the interpretation of which has bothered folk in our time in an entirely different manner. What does Paul mean by saying that some will be saved 'but only as through fire' (1 Cor. 3:15)? Those who minimize sanctification as evidence of true conversion in our time have employed this text to suggest that we can take Jesus as Saviour without submitting to the demands of his Lordship. Medieval Catholicism viewed this move as evidence of purgatory.

In embattled spirit, Calvin asks if his opponents think that Paul and the apostles had to endure purgatory? And if so, what assurance do we have that they have made it through to the beatific vision? And if not, how come their merits accrue to the deficiencies of the rest? Calvin's reasoning is devastating and his exegesis of the passage is masterful.

As for prayers for the dead (in purgatory), Calvin argues that neither Scripture nor the early church advocate any such thing. From where, therefore, does it originate? Here Calvin touches on a raw nerve: it is yet again an example of man's irrepressible default of a works-righteousness mentality, for it provides another means for attributing salvation to human merit (3.5.10). In the end, every false religion is a variation on self-justification.

DEREK THOMAS

3.6.1 - 3.6.5

Calvin begins a new section here comprising five chapters devoted to the nature of the Christian life. It has known a separate existence from the *Institutes*, published as a booklet in its own right. Referring to his love of brevity (yes, after nearly seven hundred pages!), Calvin begins by outlining his plan and method. The central point to grasp is that Christians must have a 'love for righteousness' (3.6.2). We are to be holy because God is holy. 'For it is highly unfitting that the sanctuary in which he dwells should like a stable be crammed with filth' (*ibid.*). More specifically, the shape of holiness is moulded in the imitation of Christ, who is 'the bond of our adoption' (3.6.3).

Sounding very much like the medieval Thomas à Kempis (*The Imitation of Christ*), Calvin stresses the importance of the heart, and warns against the evil of nominal Christianity. We strive toward holy perfection though we may never, of course, attain it. With language of rhetorical beauty, Calvin urges us to struggle *daily* without growing weary for lack of progress:

> No one shall set out so inauspiciously as not daily to make some headway, though it be slight. Therefore, let us not cease so to act that we may make some unceasing progress in the way of the Lord. And let us not despair at the slightness of our success; for even though attainment may not correspond to desire, when today outstrips yesterday the effort is not lost (3.6.5).

Lord, renew that vision in me!

DEREK THOMAS

3.7.1 - 3.7.7

One of the most memorable passages in all of the *Institutes* begins with the words, 'We are not our own...':

> We are not our own: let not our reason nor our will, therefore, sway our plans and deeds. We are not our own: let us therefore not seek what is expedient for us according to the flesh. We are not our own: in so far as we can, let us therefore forget ourselves and all that is ours. Conversely, we are God's: let us therefore live for him and die for him. We are God's: let his wisdom and will therefore rule all our actions. We are God's: let all the parts of our life accordingly strive toward him as our only lawful goal (3.7.1).

For Calvin, self-denial and cross-bearing are the twin (negative) marks of genuine holiness. In this section Calvin is at his most eloquent. You can hear the preacher in him: '...we are God's: let us therefore live for him and die for him. We are God's: let his wisdom and will therefore rule all our actions. We are God's: let all the parts of our life accordingly strive toward him as our only lawful goal' (3.7.1).

One can almost sense how disgusting pride was to the Reformer. The way of Christ is the way of self-denial, to think others better than himself. What might this mean in practice? Consider what Calvin has to say about 'giving' in 3.7.7. In giving we must imagine ourselves in the place of the one whom we see in need, and give as though we were giving to our own relief. Then, in answer to the question, 'How much?' Calvin responds, not with 10%, but with no less than love demands, 'to set no other limit than the end of his resources'.

Ouch! Love gives and gives again and, then, gives again.

Lord, give me a loving heart that gives and gives and gives.

DEREK THOMAS

3.7.8 - 3.8.3

The *Institutes* almost demands multiple readings. Not only because the work is so rich in doctrinal perspective, but also because it is, in fact, full of striking 'one-liners'. Such surely include these words: 'the chief part of self-denial ... looks to God' (3.7.8).

There is a verbal paradox here, and also a word that can prove to be a kind of salvation for earnest souls. *Self*-denial is not attained by self-focus, but by God-centredness. The medicine for the self-intoxication of the narcissistic self is not reflection on the self at all. It is personal reflection on God that produces the kind of self-forgetfulness that comes to expression in the beauty of Christian character.

Yet, Calvin insists, there is something deeper — or, as he says, 'higher' (3.8.1). Self-denial is not a shapeless, amorphous, notion. Since the goal of self-denial is not merely self-forgetfulness but Christ-likeness (and we cannot look to God apart from Christ), the 'higher' dimension of self-denial is bearing the cross. After all, if the Father purposes to conform his children to the image of his Son, what other instrument would he use than cross-bearing? The Saviour's 'whole life was nothing but a sort of perpetual cross' (*ibid.*). 'Why', asks Calvin, 'should we exempt ourselves ... from the condition to which Christ our head had to submit?' (*ibid.*).

This is muscular Christianity, indeed. But is it not all too bleak (as some have thought)? Not if we consider: (1) the depravity of our hearts that requires the strongest of medicines to eradicate our self-intoxication; and (2) the wonder of the goal in view — that we should become like Jesus. In the goal lies the comfort.

The implication? Do not underestimate the radical nature of the work that needs to be done in you if you are to become like Christ! Surely you didn't think that would be a small thing accomplished without pain?

SINCLAIR FERGUSON

3.8.4 - 3.8.10

Christians are crucifers, cross-bearers. The cross is laid across the back of the spiritually obese. We are 'fattened and made flabby' (3.8.5), wrote the lean and spare Geneva Reformer. We might say — keeping Calvin's universe of discourse but employing a contemporary idiom — the cross is the spiritual lap-band surgery that alone curtails our appetite for this world.

But the cruciform shape of the Christian life serves other functions. It tests our patience and presses us into the way of obedience. Only when our own natural desires for ease and pleasure are crossed will we learn fully to look to the Lord who sovereignly governs all things. Only by bearing the cross do we learn the kind of patient waiting that is the hallmark of the seasoned believer. This means both waiting *on* the Lord in humble devotion and self-abandonment, but also waiting *for* the Lord who works when, how and where he pleases.

True, it is our calling to make responsible decisions according to the will of God. But this we can do only when the sovereign purposes of God are ripe for the decision. In the meantime, we may have to 'bear patiently the cross of grief or pain'. Such a cross is laid on our shoulder at different angles. Sometimes the friction on our skin will be caused by chastisement. Thus we must learn to see afflictions as child training. If we grasp this we will immediately begin to feel that there is always something kind and gracious about the Lord's dealings with us.

But believers sometimes face persecution — 'stripped of our possessions by the wickedness of impious men...' (3.8.7). Where lies our consolation then? Here is the tender answer of someone who in his early twenties had to flee his beloved homeland as a wanted man, never to enjoy again extended residence there: 'If we are cast out of our own house, then we will be the more intimately received into God's family. If we are vexed and despised, we but take all the firmer root in Christ' (*ibid.*).

Such a strong prescription for the Christian life can be safely accepted from a soul-physician who spoke from such experience, and who, in his life, had instructed and then strengthened young men who gave their very life-blood for Christ.

SINCLAIR FERGUSON

Christians are not the only ones who have discussed the virtue of patience. But what distinguishes biblical teaching from that of the philosophers is the grand sense of purpose and design.

Granted, pagan philosophers at times saw that affliction tests us — but to what glorious end? By contrast, the Christian sees in affliction both the *righteousness* of God (I deserve affliction) and the *purpose* of God (suffering leads to glory). Only this perspective, says Calvin, can bring a truly quiet and thankful mind.

But there is more — for Calvin always has surprises for those who have misread him: thanksgiving in affliction 'can come forth only from a cheerful and happy heart' (3.8.11). May we say, on this basis, that Calvinism — which claims to point firmly to the biblical basis for thankfulness — is always meant to produce cheerful and happy Christians. What else?

The patient believer is thankful, Calvin says further, because he has a radically different perspective on life, or, we might say, on death. Looking to the glorious future promised to him in the gospel, he learns to disdain the present life by comparison.

This orientation is far from Stoicism, far from enslavement to a brutal principle of necessity. Rather, it is the perspective of the person who has seen through the dazzle of this world's riches and recognized that they are empty. Look at life through the lenses of its innumerable miseries and we realize we live in Vanity Fair. This is not a world of final happiness — for the simple reason that it is not the final world on which the believer has set his sights.

One more thought: Calvin speaks about 'contempt' for the present world (3.9.1). Is that not too strong? Certainly some have thought so. But perhaps they have never stood on the same ground as Calvin as they have assessed this world: 'If heaven is our homeland, what else is the earth but our place of exile?' (3.9.4).

What indeed? Wise words from a man who spent more than half his life in exile!

SINCLAIR FERGUSON

3.9.5 - 3.10.4

How can we happily contemplate the future life when the access route to it is by death? The natural fear of the dissolution of our bodies surely makes encouragement to contemplate the future life a 'counsel of perfection', reserved only for the most sophisticated of Christians.

Not for Calvin! The Christian, he says, does not see his physical death abstracted from the sure promise of the resurrection. Furthermore, the human craving to endure can be satisfied only by the realities offered to us in the gospel on the other side of death. Shame on us, then, if the whole creation is longing for that day but we are not! Receive Calvin's challenge: 'Let us ... consider this settled: that no one has made progress in the school of Christ who does not joyfully await the day of death and final resurrection' (3.9.5).

There is a broader context, of course, for this — reflection on the destinies of believers and unbelievers. There is comfort for the one who, in faith, looks to eternal salvation, when all tears will be wiped away and the delights of fellowship with God will be fully experienced. Apart from this there is not merely nothingness, but laughter turned into weeping, peace become torment.

But how, then, are we who await death to live in this world and to use it? Here Calvin distances himself from his beloved Augustine. The Christian does not see the world as an unavoidable evil to be used as little as possible. He views it as a great, if fallen, creation.

So, the principles of the justified sinner include:

1. Use God's gifts for the ends for which he gave them — which includes utility and pleasure.
2. Remember that you are a sinner, resisting the desires of ever-present lust.
3. Live with an open hand, possessing all you have as though it were not yours; for, after all, nothing *is* yours. Yes, it is for your use, enjoyment and pleasure; but everything you have is a trust from God, and it remains his, not yours.

Perhaps you need to apply one, or all, of these principles today?

SINCLAIR FERGUSON

3.10.5 - 3.11.4

The *Institutes* is a great work of theology. But it is difficult to find the right adjective for the kind of theology it represents — systematic, biblical-ecclesiastical, pastoral? It is certainly all of the above. Calvin engages the mind, heart, will and affections as he writes. He does not want to miss the atmosphere in which Scripture teaches the church as he in turn becomes her teacher.

Thus, as he directs us to the importance of meditating on the future life and seeing the present in the light of the future, he offers further practical counsels to teach us how to live:

1. If you have little, learn how to go without. The advice may sound a little brutal coming from so famous a man; but do not presume he was rich. He left little of this world's goods behind. He 'went without' because he had more important things to do with his life than to fuss about what he did not have.
2. Remember, you will render account for your stewardship. This changes everything. It puts in a new light 'all delights that draw man's spirit away from chastity and purity, or befog the mind' (3.10.5).
3. Reflect on your God-given calling, whatever it may be. Calvin stresses that there is no divinely given vocation that is sordid or base. What dignity the sense of God's sovereignty and providence in our lives can produce!

Calvin, dramatically, only now introduces the doctrine of the justification of sinners by the free grace of God through faith apart from works. His arrangement seems strange to the modern reader (especially if schooled in the *ordo salutis* — the 'order of salvation' — of later Calvinism, where justification precedes progress in sanctification). Why do this so late in the day, after describing the life of holiness?

Calvin is explicit about his motive: to demonstrate that the faith that justifies apart from works is never devoid of good works. Further, his order also reflects the order in which our witness vindicates the gospel and leads others to seek Christ. First they see good works in our lives. Only then do they come to discover how — or better by whom — they were produced. May that continue to be so!

SINCLAIR FERGUSON

3.11.5 - 3.11.8

Is the *Institutes* a work of systematic theology (as the prior reading asked)? Yes and no. Calvin covers many of the topics of theology in his own inimitable way, but unevenly. There is much from the patristic and medieval theology that he takes for granted. His book is an 'occasional' work, written to further the Reformation. It not written in the more timeless style of, say, Charles Hodge's *Systematic Theology*.

This comes through, for example, in Calvin's discussion of the Lutheran theologian Andreas Osiander (1498-1565), who is largely forgotten now. Osiander is best remembered, perhaps, for being the author of the anonymous preface to Copernicus' *On the Revolutions of the Heavenly Spheres*. But he is also immortalized in the *Institutes*. Calvin was stirred up by his confusions over justification.

For Calvin, justification entails the imputation of Christ's righteousness to sinners. For Osiander, Christ's righteousness is literally the believer's; beyond being reckoned to him by faith, it becomes one of his properties. For Osiander, 'Christ's essence is mixed with our own' (3.11.5), as Calvin puts it, and there are a number of reasons why this is unacceptable.

As regards justification, Osiander commits a double error. Not only does he confuse how Christ's righteousness becomes the believer's, but he misunderstands the nature of the believer's union with Christ, which is a bond established by the Spirit, not a merging of essences as Osiander envisages.

This debate has radical implications for our understanding of the benefits of redemption. By merging Christ with the believer, Osiander confounds justification and sanctification attributing both to 'the essence of the divine nature ... poured into us' (3.11.6) — a serious blunder. For Calvin, justification and sanctification are inseparable but always distinct. For him, both graces become ours through the Spirit as we are united to Christ.

However, there is one point of agreement — faith itself does not justify us before God, it is for Calvin (merely) 'a kind of vessel', 'only the instrument for receiving righteousness' from Christ, who is 'the Author and Minister of this great benefit' (3.11.7).

PAUL HELM

3.11.9 - 3.11.11

In his attack upon Osiander, Calvin adds that while 'Christ, as he is God and man, justifies us', Christ's righteousness remains a work of the Saviour's human nature, the fruit of his obedience to the Father (Phil. 2:8). This is another reason why it cannot be God's divine righteousness that is actually conveyed to us.

Calvin now brings us to the heart of his discussion of the application of redemption. Salvation comes to us by our union with Christ, a union in which we remain distinct from Christ but are bound to him by his Spirit. 'We do not, therefore, contemplate him outside ourselves from afar in order that his righteousness may be imputed to us but because we put on Christ and are engrafted into his body — in short, because he deigns to make us one with him' (3.11.10). Osiander disdains this, preferring to think of a 'gross mingling' (*ibid.*) of Christ with believers.

Calvin glances at the way in which these differences will affect how one understands the Lord's Supper, marking the Lutheran teaching that at the Supper the substance of Christ is received. For Calvin, the whole Christ is received in the Supper, but only as the Spirit imparts his graces to faithful participators.

Why quibble over such matters? The final problem is assurance. The imputation of Christ's righteousness, a righteousness that is perfect and complete, is the only ground of assurance. Osiander thinks (as many have since) that such imputation is a fiction, but this is because he fails to see that 'the grace of justification is not separated from regeneration, although they are things distinct' (3.11.11). Merge Christ and the Christian, or justification with the Christian's works, and assurance is lost.

PAUL HELM

3.11.12 - 3.11.17

After soundly refuting Osiander, Calvin returns to his mainline exposition of justification by faith alone — that the believer receives pardon, and righteousness is reckoned to him as the only ground of acceptance.

So are works of the law excluded? Certainly. But what about the works of the regenerate? Don't they count towards justification? No, not even these works count for justification, since Paul excludes works of all sorts. 'In the contrast between the righteousness of the law and of the gospel ... all works are excluded, whatever title may grace them' (3.11.14). Anything less confounds justification and sanctification.

In this regard, Calvin picks out the Roman doctrine of merit for special mention. Beginning with the early introduction of the idea of merit through Augustine, Calvin sees the idea of merit as a gift of God's grace as having gradually degenerated until it became a brand of works-righteousness, a form of Pelagianism. The biblical doctrine of justification through Christ's imputed righteousness is incompatible with such teaching. Rather than offer our own pseudo-merits, even works which are wholly the product of divine grace, we must instead 'look solely upon God's mercy and Christ's perfection' (3.11.16), since our graces are always imperfect, our obedience always tainted.

Calvin states, rather disarmingly, that what he is discussing could be set forth better than he has managed, but that it does not much matter in what order these benefits are set out provided that we are clear on the essentials. Take note, students of the 'order of salvation' (*ordo salutis*)!

PAUL HELM

If, as Paul says, the law is not of faith (Gal. 3:11-12), the one excludes the other as the instrument of justification. As Calvin puts it, if 'works are required for law righteousness ... it follows that they are not required for faith righteousness' (3.11.18). But Paul repeatedly 'denies that we are aided by works and that we attain righteousness by working; instead, we come empty and receive it' (*ibid.*) by God's mercy. And so justification is by faith alone.

Calvin is sensitive to language, particularly when it comes to the appropriateness of using non-scriptural terms when analysing scriptural doctrine (see his disdain for the term 'merit' in 3.15.2!). But he defends the phrase 'justification by faith *alone*' even though the 'alone' is not found verbatim in Scripture. The addition is legitimate, he says, because it captures Paul's insistence that the sinner is justified 'apart from the law' (Rom. 3:21). 'Does not he who takes everything from works firmly enough ascribe everything to faith alone?' (3.11.19). If faith excludes works and justification is by faith, then justification is by faith alone.

Next, Calvin tackles another 'ingenious subterfuge' (*ibid.*) — that the works in question are ceremonial Jewish works distinct from the moral law; and so moral observance is necessary for justification. But Paul is clear: 'Cursed be everyone who does not abide by all things written in the Book of the Law, and do them' (Gal. 3:10).

PAUL HELM

Justification by the imputed righteousness of Christ is the true doctrine of acceptance. But is it necessary, vital? How serious should we be about it? Does it matter? Is it really worth fighting over?

It matters more than we can say, says Calvin. For it concerns our vindication not before a human court but before a 'heavenly tribunal' (3.12.1). Therefore, it is a 'serious matter' far beyond 'frivolous word battles' (*ibid.*). Only God's righteousness is immaculate, underived, Creatorly righteousness (incidentally, Calvin's emphasis on the book of Job in asserting the immaculate righteousness of God, which first appeared in the 1539 *Institutes*, carries over from his preaching through that book in 1554-5). It is with this God that we have to do. Such righteousness will not be satisfied with any works of man. Christian theology is not a game. The Christian religion is hardly a way that we choose to spend our leisure.

Calvin finds support for this outlook in Paul, of course, but also in Augustine and Bernard of Clairvaux, the two thinkers to whom he habitually turns in matters of grace and free will.

Augustine: 'All the pious who groan under their burden of corruptible flesh and in this weakness of life have one hope, that we have one Mediator, Jesus Christ the righteous one, and he is the appeasement for our sins' (3.12.3).

Bernard: 'Merit enough it is to know that merits are not enough; but as it is merit enough not to presume upon merits, so to be without merits is enough for judgement' (*ibid.*).

Calvin bridles at the use of the word 'merit' but does not lose Bernard's main point, which is to strike fear in hypocrites.

So the recognition of the fact that we do not live before men but before God has two other practical consequences. It puts paid to hypocrisy, and to self-flattery.

PAUL HELM

For Calvin, the only possible way to receive God's mercy is with absolute humility, which he defines as 'an unfeigned submission of our heart, stricken down in earnest with an awareness of its own misery and want' (3.12.6). Without such humility, we remain persuaded of our own righteousness, when in fact we ought to be confident only in the mercy of God. We will never find sufficient consolation in Christ, Calvin observes, 'unless we have already experienced desolation in ourselves' (3.12.8). But when we are truly humbled before God, our hearts are open to receive the free gift of his justifying grace.

Chapter 13 begins by noting two goals that the biblical doctrine of justification achieves: first, it preserves God's undiminished glory; and second, it blesses the sinful conscience with full peace and assurance.

Calvin seeks to promote the glory of God at every possible point in his theology, but never more so than in his doctrine of free justification. As long as we insist on saying something in our own defence, giving some credit to our own righteousness, we detract from God's glory. 'Whoever glories in himself', Calvin insists, 'glories against God' (3.13.2).

Justification begins, therefore, with the recognition that we do not have even one single 'crumb' (*ibid*.) of our own true righteousness. Whatever righteousness we possess comes as a gift from God, who thus retains all the praise for our justification.

In addition to preserving God's glory to himself, the doctrine of free justification has the further benefit of providing the believer with full assurance of faith. Because it comes from God — not from ourselves — justifying righteousness supports the believer with steadfast confidence before the judgement of God.

PHILIP RYKEN

3.13.4 - 3.14.5

In justification, the sinner receives righteousness from God as a gift. Because this gift rests on the promise of God, received by faith, it provides complete assurance to the conscience and full peace to the soul. Our hope of inheriting an eternal kingdom is based on the solid ground of our union with Christ and his righteousness imputed to us.

To help explain this doctrine of justification, Calvin distinguishes between four categories of people, starting with those who are not justified at all. He describes such people as being 'endowed with no knowledge of God and immersed in idolatry' (3.14.1). This definition echoes two important themes from the beginning of the *Institutes*: the importance of knowing God and the pervasiveness of idolatry as the root sin of the human heart.

Calvin does not deny that unbelievers are capable of virtue, yet he insists that any virtues they possess come from God — gifts of his common grace. However, he insists that the virtues of unbelievers still merit punishment rather than reward. This is primarily because deeds that appear outwardly to be good works are tainted nonetheless by sinful motives. Here Calvin quotes Augustine approvingly: 'Our religion distinguishes the just from the unjust not by the law of works but by that of faith, without which what seemed good works are turned into sins' (3.14.4).

Before turning to the other three categories of people, Calvin restates — yet again — the core principle of his doctrine of justification by grace: we cannot be justified by our own inherent righteousness (of which we have not the slightest particle), but only by the righteousness that comes from our merciful God. He never tires of the truth; nor should we.

PHILIP RYKEN

3.14.6 - 3.14.11

Calvin continues his four-fold categorization of where people stand with respect to justification. He concludes his remarks on the first category — people who are outside of Christ and thus remain unjustified — by reiterating that justification depends entirely on God's mercy, not our works. We remain dead in our sins until we are united to the living Christ.

The next two categories get lumped together: nominal Christians (those who confess Christ with their lips, but deny him with their actions) and hypocrites (those who conceal their wickedness with empty pretence). People in both categories are not justified before God. Even worse, whatever external good works they perform are contaminated by the impurity of their sinful hearts. In people who are not truly justified, 'works manifesting even the highest splendour are so far away from righteousness before the Lord that they are reckoned sins' (3.14.8).

The fourth and final category is people who have been regenerated by the Holy Spirit and are justified by faith. Such believers make true holiness their primary concern and live as those sprinkled with the blood of Christ (1 Peter 1:2); not that their works are perfect, of course; even the best works of the best Christians are 'corrupted with some impurity of the flesh' (3.14.9).

We should never think, therefore, that we have any righteousness of our own that can justify us before God. Calvin insists, in the strongest possible terms, 'first, that there never existed any work of a godly man which, if examined by God's stern judgement, would not deserve condemnation; secondly, if such a work were found ... it would still lose favour — weakened and stained as it is by the sins with which its author himself is surely burdened' (3.14.11).

It is only through faith in Christ that our persons and our works are ever accepted by God. In his righteousness alone we find 'cleansing, satisfaction, atonement, and perfect obedience, with which all our iniquities are covered' (*ibid.*).

PHILIP RYKEN

3.14.12 - 3.14.18

Calvin borrowed generously from earlier theologians (especially Augustine) in formulating his *Institutes of the Christian Religion*. Of one group, though, he was especially critical: 'the Schoolmen', also known as 'the Scholastics'.

The Schoolmen were theologians who taught theology and philosophy at major European universities during the Middle Ages — men like William of Ockham, Duns Scotus, and, especially, Thomas Aquinas. Although Calvin valued the scholarship of these theologians, he did not hesitate to critique their theology, especially as it pertained to the grace of God.

Generally speaking, the Schoolmen conceded that human righteousness was not, in and of itself, worthy to gain salvation. Nevertheless, they believed that good works that went above and beyond the call of duty (works of 'supererogation') could merit forgiveness for sinners.

Calvin rejected this argument outright. The only righteousness perfect enough to justify a sinner before God is the righteousness of Jesus Christ, received by faith. Only a sinner clothed in the innocence of Christ has continual forgiveness before God.

The error of the Schoolmen, from Calvin's perspective, was their failure to take sin as seriously as God takes it. If they truly understood how utterly wicked it is to sin against a holy God, they would never pretend that the sum of a sinner's righteousness could ever compensate for even one little sin.

Nor did the Schoolmen truly understand the obedience that God requires, argues Calvin. Jesus said that even if we were to do everything that God commands, we would still be nothing more than 'unworthy servants' (Luke 17:10). Therefore, we should neither trust in the merit of our works nor ascribe to them any boastful glory, as the Schoolmen did.

PHILIP RYKEN

3.14.19 - 3.15.3

During recent debates over justification, it has occasionally been said that a tendency to works righteousness is merely a local problem. It was Luther's problem, and probably Augustine's too, but the Reformation has wrongly assumed that it is everyone's problem.

Calvin's treatment of works and justification in this section takes precisely the opposite position. He regards works righteousness as endemic to the idolatrous, sinful human condition. To read these sections is to see the Reformer's profound personal and pastoral passion. Here, too, we are reminded that, when it comes to the spiritual life of Christians, not much has changed in the last five hundred years.

Calvin has already abused the notion of works contributing to justification. But do good works contribute to the Christian's assurance in any sense? Yes, says Calvin, but tread carefully. Our works are 'proof of the indwelling of the Holy Spirit' (3.14.19); but, if ever we view them as the basis or even the direct proof of our salvation, their weakness will unravel our confidence.

Meanwhile, we must not despise good works as worthless. We are saved for good works (Eph. 2:10); hence, they are very precious to God. But, again relying on Augustine, Calvin argues that we must never commend our good works to God but only commend God in our good works, since praise belongs to him alone. Even in texts that appear to correlate our salvation with good works (think of Jesus' words to the sheep in Matt. 25:31f), the gracious ministry of the Spirit is always the cause of the works. (Calvin's sound treatment of good works in this section will undoubtedly help confused readers of, for example, N. T. Wright's recent writings.)

The only works capable of meriting salvation are perfect works that completely fulfil God's law — and these we sinners cannot do! Still, justified Christians should not grow weary of doing good works (Gal. 6:9) in the Spirit, for they display God's merit, not ours. Tenant farmers may enjoy the fruit that grows on their land, says Calvin, but they may not claim the deed to it. Likewise, we may celebrate works, so long as we remember that we are farming on soil of which God is the sole owner.

RICHARD PHILLIPS

3.15.4 - 3.15.8

Calvin understood that those who will not submit themselves to Scripture will always seek to impose their views onto Scripture through its misuse. When it comes to the topic of works and merit, we must exercise the greatest care in our reading. Especially in this section, Calvin is a worthy guide.

The Reformer dismisses several false doctrines invented by men and taught nowhere in Scripture. One is the idea that while eternal life is by grace alone, good works merit God's favour in a temporal way. The Lord does, of course, reward obedience and punish disobedience in his people similar to any loving father; but this hardly implies that good works accrue temporal merit before God. All our works are divine gifts that he 'examines ... according to his tenderness' and rewards according to his grace. Even to be a child of God who receives chastisement is the result of God's mercy.

Those who seek to gain merit with God through their works, whether Spirit-wrought or not, seek to build on a foundation other than Christ. Our churches today are plagued with any number of subtle doctrinal schemes that amount to 'get in by grace, but stay in by works'. Calvin unleashes a barrage of New Testament texts to deal with this false teaching as well. Righteousness, not merit, is the gift of pure grace. Therefore, we remain sinners even as we are counted righteous; we remain fools even as Christ is our wisdom unto salvation; and we remain weak, even as Christ is power to us that shatters the gates of hell.

It should not need to be said — though it does — that no Christian ever advances beyond the point of relying utterly on the grace of Christ. Sadly, Roman Catholicism directs penitents to grace-infused works as an approach to merit with God. Note Calvin's vehement response: 'O overweening and shameless impiety!' (3.15.6). For him, true doctrine (and true power) accompanies a true passion for God's glory.

So much for the argument heard today that zeal for doctrine will lead to spiritual dryness. Calvin knows that, in fact, Christian zeal rests on scriptural truth — and thus on Christ alone, through faith alone, by grace alone.

RICHARD PHILLIPS

'My, how time flies', we like to say. But, reading Calvin, we realize that while time flies, challenges to the gospel seldom change. Chapter 16 of Book 3 takes up objections to the doctrine of justification through faith alone that never seem to die (in part because they are kept alive by their original source, the Roman Catholic Church). The good news is that heresy is always the occasion for many excellent writings by orthodox Christians. Thus, these four paragraphs in the *Institutes* are worthy of consideration by every believer.

First, Calvin confronts the charge that to teach justification by faith alone is to do away with good works. How many well-meaning false teachers — including some who know the truth of justification through faith alone (hello, Richard Baxter!) — insist that some form of legalism is necessary to avoid moral laxity in the Christian life. If such a thought has crossed your lips, then read Calvin carefully in 3.16.1. Those who grasp justification (by faith alone) necessarily grasp sanctification, too, for there is only one Christ, 'who contains both of them in himself' (3.16.1). Again, 'Christ justifies no one whom he does not at the same time sanctify. These benefits are joined together by an everlasting and indissoluble bond' (*ibid.*). I love it when Calvin gets worked up in passionate prose (as he does here), because it means something vital is at hand.

A second charge is the related belief that merit through good works is necessary for inspiring moral zeal. Calvin refutes his opponents who 'stupidly reason from reward to merit' (3.16.2) by reminding us that true believers are motivated by the worship and glory of God, not just for personal (and graciously bestowed) rewards. Scripture does speak of future rewards, in part, to motivate us to good works. But many exhortations to holiness point in other directions, making no mention of rewards. A Christian's holy calling, gratitude for divine love, the example of Christ, the glory of God, and the indwelling of the Holy Spirit, for example, all impel believers to obey with joy.

Ultimately, the 'fear of God', which defines the Christian life, and which papists erroneously consider a source of merit, is itself 'founded upon the pardon and forgiveness of sins' (3.16.3). For this reason, Calvin states, 'there is no honouring of God unless his mercy be acknowledged' (3.16.3).

RICHARD PHILLIPS

3.17.1 - 3.17.5

In these sections, Calvin is clearly wearied by the ceaseless attacks on justification through faith alone. Still, he perseveres, exhorting his readers, 'Come, let us keep beating them back!' (3.17.1). He quickly offers up another classic statement: 'Justification is withdrawn from works, not that no good works may be done, or that what is done may be denied to be good, but that we may not rely upon them, glory in them, or ascribe salvation to them' (*ibid.*). It is no surprise that we are still reading Calvin five centuries after his birth!

Calvin argues that a true apprehension of the gospel requires us to understand clearly two things about works and the law. First, because we have broken the law through sin, no works of ours can absolve us of our guilt. Second, even our purest works fall short of the holy standard of God's law. When we grasp these two truths, we will understand how desperately we need 'another righteousness from faith' (3.17.2). However, lest anyone denigrates works, Calvin explains that our good works, although flawed and corrupt, please God as he embraces us as his servants in Christ.

The 'Sophists', says Calvin, distort this view of good works with their concept of 'condign merit' (this is what Calvin refers to when he writes, 'by reason of the covenant' [3.17.3] — it is papist merit theology, not Reformed covenant theology, that he is disparaging here). Condign merit acknowledges that while our good works do not *strictly* merit acceptance with God, he will accept certain good works nonetheless. Such works, of course, permeate Roman Catholic sacramental and penitential practices. Calvin utterly repudiates this, showing that the Scriptures leave no room for our works when it comes to our acceptance by God, which is by mercy alone. If God later commends our good works, it is only because of the finished work of Christ that secured our salvation 'while we were still sinners' (Rom. 5:8).

As I noted earlier, the *Institutes* speaks very directly to such controversial views of justification which seek to blend faith and human works. Calvin says, 'God's sole reason to receive man unto himself is that he sees him utterly lost if left to himself, but because he does not will to be lost, he exercises mercy in freeing him' (3.17.4).

RICHARD PHILLIPS

3.17.6 - 3.17.10

Calvin's greatness, in part, is in his enduring relevance. I believe Calvin anticipated (correctly) that attempts to attain a righteousness by works would always attack the gospel truth of justification through faith alone. His unwavering persistence in dealing with this topic is proof.

Calvin now turns to Old Testament texts that speak of God's favour to those who are faithful. Do these teach works righteousness? No, Calvin insists. Rather, such texts indicate 'what kind of servants they are who have undertaken his covenant in good faith rather than express the reason why the Lord benefits them' (3.17.6). This should remind us that there are all kinds of causal relationships within Christian salvation and, in some of them, good works are a true cause. But: (1) our works are never the instrumental cause of our justification (faith alone is the instrument); and (2) behind every other cause in our salvation is the grace of God working through faith in Christ.

Next, Calvin cites an impressive collection of Old Testament verses that mention the righteousness of works (e.g. Deut. 6:25: 'It will be righteousness for us, if we are careful to do all this commandment...') — Calvin's opponents could hardly have done better (3.17.7)! Surely now, they argue, justification cannot be by faith alone. In response, Calvin admits that a real righteousness may be found through works, so long as the whole law is perfectly kept. But this he denies exists anywhere among sinful men.

How can a man be justified by a few works when he transgresses in so many others? How can a man with unresolved guilt be accepted by God? That any of our works are called 'righteous' by God indicates that we are first justified through faith alone in Christ alone. Thus, while works are opposed to faith as the ground of justification, faith is not opposed to works as its fruit. Rather, the faith that justifies is also a faith that works in love (Gal. 5:6). Here is the biblical line that Calvin walked.

RICHARD PHILLIPS

3.17.11 - 3.17.15

Rick has carefully noted the relevance of Calvin's arguments concerning justification for today. Unfortunately, the errors that the Geneva Reformer addressed in his time persist centuries later. This section provides another opportunity to learn from him as we strive to contend for the apostolic faith.

In this section, Calvin addresses the perplexing issue of how Paul and James appear to contradict one another on justification, faith and works. But Calvin demonstrates that the two apostles harmonize once we realize that they attach different (but legitimate) meanings to the same words. For example, 'faith', for Paul, primarily indicates the genuine, living faith of a believer in union with Christ. By contrast, James uses the term to speak of a dead and demonic confession of monotheism; a faith that does not terminate on the justifying Christ. Similarly, for Paul, 'justification' refers to pardon and the imputation of righteousness by faith, whereas James speaks of a 'justification' whereby good works manifest saving faith. With these nuances in place, Calvin rightfully upholds Paul's justification in Christ by faith alone and James' insistence that believers manifest their justifying faith by good works. Nowhere does James contradict the substance of Paul's epistles.

Calvin then tackles another confusing issue: if justification is by faith alone, why do Old Testament saints occasionally appeal to God by their own righteousness (e.g. Ps. 7:8; 26:1)? Calvin helpfully draws our attention to the broader context of such claims. These saints, he says, pointed to their righteous behaviour: (1) in particular cases, not throughout their entire lives; and (2) in contrast to the wicked, not according to the perfection of God's law. Hence, believers may appeal to God to witness their integrity against the hypocrisy of the ungodly, but we must always confess that no one will stand or be justified before God through their own deeds (Ps. 130:3; 143:2).

If we dare apply the label 'perfection' to the saints, says Calvin, we must (with Augustine) remember that 'to this very perfection also belongs the recognition of imperfection, both in truth and in humility' (3.17.15). And so we cling to the Lord always.

JUSTIN TAYLOR

3.18.1 - 3.18.5

If we are justified by faith alone apart from works, how are we to understand the scriptural (including Pauline) teaching that we are to be judged and rewarded according to deeds?

We should note, first, that Calvin believes (rightly in my view) that these passages refer to eternal life itself (i.e., not some extra heavenly rewards). Therefore, they describe what will happen to believers (i.e., they are not hypothetical or applied only to unbelievers). Calvin's main point is that a Christian's good works do not strictly bring eternal life, but they are an essential preparatory step on the way to immortality. We are not servants seeking to earn our wages, but rather sons with an inheritance who desire to please our Father.

Second, Calvin points to Jesus' parable of the tenants (Matt. 20:1ff) to demonstrate the role of grace in works. The blessings of reward were promised to the workers *before* their works were accomplished; so, too, eternal life is not merited by the things we do, but rather by the adoption that our Father has bestowed (3.18.3). In every way, the blessings of eternal life are the result of divine mercy.

God has wisely designed our salvation, concludes Calvin, to bring us comfort, never to engender pride. It is humbling to remember that even our best works are unworthy in God's sight. But by his infinite mercy and goodness, he destroys what is unworthy in our works and gladly receives them in Christ.

JUSTIN TAYLOR

3.18.6 - 3.18.10

Let us focus on two points of interest in Calvin's teaching in this section: first, the relationship between God's promises and his justice; second, Jesus' answer to the rich young ruler.

Calvin argues that God's promises are effective only if they are preceded by God's free covenant mercy, without which there would be no salvation. Bound to him by covenant, we can have confidence that God in his grace will reward our unworthy works. In this case, divine justice is not expressed by his repaying us for the good we have done, but by his faithfulness to the promise he has made.

You will recall that the young legal scholar asked Jesus what good deed was required to gain eternal life (Matt. 19:16). Jesus responded that if he would enter life, he must keep the commandments. Calvin explains that a proper understanding of Jesus' statement will consider, first, the young man's character; and, second, his question. Here was a man blinded by confidence in his works and interested in a merely external obedience, asking Jesus what works of righteousness were necessary to obtain salvation. Calvin unfolds the gospel logic:

1. If we seek salvation in works, we must return to the law, the 'perfect mirror of righteousness' (3.18.9), and keep the commandments.
2. None of us keeps the commandments, much less grasps the chasm that lies between our life and divine righteousness.
3. Therefore, we must seek 'another help' (*ibid*.) apart from works, namely, faith alone, in Christ alone.

So the law is crucial to our salvation, after all. For unless we understand the hard path of legal righteousness and how far afield we have wandered, we will not cling to Christ alone. Only by seeing the impossibility of the way of works will we flee for refuge in him.

Thanks be to God who has rescued us in Christ from futile attempts at self-justification!

JUSTIN TAYLOR

3.19.1 - 3.19.7

Calvin regards a proper understanding of Christian liberty as 'a thing of prime necessity' (3.19.1). Without it, we cannot rightly know Christ, the truth of the gospel, or peace within. Sadly, many people react strongly, even strangely, to this teaching. They assume it offers licence to sin or to flaunt morally lax behaviour before those with allegedly weaker consciences. So Calvin sets himself to refute the abuse as he presents the true doctrine.

Christian liberty, Calvin argues, has three aspects:

1. A believer's conscience must look beyond the law for assurance of justification.
2. A believer's conscience, free from the tyranny of the law, freely seeks to obey the law as the will of God.
3. Believers are not bound to 'indifferent things' (Greek: *adiaphora*) such as certain foods or clothing, but are free either to use them or forego them.

Without this teaching of Christian liberty, says Calvin, our consciences may easily ensnare themselves in an unholy labyrinth of despair and terror.

Within this discussion, Calvin carefully situates the role of works in the Christian life. Now that we are no longer 'under law' (Rom. 6:14), may works be cast off? Calvin returns to one of his favourite biblical distinctions: a slave's obedience to his master differs dramatically from a son's efforts to please his Father. The one is defined by the severe demands of law, as the slave is filled with fear that he do all the requisite works. But in a family, a loving father requires obedience, but graciously accepts his son's best works, imperfect though they be.

One application may be made for today: even if we have connected the doctrinal 'dots', are we truly living as sons of a gracious Father, or do we functionally treat God as our demanding taskmaster?

JUSTIN TAYLOR

3.19.8 - 3.19.12

Romans 14:14 is an initially perplexing but significant verse: 'I know and am persuaded in the Lord Jesus that nothing is unclean in itself, but it is unclean for anyone who thinks it unclean.' First, Paul is picking up on the category of 'things indifferent' mentioned earlier, explaining that no external thing is unclean or unholy in and of itself. Second, he teaches that if your conscience deems something unclean or unholy, then to violate one's conscience in that area is a sin. Even ill-informed consciences should not be abused.

In view of this apostolic teaching, Calvin's wisdom shines. Laughing, being filled with food, acquiring possessions, being delighted by music, drinking wine — none of these are scripturally forbidden, and all are gifts from God. But, says Calvin, we must partake with moderation, since 'God nourishes [us] to live, not to luxuriate' (3.19.9).

But what if our enjoyment of God's gifts causes offence to others? To guide us, Calvin takes up the common distinction between 'offence given' (where the fault lies with the offending agent) and 'offence taken' (where the problem is with the party offended). He warns that if one callously offends the conscience of the weak, he has failed to love his brother. So Christian liberty 'consists as much in abstaining as in using' (3.19.10). On the other hand, there will always be those of 'bitter disposition and pharisaical pride' (3.19.11) who take illegitimate offence at lawful Christian behaviour. In such cases, the Christian is free of blame.

Calvin illustrates this principle by pointing to Paul's decision to circumcise Timothy, but refusing to circumcise Titus (Acts 16:3; Gal. 2:3). Paul expresses the same freedom in Christ in both cases, but with different results. He willingly restrains his liberty with Timothy according to the circumstances; but with Titus, he refuses to accommodate those who would seek to bind the consciences of others.

Our goal, Calvin says, is to 'use our freedom if it results in the edification of our neighbour, but if it does not help our neighbour, then we should forego it' (3.19.12). May God grant us wisdom to know the peace of Christian liberty and to live peaceably among men, so far as it depends on us.

JUSTIN TAYLOR

3.19.13 - 3.19.16

Our efforts to avoid giving unnecessary offence are warped, Calvin says, if we accommodate our actions to suit another person's seared conscience. Becoming all things to all men (*cf.* 1 Cor. 9:22) does not mean following them into the muck of sin. In all our engagements in the world, the person we ought never to offend is God.

To illustrate this principle, Calvin asks whether Paul would have conducted papal Mass out of love for errant believers in need of spiritual milk (*cf.* 1 Cor. 3:2). 'No,' Calvin asserts, 'for milk is not poison' (3.19.13). For him, Protestants who attended Mass out of evangelistic concern for their Roman Catholic neighbours and friends were inhaling the noxious fumes of unbelief. To deviate 'even a fingernail's breath' (*ibid.*) from God's explicit commands out of a desire to love others is to cease to love them truly at all.

The Reformation principle that God alone has the right to bind people's consciences not only regulates our relationship to human laws — something which will receive its 'longer and clearer explanation' (3.19.14) in Book 4, Chapter 20 — but in so doing reflects the work of Christ. For 'Christ's death is nullified if we put our souls under men's subjection' (*ibid.*). (How often do you think of matters of conscience in terms of the cross?!) But lest we embrace anarchy, Calvin affirms that Christian liberty is not contravened by the magistrate's God-given role to govern the 'outward behaviour' (3.19.15) of its citizens. Christians are to submit to human laws so long as they do not require us to disobey God.

So whether dealing with friends or family, the state or society, a Christian's conscience is essential. This is a far cry from the standard 'listen to your heart' nonsense. For Calvin, the conscience is 'a sort of guardian' (3.19.15), trained by God's Word to unearth our secret sins and lead us to repent. Care for yours well. It may lay you low for a season or bring worldly persecution; but in the Spirit's hands it will lead you to 'fearlessly present [yourself] before God' (*ibid.*). And no fleeting pleasure of sin (Heb. 11:25) can finally compete with that.

CARLTON WYNNE

3.20.1 - 3.20.5

Calvin's insistence that every ounce of our salvation is a product of the person and work of Christ leads naturally to a discussion of prayer. The title of this chapter in my copy of the *Institutes* calls prayer 'the chief exercise of faith' — and well it is. Calvin understands that when we engage in this God-given means of communion with the Father, we express everything the Reformer has taught us so far concerning salvation: that God is sovereign yet may be known in Christ; that he hears the sinner's cries for mercy; that every blessing we could imagine is found in the resurrected Son. This is why Calvin says that if we do not pray, we are like a man who 'neglect[s] a treasure, buried and hidden in the earth, after it had been pointed out to him' (3.20.1). The metaphor is apt: digging is hard work, but digging for a treasure known to be there is worth the effort.

Calvin then turns to address two objections to prayer. First, doesn't God know what I need before I ask (*cf.* Matt. 6:32), and know far better than I? If so, isn't prayer superfluous? Calvin answers that God not only calls us to pray that he might be glorified (which is reason enough to pray!), but, in a sense, has 'ordained it not so much for his own sake as for ours' (3.20.3). As it honours God, prayer changes us further into the image of his Son. In fact, the more we pray for God's glory to be revealed in whatever we ask, the more our hearts will be 'fired with zealous and burning desires ever to seek, love, and serve him' (*ibid.*).

But, second, what about those times when God seems not to hear us? God is never ignorant of our prayers, says Calvin; still, he 'very often gives the impression of one sleeping or idling in order that he may thus train us, otherwise idle and lazy, to seek, ask, and entreat him to our great good' (*ibid.*).

The lesson to learn here? Pray! Pray as someone who knows he is speaking to Almighty God. Pray for the Spirit to shape your prayers according to the Word and the will of God. Pray to be changed inwardly by prayer, and pray that your prayers would effect change in the world. But above all, pray.

CARLTON WYNNE

3.20.6 - 3.20.10

The first rule of prayer, according to Calvin, is reverence for the One to whom we pray (see 3.20.4); and the second is like it: a profound sense of just how needy we are before this God. Too often people offer prayers while their 'hearts are ... cold, and they do not ponder what they ask' (3.20.6); even worse, 'for the sake of mere performance men often beseech God for many things that they are dead sure will, apart from his kindness, come to them from some other source' (*ibid.*).

Just when we are crushed with conviction, Calvin offers a word of sympathy: 'If anyone should object that we are not always urged with equal necessity to pray, I admit it' (3.20.7). Even the great Calvin struggled at times to pray! But how can we cease to pray (1 Thess. 5:17) when surrounding dangers, unyielding temptations, and burdening sins never let up in this life? By God's wise design, these trials spur us to pray aright, assuming in our prayers the 'disposition of a beggar' (*ibid.*).

The first two rules of prayer (reverence for God and a keen sense of neediness) naturally lead to a third: humility. The humble prayer casts away all smugness or pretension and rests wholly in God's mercy to sinners. For this reason, Calvin argues, it is fitting that we begin our prayers to God by repenting of individual sins. As the *Westminster Confession* puts it, we are to repent of 'particular sins, particularly' (*WCF* 15:5). Do you do this, out loud if necessary? The giants of Scripture — David, Ezra, Isaiah, the Psalmists — all 'open[ed] for themselves the door to prayer with this key' (3.20.9) and found the God who graciously pardons sins.

You may ask: 'Didn't these Old Testament saints frequently appeal to their own righteousness when pleading with God?' (e.g., Ps. 86:2; 2 Kings 20:3). Yes, says Calvin, but by this they only meant to present themselves, in contrast to God's enemies, as his redeemed children 'to whom he promises that he will be gracious' (3.20.10).

Make no mistake: prayer is for wretched sinners — but sinners who seek to sin no more. 'For no heart can ever break into sincere calling upon God that does not at the same time aspire to godliness' (*ibid.*).

CARLTON WYNNE

3.20.11 - 3.20.14

Calvin continues his guidelines for prayer by giving a fourth rule: that 'we should be ... encouraged to pray by a sure hope that our prayer will be answered' (3.20.11). Such confidence is the antithesis of presumption, since we are to revere God's holiness even as we trust in God's goodness. Nor does this rule expect an absence of distress and trouble, since faith takes its highest flight in prayer when we 'groan under present ills and anxiously fear those to come' (*ibid.*). Prayer, then, is fuelled by two emotions: a holy anxiety over this fallen world, and a quiet satisfaction that our Father is ready to come to our aid.

It should be clear by now that Calvin's four rules for prayer (reverence, a sense of need, humility and trust) cohere: knowing God as he has revealed himself magnifies our helplessness; and the humility that results takes God at his Word that he will hear the prayers of his children. The crux, according to Calvin, is that if prayer is to do us any good, we must place our entire trust in God's self-revealed character, promises and faithfulness.

Friend, the more we are overwhelmed by our own unworthiness before God and the myriad, sometimes agonizing, circumstances of life, the more we ought 'to grasp with both hands' (3.20.12) the assurance that God will hear and answer our cries for help. Biblical faith, after all, does not teach us to approach God as his employees, but to pour out our hearts 'as children unburden their troubles to their parents' (*ibid.*).

Finally, Calvin adds that '[God] declares that to be called upon in the day of need is highest and precious above all else [Psa. 50:15]' (3.20.13). God loves to hear our prayers offered in the name of Jesus — even those mingled with error — not because we are worthy to present them, but because they glorify him as God. How? Through prayer we discover God's kindness, power and Fatherly goodness; and are further impelled, with increasing joy, to pray more.

If Calvin is correct that prayer is an act of worship, what are we saying about God if we refuse to engage in it?

CARLTON WYNNE

3.20.15 - 3.20.17

How is it that prayer has 'great power as it is working' (James 5:16) if God has already ordained all things, including our prayers? While God surely knows, to us it is a mystery. But rather than throw up our hands, we ought to bow our heads in worship, trusting Scripture's truth that '[God] so tempers the outcome of events according to his incomprehensible plan that the prayers of the saints, which are a mixture of faith and error, are not nullified' (3.20.15).

From such lofty mysteries Calvin descends with something to comfort every believer who longs to pray well: 'God tolerates even our stammering and pardons our ignorance whenever something inadvertently escapes us' (3.20.16). 'Indeed,' he explains, 'without this mercy there would be no freedom to pray' (*ibid.*).

But possessing freedom is one thing; exercising it is another. Calvin confesses that 'no one has ever carried this out with the uprightness that was due' (*ibid.*). How often have we set ourselves to pray, only to make irreverent requests while our hearts stay 'on the ground' and our 'minds slip away and well-nigh vanish' (*ibid.*)? How often have we brought 'new diseases upon [ourselves] in their very remedies' (*ibid.*) as we use prayer to shake our fist at God's plan for our lives? How often have we preferred to wallow in self-pity, so certain that our prayers would strike only the ceiling?

Be encouraged, repent of your lifeless prayers, and 'break through' (*ibid.*) Satan's blockades, urges Calvin, since 'the heavenly Father himself, to free us at once from shame and fear, which might have well thrown our hearts into despair, has given us his Son, Jesus Christ our Lord, to be our advocate' (3.20.17). When this thought is absent, hope for prayer wanes; but when 'Christ comes forward as intermediary, to change the throne of dreadful glory into the throne of grace' (*ibid.*), our prayers come alive! Grasp this firmly in your darkest moments: the sympathetic Saviour still stands before the Father for you. Because this is true, 'nothing we ask in his name will be denied us, as nothing can be denied to him by the Father' (*ibid.*).

CARLTON WYNNE

3.20.18 - 3.20.22

In these paragraphs, Calvin emphasizes how unique and central is Christ's mediation for his intercession, underscoring the fact that it is only through his work that any believer has ever had access to the Father. Nevertheless, since Christ has risen and ascended to the Father, believers are now more free to call upon him than in times past.

This shapes how we should understand the prayers of the church. It might surprise some to know that Calvin *does* believe in the intercession of the saints; and it is quite likely that most who will read this do so too. How often have you asked a friend to pray for you, or offered to pray for them in a time of need? If you are a Christian, you have probably done so many times, thus acknowledging your belief in the intercession of the saints. What is crucial, however, is that you understand that such intercession neither supplements the intercession of Christ with the Father (as if that were lacking in some way); nor stands over against it (as if your prayers and those of Christ were somehow in competition with each other to gain a hearing with the Father). Rather, your prayers ascend to God the Father in and through the mediating intercession of Christ. In this context, Calvin quotes Augustine: 'Christian men mutually commend one another by their prayers. However, it is he for whom no one intercedes, while he intercedes for all, who is the one true Mediator' (3.20.20).

Calvin also warns us to avoid crude conceptions of Christ's intercession, as if he were kneeling before the Father, begging him for some result or another. Rather, his intercession is inextricably connected to his death: he stands before God's presence in such a manner that the power of his death is his intercession, and it is this that allows him to bear to God our intercessions.

This is why notions of the intercession of dead saints detract from Christ's own majesty, because they imply that his mediation is not sufficient and that his death is thus somehow inadequate and defective. We have no need to call on saints as intercessors in this sense, let alone, as some do, as co-authors of salvation. The blood of Christ is the basis of all intercession — our Lord's and our own. Surely that should regulate the mind of things for which we pray, and the spirit with which we do so.

CARL TRUEMAN

165

3.20.23 - 3.20.27

In this section, Calvin continues to refute traditional notions of the veneration and intercession of the saints by surveying some of the Scripture texts and incidents typically cited in support.

Two things are particularly striking in this discussion. The first is Calvin's focus on the trustworthiness of God. For him, this is one of the key points where theology, experience and practice come together. We pray, we experience God's goodness, and our faith is strengthened because we know that, as God has revealed himself, so shall he be; and we can therefore rely on him to be the same God tomorrow as he is today. This, in turn, reinvigorates our prayer life.

The second point Calvin makes is that prayer springs from faith, and faith from hearing God's Word. Where is it we hear God's Word? It is in church, when the Word is read and then faithfully proclaimed by the preacher. Thus the church, the corporate gathering of believers under the sound of the Word, is the crucible out of which true prayer, the prayer of faith, will emerge.

A number of contemporary applications arise out of this discussion of prayer, intercession and the veneration of the saints. First, prayer has a context, a foundation and a content. Its context is the life and work of the Lord Jesus Christ; its foundation is his sacrificial blood and current intercession in heaven on that basis; and its content is the promises revealed in God's Word. This is a million miles away from the prevailing sentimentality that may talk about prayer, but entails little more than the secular hope that everything happens for a reason.

Second, it surely relativizes the cult of the celebrity that is so rife in many evangelical and Reformed circles. To be sure, the prayer of a righteous man avails much; but there is only one truly righteous Man, and he sits at the right hand of the Father. It is not the star pastor who engenders faith; it is the Word of God. It is not a famous theologian that makes intercession effective; it is Christ who does so, and he is wherever two or three Christian nobodies gather in his name. As Protestants, we need to make sure that we have not excised the Catholic veneration of saints only to replace it with the veneration of authors, speakers and other gurus.

CARL TRUEMAN

3.20.28 - 3.20.30

Here Calvin moves from his criticism of prayer to the saints, to the nature of true prayer itself. Underlying his discussion of prayer, however, is the truth that because God is the Giver of all good things, the believer's prayer is always to be directed to him, whether in petition or in thanksgiving. This is a beautiful example of Calvin's sense of piety, where both cognitive knowledge of God and practical Christian behaviour are inextricably connected: one cannot pray correctly unless one knows who God is; and a sign of one's knowing him is prayer that is correctly offered.

While private prayer is to be constant, there is also a time for public prayer. After all, the church is a corporate body, not just a collection of individuals. But beware: there are peculiar temptations associated with public prayer — vain repetition, a desire to show off, and an appetite for gathering an audience of admirers. Where these are to be avoided at all costs, public prayer reminds us that it is the people of God, not some building or area marked out for 'holy' purposes, who are God's temple (3.20.30).

What Calvin says here is brief but brilliant. In a day when many in evangelicalism are moving in directions that owe more to eastern mysticism than Christian teaching and historic practice, it is important to remember that true prayer rests upon true doctrinal content. Prayer is not emptying ourselves and entering a zen-like state; rather, it is crying out to God for his grace, depending on him for all things, acknowledging him as sovereign, and thanking him for all he has given us.

Likewise, Calvin casts light on the proper shape of public prayer, where the one praying leads the thoughts of the congregation as they enter the presence of God. This is an awesome responsibility and should be reflected in the language we use. For me, no sentence in such a prayer should ever begin, 'Oh Lord, we just want to…' Prayer is not about us, it is about God. Nor should it be clichéd; it should be shot through with awe and wonder.

CARL TRUEMAN

3.20.31 - 3.20.36

Calvin now addresses the rudiments of public worship. He sees both spoken and sung prayers as highly commendable (assuming they are organically connected to the heart's longing for God) since they exercise the mind and keep it attentive in its devotions. Indeed, he notes that public singing in church dates back to the time of the apostles, though evidence from Augustine indicates it was not universally practised in the fourth century.

The engagement of heart and mind in prayer inevitably means that public prayer should be offered in the vernacular: Greek for the Greeks, French for the French, English for the English. This is a typical Reformation rallying cry, and reflects the shift from a medieval, sacramentally oriented piety to one focused on faith in God.

As an aid to our prayers, God has provided us with the Lord's Prayer, the whole of which is designed for his glory and contains six petitions, the first three referring to God, the second three to us and our needs. The order is significant, for God always has priority, and it is through God's being and action that we become who we are intended to be. Further, the prayer's opening address to God as 'our Father' reveals much of the sweetness and tenderness of his attitude toward us as we come into his presence.

What is so striking to us today about Calvin's discussion is surely his insistence upon a God-ward focus in prayer. In a world full of books masquerading as Christian which consistently place human needs (self-image, prosperity, a happy life) at the centre, Calvin's words stand as a warning and a judgement: Christianity is not about us; it is not designed ultimately for our benefit and well-being but for God's glory. This fact ought to shape our prayer life, from the way in which we approach him, to the order of priorities, to the kind of things for which we plead. This is why cognitive knowledge of God's character is critical; without it, we cannot approach him as he desires, nor can we know ourselves aright.

CARL TRUEMAN

3.20.37 - 3.20.42

In this section, Calvin examines the first two petitions of the Lord's Prayer. First, what is the significance of calling God 'our Father'? This title signals that we approach him with confidence, knowing that our relationship with him is one of love; but also with reverence and fear, as we would approach our earthly fathers. This opening address also points us to the Trinitarian nature of the Christian life and of prayer in particular. We are God's children by adoption through Christ, his only begotten Son; and we are united to Christ by the Spirit of adoption.

In addition, by calling on God as *our* Father', we express the filial relationship that exists between all believers. We are all children of the Most High God. This shapes the way we relate to each other, and also encourages us to commend our 'siblings' to our heavenly Father as his beloved children. In this, prayer is a little like almsgiving: Christians are called to relieve the poor in their midst; and yet prayer is more liberal, because we can even pray for those who are far from us and of whom we may not know specific details.

Calvin also reflects on God being our Father 'in heaven', which emphasizes God's uniqueness and absolute sovereignty. And so the stage is set for us to approach his throne by prayer, with full confidence that he will hear us and can answer us.

Next, Calvin deals with the first two petitions. The first ('hallowed be your name') requires that we honour and reverence him as we should, and never speak lightly of him or his great works. The second ('Your kingdom come') is, for Calvin, a virtual repetition of the first, but this time almost as a reminder to us that God will finally and definitively crush his enemies and reign in glory.

Again, comparison with much prayer today, both public and private, is painful. For Calvin, every petition in the Lord's Prayer is shot through with God's glory and a longing for its manifestation. Those who do not see Christian doctrine as practical, who wonder why seminaries still teach courses on the doctrine of God because 'it doesn't connect with my ministry', have failed to understand God as they should. Only by knowing who God is can the believer do that most practical of all things — pray — in a manner which is at all appropriate and biblically informed.

CARL TRUEMAN

3.20.43 - 3.20.44

The third petition of the Lord's Prayer, 'Thy will be done on earth', is a necessary corollary of the first two. If we long to revere our Father as holy, and if our desire is truly for the expansion of his kingdom, we will wish ourselves and others to be subject to his will revealed in Scripture. The essence of the petition is that

> we may wish nothing of ourselves but his Spirit may govern our hearts; and while the Spirit is inwardly teaching us we may learn to love the things that please him and to hate those which displease him. In consequence, our wish is that he may render futile and of no account whatever feelings are incompatible with his will (3.20.43).

Together, the first three petitions of the Lord's Prayer will help us 'to keep God's glory alone before our eyes' (*ibid*.).

In the second triad of the Lord's Prayer, 'we descend to our own affairs', but we do not thereby 'bid farewell to God's glory' (3.20.44). Matters of food and drink may be mundane, but they are no less concerned with the glory of God than spiritual matters. The faith by which we pray takes into view the earthly aspects of our existence, since 'our most gracious Father does not disdain to take even our bodies under his safekeeping' (*ibid*.).

The order of the remaining petitions is not unimportant. There is, says Calvin, a move from what is inferior to what is superior, so that Christ takes us carefully from the petition for bread to the request for forgiveness. But do not pass through too quickly, for even the word 'daily' is a corrective to our insatiable appetite for things which we will, over time, squander. To pile up wealth for ourselves while, at the same time, asking for daily bread, is to mock God.

IAIN CAMPBELL

The final two petitions deal with all that pertains to our spiritual life, and Calvin sees a correlation between them and the nature of the new covenant. The petition 'Forgive us our debts', Calvin teaches, is related to the covenant promise of God to forgive the sins of his people (Jer. 31:34). Similarly, Calvin understands the petition to 'lead us not into temptation' and 'deliver us from evil' as tethered to God's promise to engrave his law on our hearts (Jer. 31:33). In this way the Lord's Prayer becomes a fitting pattern for the new covenant believer.

Elaborating further, Calvin notes that our sins are called 'debts' because they leave us accountable to God, and freedom from them can only come by way of forgiveness. Those who truly desire the consummation of God's kingdom are most aware of their own needs. Thus, 'in the first section of the prayer the highest perfection is set before us, but in the latter our weakness' (3.20.45).

The addition of the words 'as we forgive our debtors' is not meant to make our receiving forgiveness conditional on our granting it, but to show the freeness and wonder of God's grace. If we can willingly forgive others, how much more does God freely forgive us? Such grace points to the character of our forgiveness of others: 'willingly to cast from the mind wrath, hatred, desire for revenge, and willingly to banish to oblivion the remembrance of injustice' (*ibid.*).

As we noted above, the inscription of the law on our hearts corresponds to the petition that God will deliver us from evil and keep us from temptation. Calvin sees one petition here. We may be drawn away from God by the allurements of what appears good or by the difficulties of life's trials, but 'we pray that whatever is presented to us tending either way we may turn to good — namely, that we may not be puffed up in prosperity or yet cast down in adversity' (3.20.46). Not that we would wish to be completely free from such testings, says Calvin; since without them we would become lazy and sluggish in our faith. But their power is great, and we require the help of God to endure.

Finally, says Calvin, it is fitting that we conclude the Lord's Prayer with the one place where there is 'firm and tranquil repose for our faith' (3.20.47) — in the ascription of kingdom, power and glory to God for ever.

IAIN CAMPBELL

3.20.48 - 3.20.52

Calvin discusses the adequacy of the Lord's Prayer as a binding rule for his people. The prayer, he says, is a summary both of what is acceptable to God, and what, consequently, is necessary for us. To add to this, or to go beyond it, is to pray in some way other than by faith, since faith always leans on the Word of God. Prayer, therefore — our words to God — must first be rooted in God's words to us.

Calvin's treatment of prayer closes with an exhortation to believers to pray regularly and with perseverance. He knows our weakness and 'sluggishness' (3.20.50), and that we need to discipline ourselves to the exercise. He suggests times of the day particularly suited to prayer: 'when we arise in the morning, before we begin daily work, when we sit down to a meal, when by God's blessing we have eaten, when we are getting ready to retire' (*ibid.*). Not that this excuses us from prayer at other times; with 'eager hearts' we ought to 'hasten back to God' (*ibid.*) to acknowledge him in all our ways.

By naming such times as appropriate hours for prayer, neither is Calvin suggesting that we bind God to a timetable: 'we are taught not to make any law for him, or impose any condition upon him, but to leave to his decision to do what he is to do, in what way, at what time, and in what place it seems good to him' (*ibid.*).

By the same token, we learn through God's dealings with us in prayer to wait on him in faith and submit to his providence. 'Then we shall be sure that, even though he does not appear, he is always present to us' (3.20.51). Many saints in Scripture 'are almost worn out with praying and seem to have beaten the air with their prayers as if pouring forth words to a deaf God' (*ibid.*), yet they do not cease to pray.

Though God may not answer us immediately, such delays, Calvin argues, are not signs that he has abandoned us; he will resolve our suffering. 'But,' Calvin continues, 'if finally even after long waiting our senses cannot learn the benefit received from prayer, or perceive any fruit from it, still our faith will make us sure of what cannot be perceived by sense, that we have obtained what was expedient' (3.20.52). God may deny our requests precisely so that we will rely all the more upon his Word. Without that perseverance, Calvin says, 'we pray in vain' (3.20.52).

IAIN CAMPBELL

3.21.1 - 3.21.5

Calvin turns his attention from prayer to predestination, a subject that many naïvely assume to be the cornerstone of his theology, if not the sum of it. In the first edition of the *Institutes* Calvin refers to it briefly, simply describing the church as the whole number of the elect. In the final edition, however, he places it in his discussion of the means of grace as a reason — the supreme reason — why some believe and some do not.

Calvin treads cautiously; one of the great notes of this discussion is that of restraint. He advises us to remember that we are 'penetrating the secret precincts of divine wisdom. If anyone with carefree assurance breaks into this place, he will not succeed in satisfying his curiosity and he will enter a labyrinth from which he can find no exit' (3.21.1). We can keep ourselves from this danger only by a simple acceptance of the teaching of the Bible on the subject. 'The moment we exceed the bounds of the Word, our course is outside the pathway and in darkness' (3.21.2). By confining ourselves to the scope of divine revelation, we acknowledge our own ignorance.

There is, however, another danger — to simply ignore the doctrine of election. But that would do a disservice both to the Word of God and to the God of the Word. Calvin states the principle magnificently: 'Scripture is the school of the Holy Spirit, in which, as nothing is omitted that is both necessary and useful to know so nothing is taught but what is expedient to know' (3.21.3). Both the necessity and sufficiency of Scripture are set before us here: we cannot understand divine election without the Word, and we dare not ignore what the Spirit, in the Scriptures, teaches there concerning it.

Consequently, we must accept what God reveals: that he foreknows all things (that is, that everything remains under his eyes in one eternal present), and that he predestined men either to life or death: 'he compacted with himself what he willed to become of each man' (3.21.5). Calvin illustrates this latter point with God's gracious election of Israel not because of national strength or numerical supremacy, but simply because of his free delighting in the sons of Abraham (*cf.* the next reading), who received God's blessing according to his 'mere good pleasure' (*ibid.*).

IAIN CAMPBELL

3.21.6 - 3.22.3

God's sovereign election of Old Testament Israel as an instrument of blessing to the world also included a delimiting decree, by which individual Israelites were chosen to be heirs of salvation. By God's design, the covenant made with Israel was the means by which individual Israelites' predestination was realized. While the nation was, in one sense, chosen by God as a channel of salvation, individuals within the nation who broke covenant with God were cut off; and their rejection of the God of the covenant was a sign of their individual reprobation. Similarly, those who kept covenant by persevering in faith manifested their individual election. Calvin stresses the freedom of God in acting in this way: though he elects a whole nation, he is under no obligation to appropriate saving grace to every member of it. The unmistakable teaching of Scripture is that 'God once established by his eternal and unchangeable plan those whom he long before determined once for all to receive into salvation, and those whom, on the other hand, he would devote to destruction' (3.21.7).

Calvin then addresses false views of the scriptural position. First, he responds to those who argue that God merely elects those whom he foresees as deserving his grace. But this is to obscure Scripture's testimony concerning sin and charge God with the destruction of the lost. There was nothing in us worthy of God's electing of us; which is why Paul emphasizes that we were chosen IN CHRIST, qualified by him to be sharers of the heavenly inheritance (Col. 1:12).

Second, Calvin emphasizes that election took place 'before the foundation of the world' (Eph. 1:4). Foreknowledge of human merit requires a temporal election; but the New Testament affirms that election is beyond and before time, before any of the objects of election were in existence. 'God has chosen whom he has willed' (3.22.2), not those who deserved it.

Third, election is unto holiness, not because we are already holy. The implication is clear: 'if he chose us that we should be holy, he did not choose us because he foresaw that we should be' (3.22.3). It is a simple argument, but a powerful one. The godly, says Calvin, have their holiness from election, not their election from holiness.

Otherwise, who among us would ever be Christ's disciples?

IAIN CAMPBELL

3.22.4 - 3.22.7

Calvin drives home his argument that election is rooted in God's sovereign determination and not in human merit by turning to Romans 9 - 11. There he examines Paul's statement in Romans 9:6 that not all descendants of Abraham are beneficiaries of God's 'special election' (3.22.4), from which he derives a basic principle: 'If the will of God, the cause of which neither appears nor ought to be sought outside of himself, distinguishes some from others, so that not all the sons of Israel are true Israelites, it is vain to pretend that every man's condition begins in himself' (3.22.4).

This principle cuts two ways. First, no human merit through works induces God to choose some instead of others. In the case of Jacob and Esau, God's election and reprobation occurred before either man existed outside of the womb (3.22.6).

Second, and implied, there is no continuing performance through works that justifies God's choice of some instead of others. Calvin asks: 'Inasmuch as God establishes your salvation in himself alone, why do you descend to yourself? Since he appoints for you his mercy alone, why do you have recourse to your own merits? Seeing that he confines your thought within his mercy alone, why do you turn your attention in part to your own works?' (3.22.6).

At the end of the day, we can rest in God's mercy because it is rooted in God's good pleasure, not in our good works. Will you turn in your heart from your own deeds or misdeeds to revel in the free grace of God?

SEAN LUCAS

3.22.8 - 3.22.11

Even though Calvin establishes from Romans 9 - 11 his principle that God's good pleasure is the determining factor in human destiny, he also surveys the support or opposition of Church Fathers. Unfortunately, Ambrose, Origen and Jerome all believed 'that God distributed his grace among men according as he foresaw that each would use it well' (3.22.8). Thomas Aquinas engaged in theological 'subtlety' (3.22.9), suggesting that predestination is based on the foreknowledge of merits that come by predestined grace.

Against these Church Fathers stood the testimony of Augustine. 'If I wanted to weave a whole volume of Augustine,' says Calvin, 'I could readily show my readers that I need no other language than his' (3.22.8). Augustine's anti-Pelagian writings, all penned in the early fifth century, stood firmly for the principle of God's sovereign grace to whomever he wills: 'God calls whom he vouchsafes to call, and makes godly whom he wills' (*ibid.*).

The particularity and exclusivity expressed in God's electing decree does not oppose either the universality of God's invitation and promises. Divine sovereignty supplies such invitations with a full gospel. But unless God grants saving faith, 'the ears are beaten upon in vain with outward teaching' (3.22.10); and such saving faith ultimately depends upon God's purpose of election: 'Faith is fitly joined to election, provided it takes second place' (3.22.10).

All of this ought to elicit praise to our good and gracious God, who transforms goats into sheep, sinners into saints, rebels into obedient children! 'Oh, the depths of the riches and wisdom and knowledge of God!' (Rom. 11:33).

SEAN LUCAS

3.23.1 - 3.23.5

The other side of divine election is divine reprobation, which is necessary if the case for election stands. Reprobation means 'those whom God passes over, he condemns; and this he does for no other reason than that he wills to exclude them from the inheritance which he predestines for his own children' (3.23.1). It is this dark side of so-called 'double predestination' that has caused such much trouble for Christians and non-Christians alike.

Calvin defends this teaching by dealing with a number of objections. The first: 'By what right [does] the Lord become angry at his creatures who have not provoked him by any previous offence?' (3.23.2).

Calvin's answers are bracing. The Lord's will is the cause of all things that are; further, the Lord's will is, necessarily, the highest rule of righteousness. As a result, 'when one asks why God has so done, we must reply: because he has willed it' (3.23.2). Because God is God (and we are not), he is not liable to human judgement. Even further, all human beings, descended from Adam, participated by covenant in his fall into sin and misery. Calvin's response? 'If all are drawn from a corrupt mass, no wonder they are subject to condemnation!' (3.23.3). This first objection, therefore, fails to recognize that God retains the right, as God, to judge human beings who deserve judgement.

Calvin briefly deals with a related objection: are not all universally corrupted in Adam according to God's predestinating purposes? To judge a sinner depraved through a predetermined fall seems unjust. In reply, Calvin returns to 'the sole decision of God's will, the cause of which is hidden in him' (3.23.4). To search for a reason that comprehends God's righteous decree is to reach beyond our capacity for understanding — these are 'the depths' into which human reason cannot go: 'Thou seekest reason? I tremble at the depth. Reason, thou; I will marvel. Dispute, thou; I will believe. I see the depth; I do not reach the bottom' (3.23.5).

SEAN LUCAS

3.23.6 - 3.23.9

Calvin turns his attention to another objection to the doctrine of reprobation: 'Why should God impute those things to men as sin, the necessity of which he has imposed by his predestination?' (3.23.6). Simply put, if God decrees Adam's fall and the resulting corruption of humanity, isn't God the author of sin? If so, aren't we excused from deserving his wrath?

In reply, Calvin continues to affirm that God, as God, rightfully determines human destinies. 'The wonderful plan of God' determined that 'all mortals were bound over to eternal death in the person of one man' (3.23.7). Calvin himself shudders at this 'wonder-full' plan that is also a 'dreadful' decree (*ibid.*); and yet, God's omnipotence and sovereignty demand that 'he regulates all things according to his secret plan, which depends solely upon itself' (*ibid.*).

Theologians cannot successfully evade the force of this teaching by suggesting that God 'permitted' Adam's fall but did not also actively will it to occur (3.23.8). Even the 'mere permission' (3.23.8) of God is itself a positive act of ordaining! 'The first man fell because the Lord had judged it to be expedient; why he so judged is hidden from us. Yet it is certain that he so judged because he saw that thereby the glory of his name is duly revealed' (3.23.8).

But there is more to say: Adam's fall, which occurred by divine ordination, happened in such a way that 'he falls by his own fault' (*ibid.*). God is not the author of sin (James 1:13; 1 John 2:16). 'By his own evil intention, then, man corrupted the pure nature he had received from the Lord; and by his fall he drew all his posterity with him into destruction' (3.23.8). In ways that we cannot understand, nor Calvin can fully explain, the reprobate are condemned both because God perfectly willed it and because of their own culpability in the corruption of their natures (3.23.9).

SEAN LUCAS

3.23.10 - 3.23.14

In the rest of this chapter, Calvin deals with a series of lesser objections. One considers whether God exercises partiality toward persons in choosing some to be saved and leaving the rest to be damned. In reply, Calvin returns again to his basic principle: 'We admit the common guilt, but we say that God's mercy succours some' (3.23.11). God, in his mercy, and according to his own purpose, chose an unworthy people to be saved. We ought to stand amazed at the inscrutable wisdom of God (Rom. 11:33).

Another objection suggests that election undercuts holy living. After all, if someone knows they are elect, then what does it matter how they live? Calvin points out that Scripture takes a far different route: 'Paul teaches that we have been chosen to this end: that we may lead a holy and blameless life. If election has as its goal holiness of life, it ought rather to arouse and goad us eagerly to set our mind upon it than to serve as a pretext for doing nothing' (3.23.12).

A third objection focuses on whether election weakens biblical imperatives for holiness. Again, the example of the apostle Paul, as a herald of divine election, is instructive: 'Was he therefore cold in admonition and exhortation? Let these good zealots compare their earnestness with his: theirs will be found ice compared with his intense fervour' (3.23.13).

Calvin closes with a lengthy and insightful reflection on how to preach predestination. On the one hand, the doctrines of election and reprobation ought to be preached, so that 'Those who obey may not be proud as of something of their own but may glory in the Lord' (3.23.13). On the other hand, 'Those things which are truly said can at the same time be fittingly said' (3.23.14). We must preach to rebuke pride and sloth; but, in the end, such rebukes only achieve their intended ends when they extol God's grace and revere his hidden wisdom.

SEAN LUCAS

3.24.1 - 3.24.5

'What else do prophets [i.e., pastors] do but continually preach God's free call?' (3.24.1). So Calvin ends the final paragraph of this section on the thorny issue of election and reprobation. May we not just substitute for 'prophets' all who call themselves disciples of Christ? Every believer embraces and shares a gospel of mercy, 'nothing but God's free mercy' (*ibid.*) is how Calvin puts it. We cannot say it too much. This is the gospel of God's electing grace, where 'mercy appears on every side' (*ibid.*).

No doubt you and I will read over these paragraphs in order to be equipped for a good theological debate — and who doesn't like one of those? Incidentally, Calvin says discussions about predestination are 'pleasant sailing' (3.24.4) so long as we confine ourselves to the limits of God's Word.

But could we just linger over this last line of Calvin's from 3.24.1? I'll be the first to confess: it shows me how far short I fall. What a gracious God we have. What a privilege to be ministers of his gospel, whether or not we get paid for it. Why do we neglect our duty?

STEPHEN NICHOLS

3.24.6 - 3.24.11

Calvin ended the previous reading by lodging election squarely in Christ alone. He is the 'mirror wherein we must, and without self-deception may, contemplate our election' (3.24.5). Now he develops how this truth grounds, roots and anchors — pick any metaphor you prefer — our assurance in Christ.

Years ago, when I was working on my doctoral dissertation, tackling Jonathan Edwards' teaching on assurance, I remember reading these passages in Calvin (the marginalia in my copy of the *Institutes* also leaves no doubt that I was roaming around here back then). I found the doctrine to be vital; a basic essential to living fully and richly in Christ. But in the currents of American evangelical culture, with its stress on the 'decision', too often people can be paralyzed here. Did I really believe in my heart of hearts? Maybe it — the walking forward — didn't quite take!

How refreshing this old path marked off by Calvin can be for anxious Christians. Once we understand election, once we understand faith (see 3.24.3!), and once we understand Christ and his work, then we begin to appreciate and possess assurance.

After a litany of biblical texts expressing Christ's work of keeping us, Calvin the pastor brings assurance home in 3.24.6: 'What did Christ wish to have us to learn from this but to trust that we shall ever remain safe because we have been made his once for all?'

In our day of seemingly numberless uncertainties, this certainty remains. And this is the one that matters most.

STEPHEN NICHOLS

3.24.12 - 3.24.17

Now we turn back to reprobation, a topic not nearly as edifying as election and assurance. Calvin starts here where he does with election, solidly affirming the sovereignty of God over his creation to bring about his decreed will according to his eternal plan (3.24.12).

In my own discussion of 'double election' (one election to salvation and another to damnation, the latter also being called reprobation), I have expressed — with many others — that we are all damned, all under the wrath of God, all alienated from him, and all cut off from peaceful relationship with him. Augustine called us, the whole collective of humanity, 'Adam's sinful lump', playing on Paul's metaphor of the two lumps of clay in Romans 9. As we review this section, three options remain: either Calvin promotes this approach, allows for it, or proscribes it. Which is it?

In defence of the first option, Calvin refers to the damned as those whom God 'leaves in blindness' (3.24.12) and those whom God 'pass[es] over' (3.24.13). Later, he mentions the reprobate as those 'whom [God] pleases not to illumine' (*ibid*.). If you keep reading, you will find similar phrases. When they are read together, it seems to me that Calvin's view of reprobation is not something like this: Person 'X' stands before God and God decrees that person either elect or reprobate. Instead, the picture is this: We *all* stand condemned; and God, in his mysterious, free, and marvellous grace and mercy, chooses some for salvation.

The benefit of this second model? We are all reminded that our salvation is totally by grace — and that should make us both grateful and generous.

STEPHEN NICHOLS

3.25.1 - 3.25.3

With this new chapter, Calvin transitions from election to the final resurrection. As he explains, citing 1 Peter 1:8-9, the resurrection is 'the outcome of our faith' (3.25.1). In discussing election, God's sovereign purposes and plan, and the assurance that believers possess — all topics in the previous chapter — Calvin is leading us to the final resurrection. Here is a place to stand in the midst of every misery, trial, or injustice in this life. The triune God brings us into fellowship with himself through our union with Christ, our elder brother. The final resurrection brings this union to its fullest and most glorious fruition. That's hope.

In 3.25.2, Calvin displays the glory of the final resurrection along two lines: our union with God (the first paragraph) and the renewal of the 'formless ruins' of our fallen world (the second paragraph). As for the former, Calvin mentions that Plato came closest among the Greeks in understanding, though he did so only faintly, seeing union with God merely as man's highest good (*summum bonum*). The Greek philosophical discussion of the highest good was one way of asking not only what is the point of life, but what is the ultimate purpose of everything. Of course, it takes God's written revelation to properly answer this ultimate question.

Sounding very much like Jonathan Edwards (I say that tongue-in-cheek, of course — it appears Edwards was merely following the Reformer here), Calvin says the chief end, the highest good, the ultimate meaning and purpose of it all, is union with the triune God. In heaven, to use an 'Edwardsian' phrase, we will be 'unclogged', worshipping in perfect union with God in Christ.

What is more, there will be a new heaven and a new earth (Rev. 21:1). Creation, groaning as it is under the curse and reeling in 'formless ruins' (3.15.2) from the Fall, will be set right. Calvin informs us of the upshot of all this: 'Whatever hardships distress us, let this "redemption" sustain us until its completion' (*ibid.*).

Might I add one small piece? This vision of consummate union with God and the final renewal of the cosmos should not merely be a future hope, but let it serve to inspire us to anticipate it in the present.

STEPHEN NICHOLS

3.25.4 - 3.25.6

The previous reading did not cover 3.25.3 on Christ's bodily resurrection. That is probably for the best, since that portion is closely connected with this section's focus on the resurrection of all believers.

The bodily resurrection is a cardinal doctrine, making its way right into the *Apostles' Creed*. It was a topic of debate among the ancient philosophers. It was a subject of intense interest and false teaching during the so-called 'fundamentalist-modernist' controversy at the turn of the twentieth century. It was denied by the sect of the Sadducees in Christ's day, and its rejection was a significant problem in Calvin's own day.

Calvin makes an excellent point in the midst of all this. After arguing that Scripture clearly and undeniably affirms the resurrection, and even pointing to a virtually universal longing for all that is awry to be set right (a sort of existential argument, if you will), Calvin says, 'But let us remember that no one is truly persuaded of the coming resurrection unless he is seized with wonder, and ascribes to the power of God its due glory' (3.25.4).

Calvin adds that the 'pagan denial' (3.25.5) of the resurrection produces a most bleak outlook on everything. Read Job 10:18-22 ('the land of gloom like thick darkness') to get the picture. But the Christian hope of the bodily resurrection changes everything! Now read Job 19:23-29. I mention these two passages because I still remember my pastor preaching a wonderful sermon on these two texts. And of course, Calvin himself enlists Job's line: 'I know that my Redeemer lives' (Job 19:25).

As one who is 'seized with wonder', Calvin links our bodily resurrection to Christ's bodily resurrection: 'Christ rose again,' he tells us, 'that he might have us as companions in the life to come' (3.25.3.).

If you would like to add some poetry to your theology, look up John Updike's 'Seven Stanzas at Easter'. It is well worth it.

STEPHEN NICHOLS

3.25.7 - 3.25.8

Calvin begins this section by stressing that the bodily resurrection will not break with the present creation, but complete its renovation. In the resurrection, God proves himself as the 'Author of life' (3.25.4).

The notion that the resurrected soul will not receive the *same* body but something 'new' and 'different' is, for Calvin, 'monstrous' (3.25.7). Strong language for sure. In Calvin's sights is Lelio Sozzini (Socinus, as we know him in a Latinized version), who had advocated the errant view. Continuity between this body and the resurrected body is essential: 'as to substance we shall be raised again in the same flesh we now bear, but that the quality will be different' (3.25.8).

Why the insistence? The answer is Christological. The body that was crucified on the cross must be the same body that enters into heaven and remains there for our sakes: 'He received again the mortal body which he had previously borne. And it would not profit us much if the body which had been offered as an atoning sacrifice had been destroyed and replaced by a new one' (3.25.7). Our present union with Christ consists of a union with him in his death *and* resurrection. The cases of Enoch and Elijah confirm Calvin's thesis. Their bodies were immediately taken into heaven — their quality was changed but not the essence of the flesh.

Behind Calvin's defence of the nature of the resurrection body lie sixteenth-century reformulations of Platonist, Gnostic and Manichaean heresies which viewed the present world as a prison-house for the soul and cast the material universe itself as evil; goodness, it was said, was only to be found in the spiritual or non-material realm. Instead, Calvin saw this world as yearning for consummation and fulness. Are you, too?

DEREK THOMAS

3.25.9 - 3.25.12

The annihilation of the wicked (dissolving their existence) was not a popular thought in the sixteenth century. Therefore, when Calvin discusses the resurrection of unbelievers, it is not so much the fact of their resurrection that he has in view, but the implications of it. If unbelievers, too, are resurrected to 'life', does this imply that Christ came 'to give life to all mankind without distinction' (3.25.9)? Is Origen's universalism true after all (which was labelled a heresy by the Synod of Constantinople in AD 543)?

To speak of a resurrection of both believers and unbelievers seems to suggest that the resurrection is a common benefit of the cross. Had the discussion taken place half a century later, we might have expected Calvin to address Arminian views concerning the efficacy of the atonement. But this is the mid-sixteenth century and, for Calvin, the discussion takes a different turn: 'What would be less fitting than that they in their stubborn blindness should attain what the pious worshippers of God receive by faith alone?' (3.25.9). We are to understand, therefore, that the resurrection of unbelievers is a 'resurrection of judgement' (*ibid.*). It is an 'incidental resurrection' in which they are 'unwillingly hauled before the judgement seat of Christ' (3.25.9). The God-man is not only the Mediator of the elect, but the Judge of the wicked.

However, when Scripture speaks of the resurrection, it most commonly refers to the resurrection of believers. It is the promise that what now seems 'wrapped in obscurities' will eventually be revealed in 'his glory, that we may behold it face to face' (3.25.10). Here Calvin becomes lyrical, suggesting that we meditate on heaven and remember at all times our finite capacities, 'lest we be overcome by the brightness of the heavenly glory' (3.25.10).

Alas, too few care how they get to heaven, only that they do so. They do not adequately consider the vengeance of God against the wicked. We need to strive to make our calling and election sure (2 Peter 1:10).

DEREK THOMAS

BOOK FOUR

'The Society of Christ'

Introduction

The Institutes *unfolds how God has 'accommodated himself to our capacity' (4.1.1) by creating (Book One), by redeeming (Books Two and Three), and, now, by sustaining a people to worship him (Book Four). The full title of the final Book ('The External Means or Aids by Which God Invites Us Into the Society of Christ and Holds Us Therein') speaks of a definite community of faith, proving that one cannot be Calvinistic in the truest sense without possessing a high view of the church.*

As Calvin explains, Scripture speaks of the church in two ways: sometimes as a visible body of professing worshippers, but other times as the hidden multitude who are objects of God's electing love. Until Christ returns, and the redeemed from every time and place are revealed, the visible church is crucial. Why? It is there, says Calvin, that repenting saints find the 'outward helps' (4.1.1) they need to run the race of faith. Book Four, therefore, flows from Book Three insofar as an individual's salvation in Christ entails a corporate identity we cannot do without.

Calvin is a lover of the church, but he writes Book Four with a brutal honesty about her make-up and history. A church, storm-tossed and sin-plagued as she is, may be either true or false (Chapters 1 - 2). In the first four centuries after Christ, the scriptural pattern of government (Chapter 3) generally marked the early church (Chapter 4). But, Calvin argues, the medieval Roman Catholic Church soon corrupted her (Chapters 5 - 6) with unbiblical leadership (Chapters 7), false doctrine (Chapter 8), errant councils (Chapter 9) and destructive traditions (Chapter 10). That such travesties 'crept in gradually' (4.10.18) only heightens the need to maintain proper church discipline (Chapter 11) and vows (Chapter 12).

Despite her failures, the Bride of Christ has a Husband who remains faithful to strengthen her where she is weak. A healthy church, therefore, not only hears the gospel preached, but also sees the gospel pictured in the sacraments of the Lord's Supper and baptism (Chapters 14 - 18). Because believers belong to the church but still live in the world, the final chapter of Book Four deals with the civil government (Chapter 20). Appropriately, Calvin closes his work with a word of praise to God. May the Institutes *lead us to do the same!*

4.1.1 - 4.1.4

And thus we turn to Book 4 of the *Institutes*, the longest of the four. How is the work of Christ on behalf of the elect appropriated? Answer: by faith in the gospel (Book 3). But since we are ignorant and slothful (Calvin's words), 'We need outward helps to beget and increase faith within us' (4.1.1). These 'helps' are to be found in the church. Citing Cyprian, Calvin makes the following statements (which to twenty-first-century individualists sound Roman Catholic): 'For those to whom [God] is Father the church may also be Mother' and 'There is no other way to enter into life unless this mother conceive us in her womb, give us birth, nourish us at her breast, and lastly, unless she keep us under her care and guidance until, putting off mortal flesh, we become like the angels' (4.1.1; 4.1.4).

'I believe in the holy, catholic church,' we affirm as we recite the *Apostles' Creed*; but do we really mean it? Lest we forget, in the *Creed* we confess our belief in the church before affirming our belief in personal salvation ('the forgiveness of sins'). Calvin's words above strike the modern evangelical as obscure at best and sacramental at worst. Twenty-first-century evangelicalism knows the language of personal faith and personal 'quiet-times', but baulks at the corporate dimension of salvation and the means of grace. But *extra ecclesiam nulla salus* ('outside the church there is no salvation') was only slightly modified by the Westminster Divines to allow for the possibility of salvation for 'elect infants' dying in infancy and those whose mental abilities make it impossible for them to rationally understand the gospel (*WCF* 10:3). In doing so, the Divines in no way wished to distance themselves from Calvin's robust affirmation that the way to salvation is appropriated through the instrumentality of the church.

'I believe in the holy, catholic church.' Do you?

DEREK THOMAS

4.1.5 - 4.1.8

The Reformers affirmed the necessary distinction between the visible and invisible church; that is, between the church of Christ on earth, as men see it, and the church in heaven and earth, as God sees it. The one is related to the other, but they are not identical. The overlap between the two is partial at best, indirect and constantly varying in degree. The point is important. The church as God sees it consists 'not only of the saints presently living on earth, but all the elect from the beginning of the world' (4.1.7). The church as humans see it 'designates the whole multitude of men spread over the earth who profess to worship one God and Christ' (*ibid.*). In this company 'are mingled many hypocrites who have nothing of Christ but the name and outward appearance' (*ibid.*).

We often speak of the visible church as a 'mixed' body. Some who belong to it are not true believers — not, that is, true members of the church as God knows it — and are in need of conversion. Calvin and the other Reformers affirmed this in order to safeguard against the notion that a person may be saved simply by joining the church apart from personal faith (i.e., through baptism).

This distinction between the church visible and invisible preserves another important feature — the true nature and responsibility of church unity. We are to strive for the unity of the church lest we become guilty of schism. But how are we to discern a true church from a false one? The answer: certain 'marks' form the telltale means of our affirming, 'by charitable judgement' (4.1.8), those who are members of the church. These are 'confession of faith', 'example of life', and the 'partaking of the sacraments' (*ibid.*). We are obligated to accept those who demonstrate such marks as fellow members of the church of Christ.

The proper ecumenical task, therefore, is not to create church unity by denominational coalescence, but by recognizing these marks as demonstrative that unity already exists.

DEREK THOMAS

4.1.9 - 4.1.14

'Wherever we see the Word of God purely preached and heard, and the sacraments administered according to Christ's institution, there, it is not to be doubted, a church of God exists' (4.1.9). Thus Calvin identifies the two (not three, by other counts) marks of a true church of Christ. By omitting the distinctive of 'church discipline', Calvin is often cited as differing from his father figure, Martin Bucer, as well as the *Scots* and *Belgic Confessions*. We need to be careful lest we draw false conclusions here. Calvin did believe in church discipline (see 4.11.1 - 4.12.28) and we misunderstand Geneva in Calvin's time if we think he did not.

Calvin's reason for omitting discipline (a difficult issue in Geneva) was to deny the right of individuals to abandon the church where such discipline was deemed absent. 'Schism is the worst and most harmful evil in the church of God,' Calvin wrote in his commentary on John 9:16. It is always 'disastrous to leave the church' (4.1.4). So long as the marks of the true church are recognizable, even though not perfectly, the church cannot be rejected 'even if it otherwise swarms with many faults' (4.1.12).

In a letter dated 13 January 1555, Calvin wrote to English exiles in Frankfurt: 'In the Anglican liturgy, such as you describe it to me, I see there were many silly things ... [However] if there lurked under them no manifest impiety [they are] to be endured for a time' (*Tracts and Treatises*, ed. Jules Bonnet, 7 vols [Edinburgh: Banner of Truth, 2009], 6:118).

Here is perhaps a different portrayal of Calvin from the typical caricature of him. Calvin — the ecumenist!

DEREK THOMAS

4.1.15 - 4.1.21

John Calvin's teaching has never been for shrinking violets, nor is he to be thought of as 'soft'. He uses strong language about those who are enemies of the gospel ('pigs', 'dogs', etc.).

In discussing church discipline, he notes the special responsibilities borne by pastors (some of whom are not sufficiently watchful, others tend to be over-lenient — but he also grants that pastors are often hindered in their labours by those who belong to the churches they serve). The truth is that elders can turn down the thermostat of a congregation virtually at will.

Yet Calvin is also concerned about Christians who act in haste and without grace by precipitously separating from the church because of its faults. The individual member dare not do that simply out of personal whim or a unilateral declaration of independence. He is, after all, a member of the church, not a 'Lone Ranger' believer. Misguided zeal, pride and arrogance, false views of holiness (or, more accurately, false views of others' holiness or lack thereof) themselves need to be disciplined.

Separation from the visible church is, therefore, to be considered only when it has actually ceased to be the visible church altogether — for in its very nature its sanctity is mixed with ongoing sin and failure. Thus, when the prophets, the apostles and the Saviour himself are considered, we learn a biblical balance of commitment to truth and commitment to the imperfect community. It is inexcusable for an individual to abandon the church so long as it remains a real church.

Forgiveness, therefore, is always a watchword in church life. Calvin strikingly points out the significance of the words many of us recite every Lord's Day: 'I believe in the holy catholic church, the forgiveness of sins...' The former (church) is the context in which the latter (forgiveness) is realized. The very forgiveness by which we enter the church is the forgiveness in which we are ever and again sustained.

SINCLAIR FERGUSON

4.1.22 - 4.1.29

The sixteenth-century Reformers fought to win back the 'keys of the kingdom' (Matt. 16:19) from medieval abuses (see Phil Ryken's reading on 4.6.4 - 4.6.9). Calvin held that, ordinarily, there is no salvation outside of the church, but he did not hold that the church itself was the repository of forgiveness. No, forgiveness comes through the preaching of the gospel and its application to the conscience through the ministry of the Holy Spirit. Rome, therefore, had usurped the role of the Word and Spirit of God.

God's people stand daily in need of forgiveness and an ever-deepening assurance that they are forgiven. All sins repented of may be forgiven. This is the testimony of the patriarchs, of David, of the prophets, of Simon Peter and of the rest of Scripture. There is forgiveness of sins at the entry into the Christian life; but it is ever and again available to us.

Especially when the church engages in the discipline of sinners we need to remember that its function is to lead to a fresh sense of divine forgiveness and church restoration. For that reason, its rigour must not endanger, much less destroy, the very pardon and reconciliation it seeks to produce.

Believers in the church still do battle with indwelling sin and are in need of God's mercy. 'Therefore,' says Calvin, 'in the communion of saints, our sins are continually forgiven us by the ministry of the church itself when the presbyters or bishops to whom this office has been committed strengthen godly consciences by the gospel promises in the hope of pardon and forgiveness. This they do both publicly and privately as need requires. For very many, on account of their weakness, need personal consolation' (4.1.22).

SINCLAIR FERGUSON

When is a 'church' not a church? How do we recognize the true church of Jesus Christ? And how do we discern the false? Calvin's answer to what was in his day — and remains — an important question, is, essentially: the ministry of the Word and of the sacraments of baptism and the Lord's Supper are the hallmarks of the true church. Where these are lacking, 'surely the death of the church follows' (4.2.1).

Why should this be so? Because the church is built on the prophets and apostles (Eph. 2:20). The servants of God enjoyed a primacy of role in person in the course of redemptive history; but their teaching is the foundation for every expression of the Christian faith. If you substitute another foundation for the church, the whole building will crumble. In Calvin's eyes, Roman Catholic theology failed to grasp this when it effectively transferred the authority of the once-for-all, written and apostolic Word to the questionable strength of a chain of bishops marked by varying degrees of orthodoxy and reliability.

A physical succession of church leaders may be attractive, but it guarantees nothing. That is precisely why we have the written Scriptures, so that the truth of God may be carefully preserved and passed on intact from believing generation to believing generation. Neither the biblically instructed Christians of the sixteenth century nor the Fathers of the church in the early centuries believed that a mere succession of bishops guaranteed that the gospel message would be kept in pristine purity. Nor should we today.

This is why Calvin's departure from the ecclesial community of physical succession was not schism. For how could agreement with the Word of God be regarded as schism from the church of God?

SINCLAIR FERGUSON

4.2.6 - 4.2.12

The episcopacy or headship that holds the church together in unity, says Calvin, is not man's, but Christ's. The unity of the church, therefore, is not a formal, historical reality made concrete in an institution (e.g., the college of bishops or the pope). Rather the one church is a dynamic reality, born out of living union and communion with the one true Bishop of our souls, the Lord Jesus Christ. Rome's fault was not only its boast in a historical episcopacy, but in its failure to make confession of biblical truth and its anathematizing of those who did.

If truth be told, it is not Geneva but Rome that is schismatic. More than that, Rome harbours idolatry within its bosom in its celebration of 'the Mass, which we abominate as the greatest sacrilege' (4.2.9).

Yet it remains true, Calvin acknowledges, that there are genuine believers — however confused — within the pale of Rome. Correspondingly, there we find 'traces of the church' (4.2.11). But Rome itself cannot be considered a true church or part of the one true church, since the marks of the church have been all but eradicated. In fact, Rome gives expression to the spirit of antichrist (4.2.12).

Here again is Calvin's ability to see with both eyes. In some Roman communities he was sure there were true believers; in that sense they are churches. Even major distortions of truth and failures with respect to grace do not necessarily mean God has not preserved a remnant of survivors.

The truth is that the heart may be regenerated while the head is not finally cleansed. Hence, Calvin appears to have thought that some under the papacy were, in fact, true believers, however inconsistent their theology and perhaps personally intimidated they were. Despite his disapproval of Rome, Calvin struggled to exercise wisdom and patience with her members.

In the end, however, Christ was being obscured. And if Christ is obscured for long, man-centredness, self-industriousness and ritualism inevitably seem to follow. That is always an explanation for the (ongoing) necessity of reformation.

SINCLAIR FERGUSON

4.3.1 - 4.3.7

For Calvin, God's glorious calling of someone to the Christian ministry is never grounded in the superior qualities of the minister himself. This raises a question for Everyman the church member: 'Why should I listen to this man who is, in many respects, inferior to me?' Calvin's answer is full of insight. What greater proof of, and challenge to, our teachability could there be than that we hear the Word of God preached by 'even ... those of lower worth than we' (4.3.1). This is the divine way. God takes ministers in their 'weakness' and their ongoing ministry of the Word and transforms them into the powerful 'knot' by which the whole church is held together (*ibid.*). Such Word ministry is essential for the church's life and growth — even more so, Calvin comments daringly, than the light and heat of the sun, and the provision of food and drink are for sustaining natural life (4.3.2).

The New Testament knows of five core, Word-centred ministries: apostle, prophet, evangelist, pastor and teacher. The first three, in Calvin's view, belonged to the earliest epoch of post-Pentecost revelation. The apostles of Christ were personally called by him; prophets brought revelation as they spoke; evangelists acted essentially as apostolic lieutenants. Now and again, Calvin holds, God may revive these ministries or, perhaps, more accurately, ministries that bear certain similarities to them. But only the ministries of pastor and teacher continue. The latter's task is education and the former's duties include biblical exposition and exhortation, and sacramental administration.

Theodore Beza, Calvin's successor, recorded that at the apex of Calvin's preaching powers in Geneva, over a thousand people might crowd into the Church of Saint Pierre each weekday to hear him. In the pulpit, Calvin grew to his full height and engaged in a Word ministry fuelled by the power of the Spirit, transforming the lives of multitudes.

May his tribe increase!

SINCLAIR FERGUSON

4.3.8 - 4.3.15

These pages of the *Institutes* make it clear that preserving order is a central Calvinian criterion for ecclesiastical government. For example, the church is permanently required to establish governors, that is, elders or overseers, since 'this sort of order is not confined to one age' (4.3.8) (in contrast to the impermanence of certain other apostolic arrangements).

Similarly, the organization of deacons (and deaconesses) and especially the calling of a pastor require diligent attention to order. An inner call (from God to the conscience) and outer call (through the church's witness) must concur. Here is another example of Calvinian order. The outward call to the pastorate is to involve ministers of the church cooperating with congregations, under the chairmanship of another pastor, 'in order that the multitude may not go wrong ... through disorder' (4.3.15). Even in the apostolic era, an extraordinary time, 'church order was in no respect neglected' (4.3.14).

To secure such order, Calvin was prepared to tolerate, or even to encourage, a certain flexibility in arrangements, particularly in areas where there was, in his judgement, not so much apostolic teaching as apostolic precedent.

Although church order is necessary, it is not sufficient, of course — a cemetery is the very model of orderliness.

PAUL HELM

4.3.16 - 4.4.4

Part of Calvin's idea of order in the church follows apostolic precedent (for example, of ordination by the laying on of hands) where there is no explicit New Testament command. Such historical patterns 'ought to serve in lieu of a precept' (4.3.16).

As in several other places in the *Institutes*, Calvin plots in a rather laid-back way the administrative developments in the early church, offering a generously reasoned defence of them. (This generosity will enable him, when the time comes, to trace more dramatically the decline of the church into legalism, tyranny and superstition.) He notes, for example, that the office of bishop first arose to meet what was simply an administrative need to head up bodies of ministers in urban areas 'for the preservation of [the church's] organization and peace' (4.4.2). Despite the changes that led to the elevation of one man, the bishop remained the first among equals, and also, through his tenure of office, a minister of the Word of God.

Perhaps there is more to what Calvin writes than a mere defence for the early church's way of doing things. Perhaps he sees their way as *his* way.

A final question: how is Calvin to advise on the divergent ecclesiastical arrangements in the various countries of Europe where the Reformation was beginning to develop? (See the next reading.)

PAUL HELM

4.4.5 - 4.4.10

The previous reading ended with an interesting question. The answer is that Calvin offers ecclesiastical advice to places other than Geneva by distinguishing between what is necessary for the *being* of the church and what is necessary for its *well*-being. His primary aim is to secure the existence of churches, and he seems prepared to compromise as to its well-being, at least in the short term.

After discussing ordination to the ministry of the Word of God, he proceeds to the office of deacon, and tells a similar story. Deacons were to devote themselves, by apostolic precedent, to attend to the financial needs of the poor. The archdeacons and staffers who followed them enjoyed offices that served the same purpose. Gifts to the church were to be distributed fairly for the benefit of the poor. Originally, gold was not for the adornment of the church but to raise cash for the poor.

Other ecclesial ministries were preparatory. So-called 'acolytes' were simply young men who were receiving in-service training to fit them for the ministry of the Word. Calvin repeats the theme: the bishop was (merely) the administrative head of all these offices. He was not to be personally wealthy; the gifts for the church were not for his own use except to cover his basic needs. Ostentation and luxury were rebuked.

Once more, Calvin is both (1) offering a justification for the *ad hoc* arrangements in Geneva for which there was not strict biblical precedent; and (2) preparing us for the post-apostolic history of the church and her decline into various kinds of corruption.

PAUL HELM

4.4.11 - 4.5.1

Another aspect of ecclesiastical order is the election of bishops. Here Calvin reveals his impressive knowledge of the early church (perhaps reflecting the days when his father had him trained as a canon lawyer?). Once more, his aversion to disorder disturbs the mind of this aristocratically-minded Reformer. The problem with the popular election of bishops is that 'it scarcely ever happens that so many heads can unanimously settle any matter' (4.4.12). The 'excellent remedy' (*ibid.*) for such a potentially disorderly state of affairs was for the bishops and clergy to take their candidate-bishop first to the magistrates or senate and leading citizens, and then present their preferred choice to the people. Bingo! (Do magistrates and leading citizens never disagree?)

This combined clergy-laity model of election continued until Gregory I and probably beyond that time. Then begins the descent to the corruption of the Roman see (i.e., the papal office), and the establishment of a hierarchy — so much for the bishops of the ancient church and their elections!

Now Calvin's mood changes, and the reader braces himself for the Reformer's account of the decline and fall of the Roman Church. What of the Roman Catholic bishops of Calvin's own day? Bishops are no longer ministers of the Word: '...scarcely one man in a hundred has been elected who has comprehended anything of sacred learning' (4.5.1). No longer ministers of the Word, but the ignorant, the dissolute, the playboy — even a ten-year-old boy (!) — these are now the bishops of the church of Jesus Christ. These are the depths to which, under the corrupting influence of the see of Rome, the office of bishop has sunk!

PAUL HELM

4.5.2 - 4.5.7

The Protestant Reformation was not a renewal of doctrine only, but just as much (if not more so) a renewal of practice. This helps to explain why Book 4 — which primarily concerns the sacraments, government and ministry of the church — is by far the longest in the *Institutes*.

Calvin contends that the medieval Roman Catholic Church has departed from the authentically biblical form of government that was practised in the early church. Rather than protecting the right of a congregation to elect its own pastor, the Church in Rome appoints bishops of their own choosing.

The result, according to Calvin, has been nothing less than disastrous. On occasion, notorious sinners are promoted to the pastorate, in direct contradiction to biblical standards for purity in the ministry (e.g., 1 Tim. 3:1-7).

Just as bad, in Calvin's view, is the widespread medieval practice of assigning 'benefices', or revenue-producing parishes, to absentee pastors. In some cases, he says, men receive multiple benefices without ever having the intention to discharge any pastoral duties for people who live in the parish.

Calvin argues that such practices are 'utterly contrary to God, nature, and church government' (4.5.7). His attacks on these 'monstrous abuses' (*ibid.*), as he calls them, are motivated by strong, simple convictions about the proper government of the church: churches should call their own pastors; pastors should take seriously their God-given duty to lead holy lives and take good, spiritual care of the churches they are called to serve.

PHILIP RYKEN

Calvin's broad-scale attack on the abuses of the Roman Church continues with his criticisms of monks, priests, deacons and other clerics.

The Geneva Reformer has little time for monks who claim to fulfil a priestly function. Whatever virtues monastic life may hold, he says, it is not a pastoral ministry in the biblical sense; nor was it ever treated that way in the early church. Because monks generally do not preach, exercise church discipline, or administer the sacraments, Calvin does not regard their work as priestly ministry.

Calvin is equally impatient with most of the bishops of his day. Although he recognizes the validity of their office, he has rarely seen them fulfil it. A list of grievances follows: many fail to reside in the parishes they serve; they do not preach or exercise pastoral care. In short, they 'act just as if the pastor's function were to do nothing' (4.5.11). The only thing Calvin says they do well is to collect money from their parishioners.

Calvin also criticizes the priests and bishops for their low standard of morality. His long list of clerical vices include excess, effeminacy, fraud, lust, greed, cruelty, treason, and the like. As far as Calvin can see, scarcely one bishop in a hundred, 'if his conduct were to be judged according to the ancient canons, would not be subject either to excommunication or at least to deposition from office' (4.5.14).

Then there are the deacons of the medieval church, he explains, who are called to give alms to the poor, but usually view the diaconate as a good career move, a stepping-stone to the priesthood.

None of these men have any business serving in ministry, Calvin argues. Whatever authority they are granted by the Roman Catholic Church, they fail to have the support of the apostles, the endorsement of the early church Fathers, or the approval of Jesus Christ.

PHILIP RYKEN

4.5.16 - 4.6.3

In critiquing the Roman Catholic Church for pursuing earthly riches, Calvin employs an interpretive principle that holds the Old Testament and the New Testament in proper relationship.

Calvin is critical of the medieval Catholics for the magnificence of their churches and opulence of their living arrangements. Part of the Catholic rejoinder was that the worldly splendour of the church fulfilled the Old Testament prophecies of a glorious kingdom: 'kingly magnificence is beheld in the priestly order' (4.5.17).

Calvin demurs because he sees the prophecies of glory fulfilled in spiritual — not material — realities. 'We know', he says, 'that the prophets sketched for us under the image of earthly things God's heavenly glory, which ought to shine in the church' (*ibid.*). For further support, Calvin also points to the example of the apostles, who established the kingdom of God in their poverty. Thus, the true glory of a bishop is to cultivate 'humility and modesty' (*ibid.*).

Chapter 6 addresses the capstone of the Catholic argument for the supremacy of its hierarchy, namely, the primacy of the Roman see. Because Rome was the foremost church in the world, it was argued that its bishop (i.e., the pope) held exclusive authority over the catholic and universal church.

Calvin denies that the primacy of Rome was established by Christ or practised by the ancient church, and thus he believes that the Rome of his day is attempting to hold the church captive. Catholics pointed to Israel's high priest as an example of the need for a spiritual body to have a single head, but Calvin denies that what held true for one nation should or even could be extended to the whole world. Nor does Calvin accept that Christ's command to Peter — 'Feed my sheep' (John 21:17) — gave that apostle (or his so-called successors) any exclusive claim to govern the worldwide church.

PHILIP RYKEN

4.6.4 - 4.6.9

In defending the prerogatives of the pope as Peter's successor, Roman Catholics commonly appeal to Matthew 16:19, where Jesus says to Peter, 'I will give you the keys of the kingdom of heaven, and whatever you bind on earth shall be bound in heaven, and whatever you loose on earth shall be loosed in heaven.'

On Calvin's interpretation, the 'key' to heaven is simply the gospel of Jesus Christ, to which people are bound by faith or else loosed by unbelief. This gospel key was not given to Peter alone, however; it was also given to his fellow apostles (see John 20:23). Therefore, the Catholics are mistaken when they give to Peter (still less, the pope) personal authority over heaven and hell.

Roman Catholics also appeal to Matthew 16:18, where Jesus says to Peter, 'On this rock I will build my church.' Calvin is willing to grant that in the building of the church, Peter was given the honour of first placement as a living stone. Yet he denies that this honour gives him any primacy over other members of the church. According to Peter himself, we are all 'living stones' that are built on the cornerstone of Christ (see 1 Peter 2:5-6).

As we read the Gospel accounts of Peter and the other disciples, or consider the relationship between Peter and the apostle Paul (see especially Gal. 2:7-14), or observe Peter's role at the Council of Jerusalem (see Acts 15), it is clear that Peter was equal to the other apostles.

But even if we grant that Peter was the first among equals, or that the other apostles yielded primacy to him, the Roman Catholics have no warrant for extending his leadership to the whole world. The church has only one head: the Lord Jesus Christ.

PHILIP RYKEN

4.6.10 - 4.6.16

To demonstrate the unique headship of Jesus Christ over the church — a headship he does not share with the pope or any other earthly figure — Calvin makes an argument from biblical silence.

Ephesians 4 celebrates the ascension of Jesus Christ, who is always and everywhere present with his church. In ascending to heaven, Christ has left his church with apostles, prophets, pastors, teachers and evangelists. But why, asks Calvin, does the Scripture not also say that the ascended Christ has left his church with one supreme pontiff? Surely this would be the ideal place for the Bible to mandate the papacy! Instead, Ephesians 4 presents a shared ministry of the church, under the solitary headship of Christ.

Then Calvin turns from the Bible to history, in order to refute Catholic claims to the supremacy of Rome. Even if Peter happened to be the earthly head of the visible church (a view Calvin has already refuted on biblical grounds), this would still fail to prove that the Bishop of Rome had any right to procide as ruler over the worldwide church.

According to Catholic tradition, Peter transferred ecclesiastical primacy from Antioch to the church of Rome. But Calvin finds Peter's connection with Rome to have been very minimal. For example, in describing Paul's imprisonment in Rome, the book of Acts fails even to mention Peter's presence there. Why, then, should the church grant perpetual supremacy to Rome as the seat of Peter's authority?

PHILIP RYKEN

207

History is always important to Christians. Our faith rests on God's saving deeds in history and the true church passes on revealed truth from one generation to the next. For this reason, Calvin and the other Protestant Reformers urgently addressed the question of history.

In particular, Rome charged the Reformers with breaking with the tradition of Roman papal authority, the centrepiece of what they regarded as *the* Catholic Church. Calvin's withering reply — a cogent account of church history in Book 4, Chapter 7 — is just as valuable now as it was five centuries ago as a tool to liberate the church from tyranny to her rightful place under the sole headship of the living, reigning Jesus Christ.

Calvin begins by assailing the claims of Rome with the record of the ancient church, proving that Rome did not possess primacy in the early days nor even dared to assume it. True, the Council of Nicaea (AD 325) listed Rome as a patriarchy, but only as the fourth of four. In later councils, the Bishop of Rome generally did not preside except on unique occasions and never because of his primacy as pope.

Soon emerged the 'proud titles' (e.g., 'primate', 'supreme pontiff') with which 'the Romanists wonderfully vaunt themselves' (4.7.3). Few early popes would have dared assert themselves over the other bishops, Calvin argues; and any such move was vigorously opposed. In fact, when the patriarch of Constantinople sought to claim superior status over him, Pope Gregory I (AD 540-604) described his attempt to rule the whole church as an action of antichrist.

Calvin must have seen the similarities between the equality practised by the early church bishops and patriarchs, and the faithful partnership of the Reformation leaders in his own time. If he did, he never belabours or even mentions them; nor did he use himself as the eminent example that he was of godly leadership among brothers in gospel ministry.

RICHARD PHILLIPS

4.7.5 - 4.7.10

As Calvin continues his refutation of papal claims to supremacy, one marvels at the sheer volume of facts he is able to recount. Calvin's casual recitation of history rebukes our intellectual sloth and calls us to master the fields in which we serve.

Calvin turns to the matter of Rome's claim of jurisdiction over the whole church of Christ. His refutation works through four matters in which ecclesial jurisdiction is comprehended (ordination of bishops, infliction of censures, calling of councils, and the hearing of appeals), proving that Rome never enjoyed supremacy in the ancient church.

1. *Ordination*: 'All the ancient councils order bishops to be ordained by their own metropolitans; nowhere do they order the Roman bishop to do this except in his own patriarchate' (6.7.6). Moreover, new patriarchs typically 'gave an accounting of their faith' to the others, 'a sign of fellowship, not of lordship' (*ibid.*).
2. *Censures*. Cyprian is quoted: 'The brotherly fellowship which binds us together requires that we should mutually admonish each other' (4.7.7). 'Therefore,' Calvin notes, 'it does not yet seem in this respect that the Roman bishop was endowed with any jurisdiction over those who were not of his province' (*ibid.*)
3. *Councils*: Under the empire, 'only the emperor could call a universal council' (4.7.8). Therefore, says Calvin, 'we refuse to accept what the Romanists now contend — that he had dominion over all' (*ibid.*).
4. *Appeals*: The Roman pontiff was 'laughed at' (4.7.9) whenever he claimed the highest jurisdiction. Some bishops 'stoutly resisted' (*ibid.*) Rome's pernicious interference by even threatening to excommunicate anyone who appealed to the pope. Calvin condemns the fraudulent attempts by Rome, including the use of faked documents, to claim jurisdiction over appeals.

Calvin renders his verdict on papal jurisdiction: 'We therefore see how far the Roman pontiff then was from that supreme dominion which he declares to have been given him by Christ over all churches, and which he falsely asserts that he held in all ages by the consent of the whole world' (4.7.10).

RICHARD PHILLIPS

4.7.11 - 4.7.17

The besetting sin of Rome, Calvin asserts, has been its desire for dominance over all bishops, as attested by many Roman pontiffs.

So how did Rome succeed in gaining jurisdiction over the other churches? Calvin traces this progression back to Leo the Great (AD 440-461). The presenting issue was the status of the patriarchy of Constantinople, which, as Constantine's new imperial city, did not enjoy pride of place as one of the original church centres. However, if the ecclesial map was to mirror the political map of the Roman Empire, Constantinople, as capital city, demanded a prestigious patriarchal see. The motion was made: Constantinople became only second to Rome. Leo opposed this out of fear that Constantinople's growing power might enable it to overtake Rome as the chief bishopric.

Rome finally consolidated power in the West under Gregory the Great (pope from AD 590-604), and then, under Boniface III in AD 607, gained acceptance as head over the other churches. Interestingly, though Gregory was a key figure in this transition, he himself was a committed moderate. Calvin makes much of this most influential pope's reticence to assume supremacy. But the empire was 'shaken and torn apart' (4.7.12), with France and Spain suffering and Northern Africa reeling, and bishoprics that formerly resisted Roman control were soon willing to compromise to achieve stability.

Ultimately, it was the peddling of influence that earned Rome the chief position among all the churches. In AD 607, the emperor Phocas, who came to the imperial throne by murder, appointed Rome the chief metropolitan in return for political support. In later generations, this same pattern would consolidate Roman power as the pope allied himself with Pepin (AD 714-768) and his son Charlemagne (AD 742-814) in the forging of the new Holy Roman Empire.

As is too often the case today, historical circumstances dominated the affairs of the church more forcefully than biblical reflection. It took nine centuries — from Boniface III until Martin Luther — before the church successfully enforced biblical reform against papal supremacy. Surely one of the lessons for contemporary church leaders is to refuse to allow historical pressures to determine the message and model for the church; especially since it may be many long years before a more wholesome and biblical restoration arrives.

RICHARD PHILLIPS

4.7.18 – 4.7.22

Calvin might have drawn upon Lord Acton's famous dictum, 'Power corrupts, and absolute power corrupts absolutely', to summarize the papacy's successful bid to usurp all ecclesial authority. The earlier days of popes Leo and Gregory occasionally receive Calvin's praise. But, despite Gregory's violent opposition to the idea, Rome's newfound jurisdiction over the other bishops introduced tyranny, and tyranny by corruption. Calvin reports that Bernard of Clairvaux (1090-1153) 'complains that there converge upon Rome from the whole earth the ambitious, the greedy, the simoniacs, the sacrilegious, the keepers of concubines, the incestuous, and all such monsters, to obtain or retain churchly honours by apostolic authority; and that fraud, deception, and violence have prevailed' (4.7.18). The situation was exacerbated by the decline in prosperity and learning during the Early Middle Ages, sometimes known as the Dark Ages (roughly AD 500-1000).

Calvin's aim is, of course, to assail the Roman claim to papal authority and infallibility, made during a period described by Bernard as the most corrupt and debased ever. Now, Romanists living in a day 'a hundred times more corrupt than it was in the times of Gregory and Bernard' who seek to ground papal supremacy in the ancient age of Leo and Gregory 'lack all shame' (4.7.22).

This discussion provides some fertile reflections for churches today, and especially for ministers of the gospel, to wit:

1. Owing to our sinful nature and Satan's wiles, Christian institutions that attain to great power and wealth are ripe for corruption.
2. Christian leaders should never operate above accountability to some body of equals or superiors.
3. The more power a church body accumulates, the more its focus will be on secular matters to the exclusion of spiritual matters. The prime example is none other than the papacy: 'Here there is no preaching, no care for discipline, no zeal toward the churches, no spiritual activity — in short, nothing but the world' (4.7.22).
4. Therefore, in today's parlance, ministers of Christ should avoid excessive committee obligations, fund-raising and worldly obligations, and devote themselves to the far more wholesome and valuable ministries of the Word, prayer and pastoral care.

RICHARD PHILLIPS

4.7.23 - 4.7.30

Now Calvin goes for the jugular in his battle against papal supremacy. Throughout this chapter, he has steadfastly refuted Rome's chief arguments: that Christ appointed Peter head of the church; that Peter deposited this honour in the Roman see; that the ancient church sanctioned papal supremacy and confirmed it by long use; and that the supreme power had 'always' been in the hands of the Roman pontiff (4.7.23). But now he delivers the *coup de grâce*: even if these things were once true, they were not true now because there is no true church at all in Rome! 'What is not a church cannot be the mother of churches; he who is not a bishop cannot be the prince of bishops' (*ibid.*).

How far was Calvin from today's political correctness of 'charity above all' in doctrinal disputes! He fought ferociously because he knew that life or death issues were at stake. So he asks: 'I should like to know what one episcopal quality the pontiff himself has?' (*ibid.*). The pope neither teaches God's Word nor rightly administers the sacraments, nor properly exercises church discipline. He is, therefore, not a pastor at all, much less the ruler of all bishops. We do well to reflect on Calvin's comments, and consider their relevance today:

1. Church leaders, unlike civil leaders, do not retain their office even if they are unfit. They retain their authority only as they teach sound doctrine, faithfully administer the sacraments, and govern biblically. As the popes made an abomination in all these categories (4.7.24), so today the mere possession of office does not qualify anyone to bear authority in the church.
2. No claim to antiquity or apparent success in ministry justifies a failure to teach the true gospel, faithfully administer the sacraments, and exercise proper church discipline. Churches that fail to display these marks, whatever other qualifications they possess (including good intentions), should not be lauded as true churches.
3. Calvin's assessment of Roman Catholicism should inform the thinking of Christians today who belong to apostate or corrupt denominations. What would the writer of these paragraphs say to ministers and congregations who remain under the authority of spiritual leaders who assail the gospel and practise moral abominations, especially because they fear losing retirement funds or real estate?

RICHARD PHILLIPS

4.8.1 - 4.8.7

Calvin insists on two presuppositions for thinking about the spiritual power of the church:

1. It must be exercised for the edification of God's people;
2. It must recognize Christ's authority as head of his church.

In the Bible, when people are granted authority in the Holy Spirit, God does not invest that person with inherent power, but confers authority upon the Word-centred office and ministry to which he has called them.

Hence, ministers of the Word are 'not to bring anything of themselves, but to speak from the Lord's mouth' (4.8.2). Though revelation is always from the Father through the Son in the Spirit, God has spoken in various ways throughout redemptive history (Heb. 1:1-2). It was often recorded in writing, in part, so that God's people could test the words of prophets and priests against a standard from the mouth of God. Finally, the climax of divine revelation appeared in Jesus Christ, the Son of God. If he is the 'final and eternal testimony' from God, the church must never submit to a 'word from God' that is not sanctioned by God, contained in the Old (the Law and the Prophets) or the New (the Apostles) Testaments.

What freedom the written Word brings to God's people! Servants in the church today discharge the same clear duty as the ancient prophets, priests and apostles: to reveal the glory of Christ in dependence on the Holy Spirit by expounding the Father's revelation.

Life is hard, and Christian ministry can be complex, but let us remember our great calling as we seek to be disciples who rightly handle the Word of truth in order to build up other disciples for Christ.

JUSTIN TAYLOR

4.8.8 - 4.8.12

Christians can have full confidence in God's Word as the inspired message of the Creator to his world. As we minister in the world, our weapons of warfare are not the inventions of our minds but the decrees of God. Only in Scripture, alive in the Spirit, do we find 'the sovereign power with which the pastors of the church ... ought to be endowed' (4.8.9).

Pastors, then, are equipped and called to: (1) 'dare boldly' (*ibid.*) to do all things by the Word of God, compelling all the virtue, glory, wisdom and rank of the world to yield and obey his majesty; (2) command all with the Word of God, from the highest to the lowest, trusting its power to build up the house of Christ and overthrow the house of Satan; (3) feed the sheep and chase away the wolves; (4) instruct and exhort the docile; and (5) accuse, rebuke and subdue the rebellious and petulant.

If this be the case, then we are all obliged to stick to the decrees, the doctrines, the declarations of God's revealed will recorded in holy Scripture. We are liberated to guard and promote the truth by pointing people again and again to the apostolic testimony.

Calvin goes on in these sections to refute a few of the Roman Catholic arguments for the power of church councils to pronounce doctrine by their own authority. It would be good for us to apply his discussion to ourselves as well. How do our churches or philosophies of ministry subtly — or overtly — undermine the power and sufficiency of the Word? May God give us the humility and courage to return again to the old paths.

JUSTIN TAYLOR

4.8.13 - 4.9.3

Calvin closed the previous section by arguing for the church as the 'faithful custodian' (4.8.12) of the authoritative Word upon which she is built. Now he focuses on Rome's arguments for the infallibility of the church and tradition as a supplemental authority to Scripture.

First, has not God promised the Spirit to guide us into all truth (John 16:13)? Yes, says Calvin, but only in and through the Word, never without it, since 'the Spirit wills to be conjoined with God's Word by an indissoluble bond' (4.8.13).

Second, did not Jesus promise his disciples additional teachings still to come (John 16:12)? Yes, but the Spirit provided 'the fruit of that revelation' (4.8.14) to them as they recorded God's holy Word.

Third, if one contradicts the church, isn't such a person to be excommunicated (Matt. 18:17)? This well-known text, Calvin responds, refers to the church's authority to correct and censure according to God's Word, not to pronounce new and extra-biblical doctrines.

After dispensing with these objections, Calvin considers the role of church councils (4.9.1). He honours the councils, but only as they are governed by Christ, who presides over them only when the assembly submits to his Word and Spirit.

But if two or three are gathered in Christ's name (Matt. 18:20), isn't he in the midst of them? Yes, but only if they are truly gathered in his name (i.e., in full submission to his Word)! How can those who 'concoct novelty out of their own heads' (4.9.2) expect his blessing?

Calvin returns repeatedly to the same theme from various angles: our life and doctrine must be built on God's Word alone and determined by his Spirit alone. Councils and teachers have their role, but only as they adhere to God's sure revelation. May he produce in us a spirit of joyful submission.

JUSTIN TAYLOR

4.9.4 - 4.9.11

Calvin's entries here continue his discussion about councils — insisting on their value, yet refuting the idea that they are doctrinally infallible. Scripture foretells that there will be pastors who invite danger and destruction into the church; therefore we must always be on guard. As it relates here, we must always evaluate the councils by the standard of the Bible.

Calvin provides us with a window into his own process for judging the decree of a council. Ever the careful, contextual exegete, he first determines the particulars:

1. When was the council held?
2. What was its occasion?
3. What was its intention?
4. Who was present?

Calvin then evaluates the council's decree by the teaching of the authoritative Word. If the two are agreed, then the council is to be revered as sacred. He holds that the councils at Nicaea, Constantinople, the first of Ephesus, Chalcedon, etc., pass the test in this regard. But those spanned the golden age, as it were, of councils, and things soon went from bad to worse. As 'opinions were counted, not weighed' (4.9.8), various councils made pronouncements out of accord with the Word of God.

We would do well to follow Calvin's method when examining any teaching from church history: first seek understanding (who? what? when? where? why? how?) and then make an evaluation. At the end of the day, we have no higher standard than the Word of God.

JUSTIN TAYLOR

4.9.12 - 4.10.2

Not only does Calvin attack the Roman Church's attempts to set up new doctrines through councils, he objects to his opponents' habit of calling every ecclesiastical decree an 'interpretation', no matter how badly it abuses Scripture.

Calvin's opponents also claimed that the church has the power to enact laws that bind the consciences of men. These laws, such as auricular confession, they said, are both spiritual and necessary. Calvin's concern in battling them here is twofold: to preserve the pure worship of God; and to secure the spiritual liberty of his children.

Since God is the only Lawgiver, to elevate 'human traditions' (9.10.1) above Scripture is to usurp his authority and to hurt his people. In order to have peace with God, we must be free, and in order to be free we cannot be under the burden of laws that are not prescribed by God. Therefore, the church must not make necessary that which Christ has left free to man's conscience. If we ignore this rule, the result will be anxiety, pain, terror and grief.

It is easy to condemn this in sixteenth-century Roman Catholicism. But what about in our own families, churches, ministries? Are we prescribing rules and binding consciences in areas beyond or against the stipulations of God's holy Word?

JUSTIN TAYLOR

4.10.3 - 4.10.8

Calvin defines the conscience as 'an awareness of divine judgement ... [that] does not allow man to suppress within himself what he knows, but pursues him to the point of making him acknowledge his guilt' (4.10.3). But if the conscience relates to God alone (*cf.* 3.19.16), as Calvin insists, why does Paul enjoin Christians to submit to human rulers 'for the sake of conscience' (Rom. 13:5)?

Calvin's answer is two-fold: God commands us to honour the magistrate as ordained by him (Rom. 13:1), so our conscience is still ultimately bound to God, not men; besides, human laws of themselves do not bind the conscience, since they do not apply to 'the inward governing of the soul' (4.10.5). The same goes for the church: even if the medieval bishops were to possess legitimate authority in the church (an idea Calvin vigorously rejects), they would have 'no right to command the church to observe as obligatory what they have themselves conceived apart from God's Word' (4.10.6).

Our God is generous beyond measure, but he guards 'one prerogative as his very own — to rule us by the authority and laws of his Word' (4.10.7). One benefit to this is that God's revealed will for our lives remains abundantly clear in the pages of Scripture. Human innovations not only deny the sufficiency and authority of God's Word, they also obscure it for other people. Even the ways we worship God — *especially* the ways we worship God — are to be weighed in the balance of Scripture as a 'sure test' (4.10.8) for the health of the church and her obedience to God.

Many pastors or church leaders have felt the relentless pressure to elevate human preferences above God's Word when crafting a worship service. What will fill the seats? What do the people want? What can we add to enhance their 'worship experience'? Calvin would remind us that such questions, however sincerely asked, prop up a 'self-made religion' that usurps God's honour as 'the sole lawgiver' (4.10.8).

CARLTON WYNNE

4.10.9 - 4.10.16

What Calvin has said thus far concerning the unlawful binding of people's consciences he applies directly to the medieval church practices of his day. The pope and 'his minions' (4.10.9), he asserts, have reduced the worship of God to man-made 'constitutions' (or traditions and practices) that minimize true wickedness while they esteem papal precepts. The Reformer then unloads a barrage of examples: for Rome, it is better to foul a whole body than indulge 'a taste of meat on Fridays', or for a priest to commit 'a thousand adulteries' than enjoy 'one lawful marriage', or to insult everyone you meet than fail to venerate an icon — his list goes on and on (4.10.11).

In their overthrow of God's law, Roman constitutions are 'for the most part useless and sometimes even foolish'; they even lead people to 'so cling to shadows that they cannot reach Christ' (4.10.11). The church's elaborate ceremonies may dazzle the masses, but, says Calvin, such 'tricks' substitute 'ill-patched hodgepodge' (what a word!) for genuine piety (4.10.12).

There is a parallel between the Roman Church's practices and the yoke of the Old Testament Mosaic law: both of them relentlessly hammer the conscience. But there is one crucial difference: whereas the ancient Jews were led by the law to find Christ (*cf.* Gal. 3:24), the 'great heaps of ceremonies' (4.10.14) of the Roman Church hide him from view. Here Calvin primarily has in mind the sacraments, which were designed by God to be 'very few in number, very excellent in meaning, [and] very easy to observe' (*ibid.*). The Supper, for example, is meant to seal to us by faith the grace of God in Christ. By contrast, Rome's elaborate rites, however noble their original intent, 'let the poor folk seek in these outward trifles a righteousness which they may offer to God' (4.10.15). Even more, many of these practices conveniently serve as money-makers for 'greedy priestlings' (*ibid.*).

The words in this section are sharp and perhaps, for some, difficult to read. But Calvin assures us that 'nothing has been said that would not be profitable for all ages' (4.10.16). Why? There is a simple answer: our sinful hearts still harbour the subtle tendency to worship God according to our own inventions rather than his Word.

Praise God for the Spirit's work to form Christ in us (Gal. 4:19).

CARLTON WYNNE

4.10.17 - 4.10.22

For Calvin, Rome's appeal to the Holy Spirit as the Author of extra-biblical traditions flies in the face of the Spirit-breathed Scriptures. One can almost see Calvin holding up his tattered Bible and declaring: 'There is nothing involved, nothing obscure, nothing ambiguous in these words which forbid the church universal to add or take away anything from God's Word, when the worship of the Lord and precepts of salvation are concerned' (4.10.17). The church's power lies in the Word, and the Word commands her obedience.

The endless unbiblical traditions of the medieval Roman Catholic Church may lead us to think that its practices were always a part of ecclesiastical life. Not so, says Calvin. Bit by bit, the erosion of God's authoritative Word took its toll until 'empty little ceremonies' and 'novelties' permeated the church (4.10.18); but it was not always the case. The Lord's Supper, for example, was administered by the apostles with 'great simplicity' before it was drowned in priestly 'gesticulations' and ornamentation (4.10.19).

To prove his point, Calvin dives into the true meaning of Acts 15:20, a text some were using to claim that the apostles issued commands apart from Christ's direction. If such was the case, so the reasoning went, the Roman Church had a precedent for introducing binding traditions 'as the situation requires' (4.10.21). Calvin demurs. When the church leaders in Jerusalem wrote to the Gentiles proscribing meat offered to idols, blood and strangled things, he explains, they were doing two things: (1) liberating the Gentiles from the oppressive yoke of the Mosaic law (*cf.* Acts 15:10); and (2) calling them to show compassion toward weaker Christians in their use of Christian freedom. The apostles' letter may have had its nuances, but they brought 'nothing new of their own to God's eternal law, which forbids the offending of brethren' (4.10.21).

The Jerusalem council (Acts 15:1-35) had special relevance for Calvin, who, in the midst of the Protestant Reformation, saw the need to make an extra effort in matters indifferent not to wound the consciences of those for whom Christ died (1 Cor. 8:11). Here, then, is Calvin the pastor-theologian: preserving the weak while battling those who would make the apostles 'a pretext for their tyranny' (4.10.22).

CARLTON WYNNE

4.10.23 - 4.10.28

Calvin never misses a chance to drive home the biblical warrant for what Protestants have called the 'regulative principle'; namely, that God is to be worshipped 'as he commands, mingling no inventions of our own' (4.10.23). The imposition of human laws on the church not only sanctions theological error and torments people's consciences 'like slaves', it also robs God of his kingdom 'in as much as he wills to be accounted the sole lawgiver of his own worship' (*ibid.*).

Scripture is filled with examples of divine vengeance against false worship practices (see, for example, Lev. 10:1-3; Isa. 29:13-14; 2 Kings 17:24-25). Reading these texts might lead some to ask, 'Why is God so particular about how people worship him? I mean, at least he is being worshipped, right?' But is he? Calvin says that all worship devised by man rather than God — what he and Paul call 'will worship' (*cf.* Col. 2:23) — represents 'a sham obedience which is paid actually to men' (4.10.24). Behold the horror of idolatry when, in the name of sincerity, we offer to God 'all carnal and fatuous things which truly resemble their authors' (*ibid.*). The true worship of God is the worship that he prescribes, and no other.

Calvin's stern warnings against unbiblical church laws might lead one to spurn ecclesiastical structures altogether; but this is to construct the same man-made religion as Rome, only in a different form. To teach us a better way, he points out, first, that 'some form of order is necessary' (4.10.27) to secure a peaceful society; and the same is true in the church. When churches fail to maintain carefully crafted procedures and customs, 'their very sinews disintegrate and they are wholly deformed and scattered' (*ibid.*). But, second, and just as important, obedience to church laws must never be construed as necessary for salvation, but only 'for the sake of public decency' (4.10.28).

CARLTON WYNNE

4.10.29 - 4.10.32

How is a church to preserve God's right to determine her worship practices and still deal with the practical details of her particular context? After all, someone must decide when the service will begin and end, whether there will be pews or chairs, what songs to sing, how often to take the Supper, and so on. Calvin's answer: because God in his wisdom has not explicitly spoken to every aspect of church life, each congregation's context may call for different forms of worship, dress, and, yes, music. But all churches should maintain a sense of decorum and decency that befits God's people and 'takes away all confusion, barbarity, obstinacy, turbulence, and dissention' (4.10.29).

And what exactly constitutes proper decorum, you ask? Whatever promotes modesty, piety and reverence for the things of God and, above all, leads us to Christ (*ibid*.). If this is still too vague, I remember a seminary professor telling the class that when we enter into corporate worship with God's people, we ought to recognize that we are welcomed there only by the blood of Christ. Do this, and questions of decorum in worship will become clearer.

As you might expect, Calvin reminds us that we are to undertake these 'outward rudiments for human weakness' with a free conscience since they are not necessary for salvation. Nevertheless, we ought to approach them 'with a pious and ready inclination to obey' (4.10.31) since 'we all use them, for we are mutually bound, one to another, to nourish mutual love' (*ibid*.). Can you imagine the chaos that would ensue if everyone were to decide for himself what time the worship service should begin?

There is a wealth of practical wisdom for church members in these pages. Honour the decisions of your pastors and leaders with a clear conscience when Scripture has not been violated. Take care not to establish customs or plan activities that will unduly exclude certain members (e.g., the handicapped). 'That's the way we've always done it' is a bad reason to retain an outdated practice. Finally, don't begrudge another church for doing things a bit differently as they heed God's Word.

Calvin finally sets the course in all church matters: 'if we let love be our guide, all will be safe' (4.10.30).

CARLTON WYNNE

4.11.1 - 4.11.7

As we have seen, Calvin's interpretation of the 'keys of the kingdom' (Matt. 16:19; 18:17-18) contends with Roman views advocating the primacy of the Roman see. 'They know so well', Calvin comments, 'how to fit their keys to any locks and doors they please that one would say they had practised the locksmith's art all their lives!' (4.11.2).

Now Calvin weighs in on what today might be called the 'spirituality of the church', proposing a view which sees the function of the church and the state as separate but mutually supportive: 'As the magistrate ought by punishment and physical restraint to cleanse the church of offences, so the minister of the Word in turn ought to help the magistrate in order that not so many may sin. Their functions ought to be so joined that each serves to help, not hinder, the other' (4.11.3). Within this relationship, the 'keys of the kingdom' belong to the church (as part of the disciplinary responsibility of the visible church)

Calvin's view seems at odds with the traditional (Southern Presbyterian) defence of the separation of the church and state — one which may advocate that the state has no right to involve itself in the maintenance of piety. Whilst Calvin did not advocate a 'theonomic' view of the role of the civil magistrate in upholding and enforcing God's moral law, he did see an obligation on behalf of the state to enable true religion to flourish. Additionally, Calvin applied the brakes to any view that supported the granting of civil powers to the church. Thus, the church cannot baptize the state (or a particular political party), nor can the state (literally) baptize church members.

Later, we will see Calvin deny the state the right to persecute on the grounds of irreligion. But he will not withdraw from the state the right — the duty — of the magistrate to administer 'punishment and physical restraint to cleanse the church of offences' (4.11.3).

Calvin fails to gladden those on the left and right of this issue.

DEREK THOMAS

4.11.8 - 4.11.13

Should ministers of the gospel also be found in the world of civilian politics? No, according to Calvin, citing Ambrose: 'to the emperor belongs the palaces; to the priest the churches' (4.11.8). With this the Geneva Reformer takes aim at the aggregation of civil power by the bishops and especially the pope of the Roman church. The two offices of minister and magistrate operate in distinctive spheres; the magistrate does not exercise its power 'over consciences' and the church ought not to usurp 'the right of the sword' (*ibid.*). Whereas spiritual government is concerned with instructing the conscience in piety, political government is concerned with educating citizens in 'the duties of humanity and citizenship' (as he says back in 3.19.15). This enables Calvin to say (later in the *Institutes*): 'It makes no difference what your condition among men may be or under what nation's laws you live, since the Kingdom of Christ does not at all consist in these things' (4.20.1).

Calvin anticipates an inward Christian freedom undisturbed by the external relations of humanity in social-political life. It is in this light that Calvin can uphold obedience to the magistrate even under conditions of tyranny.

For Calvin, then, there are two interrelated, but distinct, realms of administration and government: the church and the state.

DEREK THOMAS

4.11.14 - 4.12.4

It is a fact often (too often?) cited that Calvin did not regard church discipline as a mark of the church, insisting instead on only two marks: faithful preaching and the right administration of the sacraments. This is sometimes said to make Calvin differ from, among others, the Scottish brothers as seen in the *Scots Confession*. But this conclusion is premature. In insisting upon the right administration of the sacraments, Calvin presupposes a measure of discipline.

Calvin could not be clearer as to the need for church discipline (4.12.1). It is the duty of pastors and presbyters (two separate offices in Calvin's view) 'not only to preach to the people, but to warn and exhort in every house, wherever they are not effective enough in general instruction' (4.12.2). If the errant believer refuses to heed a second time, in the presence of witnesses, he is to be called before 'a tribunal of the church' (*ibid.*) (e.g., Calvin and Geneva's consistory). In a day when democratic religion permeates the church, the very mention of church discipline conveys something intrusive and a violation of personal freedom. There were no such qualms in Calvin's day; nor in Paul's day either!

For a healthy church, Calvin advocates both formative and corrective discipline. Its formative form includes teaching, instruction and the blessings of the ordinary means of grace. In its corrective form, it includes warning, correction, rebuke, admonition and, ultimately, excommunication. Its goal at every point is the restoration of holiness. With some irony, Calvin concludes: 'Those who trust that without this bond of discipline the church can long stand are, I say, mistaken; unless, perhaps, we can with impunity go without that aid which the Lord foresaw would be necessary for us' (4.12.4).

And what would Calvin say of the church today?

DEREK THOMAS

The purpose of discipline is three-fold: to maintain the church's purity, to prevent temptation among the saints by the unchallenged actions of the ungodly, and to encourage repentance.

He sounds a special note for the significance of discipline for the sacraments. Common as it is today to cast the burden of examination prior to participation at the Lord's Supper upon the participant, Calvin saw it otherwise: a pastor who knowingly and willingly admits to the table 'an unworthy person whom he could rightfully turn away, is as guilty of sacrilege as if he had cast the Lord's body to dogs' (4.12.5).

Calvin is clear as to the restorative aim of discipline, particularly its severest form — excommunication: 'although excommunication ... punishes the man, it does so in such a way that, by forewarning him of his future condemnation, it may call him back to salvation. But if that be obtained, reconciliation and restoration to communion await him' (4.12.10).

The absence of church discipline in today's church goes unnoticed. Al Mohler writes: 'Regulative and restorative church discipline is, to many church members, no longer a meaningful category, or even a memory. The present generation of both ministers and church members is virtually without experience of biblical church discipline.'[1]

DEREK THOMAS

---

1. Albert Mohler, 'Church Discipline: The Missing Mark', at http://www.the-highway. com/discipline_Mohler.html (accessed 21 May 2011).

4.12.11 - 4.12.18

It is a dangerous and impious zeal that seeks to 'unchurch' a brother or sister because they do not meet our standards of perfection. Discipline in the church, Calvin argues, must be done with a measure of grace and understanding; it must be on biblical grounds and not out of a rigid severity. In the crosshairs for Calvin are the ancient Donatists and the contemporary Anabaptists. Calvin's model is Augustine (whom he cites often in these sections).

Even Calvin, it seems, encountered Christians who were prepared to leave the church if they deemed the eldership too lenient in their discipline of an errant brother. Such a prompting to 'merciless cruelty' (4.12.12), Calvin suggests, proceeds from a messenger of Satan rather than an angel of light.

Calvin (as did Augustine) underscores that the best form of discipline is a careful and faithful preaching of the Scripture, with due application to the conscience and personal admonition. Writing to Aurelius, Bishop of Carthage, Augustine complains that drunkenness (so severely condemned in Scripture) is raging unpunished in Africa, and he advises calling a council of bishops to provide a remedy. He then adds: 'These things, in my judgement, are removed not roughly or harshly, or in any imperious manner; and more by teaching than by commanding, more by monishing than by menacing. For so we must deal with a great number of sinners. But we are to use severity toward the sins of a few' (4.12.13). The use of severe discipline must be rare and only towards those whose wilful sin is especially heinous.

This is good advice, then, from the Reformer. We must not, of course, use this advice as a licence to withdraw from all discipline for fear that any judgement violates the principle of grace. A Scylla and Charybdis, then, and the path lies straight down the middle!

DEREK THOMAS

Calvin moves from the subject of church power and discipline into a consideration of fasting. He has a marvellous three-point directive to ensure that the practice does not degenerate into religious superstition.

First, we must remember the words of Joel, who counsels us to rend our hearts rather than our garments (Joel 2:13). Fasting, in and of itself, is of no value to God unless the heart is affected. It is only useful as it assists us to grow in dissatisfaction with sin and self. The fasting of hypocrites, therefore, is a gross abomination, according to Calvin.

Second, we must avoid the idea that fasting is a work of merit, or even that it is a necessary element of worship. In itself, says Calvin, it is 'a thing indifferent' (4.12.19); to mix it with what God requires in worship is to both dilute the worship and exaggerate the importance of the fasting.

Third, we must take care not to be so strict in our fasting that we give men the false idea that they have done something worthwhile merely by having fasted. Calvin alleges that by heaping praise on the practice some of the early church writers have done more harm than good.

The basis of Lent, therefore, is tenuous: the medieval church has called on people to imitate the example of Christ for a specific period by refraining from eating food. But, as Calvin points out, Christ did not fast habitually, and what he has done he has done that we may admire him, not necessarily imitate him. For Calvin, therefore, it is not always pertinent to ask 'WWJD?' ('What would Jesus do?'). It is perhaps enough to ask 'WDJD?' — 'What DID Jesus do?' — that we might admire him.

The excesses of fasting are seen in the way in which, over time, the church bound the consciences of men by insisting on the practice on many different occasions, all of which quickly became occasions to praise fasting, rather than God.

IAIN CAMPBELL

4.12.23 - 4.13.3

In this section of the *Institutes*, Calvin addresses two issues that reveal the prevalence of corruption in the church of his day. First is the issue of clerical celibacy. The insistence that priests remain unmarried has, says Calvin, 'not only deprived the church of fit and honest pastors, but has introduced a fearful sink of iniquity, and plunged many souls into the gulf of despair' (4.12.23).

Calvin rightly draws our attention to 1 Timothy 4:3, with its declaration that in the latter days, impiety would evidence itself in a proscription of marriage. This not only demeans marriage itself, which Christ has made 'an image of his sacred union with the church' (4.12.24), but also demeans the Christian ministry.

Attempts to justify priestly celibacy, for Calvin, involve a gross mishandling of the Old Testament, an ignoring of apostolic example, and a lack of awareness of early church practice. Those who advocate celibacy, therefore, have 'a too superstitious admiration' of it and attend it with 'rhapsodic praises of virginity' (4.12.27). But what is truly abhorrent to Calvin is the immorality and lust of which he is aware in the priesthood, which leads him to quote a moving statement from Chrysostom: 'The first degree of chastity is pure virginity, the second, faithful marriage' (4.12.28).

Then Calvin turns to the topic of vows. His argument in these sections, it will be recalled, is against the tyranny of an unwarranted church government that robs the church of her freedom in Christ. One of the ways in which this is done is by devising unbiblical vows.

Calvin begins by discussing the nature of vows: 'What is called a "promise" among men is a "vow" when made to God' (4.13.1). Remembering that God goes before us and that his Word must circumscribe our religious behaviour will keep us from making rash vows we cannot pay. 'You are to temper your vows to that measure which God by his gift sets for you' (4.13.3). God not only gives us the opportunity to vow to him; he also gives us the means by which to do so.

In an interesting application of this principle, Calvin again refers to priestly celibacy, and almost suggests that the vow to remain celibate is a vow to give what is not in one's means to give. It is 'to tempt God: to strive against the nature imparted by him' (4.13.3).

IAIN CAMPBELL

One of Calvin's principles for biblical vows is the mind in which such vows are undertaken. God looks on the heart. In this light, Calvin sees only four reasons why vows may legitimately be taken: to give thanks for God's goodness; to make amends for our own past sins; to cut off inducements to sin in the future; and to stimulate us to greater obedience. Vows, therefore, may be acts of thanksgiving, repentance, caution or consecration.

A vow common to all believers involves the sacraments, which Calvin compares to 'contracts by which the Lord gives us his mercy and from it eternal life; and we in turn promise him obedience' (4.13.6). This is a holy vow, and therefore ought to be taken with care and — remarkably, one would think — infrequently and temporarily. Calvin is nothing if not a pastor at this point: 'If from time to time you go to excess in making vows, the whole religious character of it will be cheapened by the very repetition, and will tend to lapse into superstition' (4.13.6). Where there is superstition, merit will follow, Calvin alleges. The stricter the vow, the more pleasing it was thought to be to God, 'in order to obtain more merit through their weariness' (4.13.7).

This leads Calvin into a discussion of monasticism, since the monastic vows are held in high esteem and veneration in the church. Calvin begins by agreeing that monasticism has a long and ancient pedigree, but asserts that the original monasteries were seminaries rather than the places of superstition they have become.

He continues to highlight passages from Augustine that describe ancient monasticism, such as the following:

> In contempt of the allurements of this world, gathered into a most chaste and holy common life, they spend their time together, living in prayers, readings, and discussions, not swollen by pride, not disorderly through stubbornness, nor living with envy. No one possesses anything of his own; no one is burdensome to any man. With their hands they earn that which may feed the body yet not keep the mind from God (4.13.9).

Does that have any resemblance to a theological seminary near you?

IAIN CAMPBELL

4.13.11 - 4.13.17

The corrupted monasticism of Calvin's day exhibited a boastful promise of perfection and a superior spirituality. When men allege that their lives aspire to perfection more than others, and people admire monasticism as if it represented a life as pure as the angels, something is very wrong. 'And how great an injury', says Calvin, 'is done to God when some such forgery is preferred to all the kinds of life ordained by him and praised by his own testimony?' (4.13.11).

There are several strands to monasticism's insult to God. First is the pretence to bear a greater burden than Christ has imposed on his followers, as if some of Christ's commandments had a special reference to monks and were not applicable to all Christians everywhere. To be a Christian is to follow a common rule imposed by Christ on all his followers. Anything else is impiety.

Second is the boast of monks that they are more pleasing to God since they have forfeited all they own. When Christ told the rich young ruler to sell all his possessions (Matt. 19:21), it was not to lay down a rule for all, but to show this man his besetting sin: 'If he had been as good a keeper of the law as he thought, he would not have gone away in sorrow on hearing this word' (4.13.13). It is no virtue to sell all that we have; our special case may require some other admonition.

Third is the divisive nature of the monastic life. Here are men who separate themselves not only from the world, but also from the church, declaring that the common ministry and pulpit is not sufficient for their piety. Instead of simply being called Christians, the monks name themselves after their leaders, calling themselves Dominicans or Franciscans, just as the church at Corinth was divided by a false allegiance to apostles. The differences between ancient and contemporary monasticism, according to Calvin, are striking; and he sees nothing praiseworthy in a religious life of seclusion from the ordinary, daily routines of our respective callings.

As Calvin considers monasticism in his own day, he concludes that all their vows are an abomination to God. The monastic lifestyle has no respect for the calling or approval of God, being consecrated more to the devil than to him. Finally, these orders profess to be wiser than God as they despise the means he has ordained for dealing with sin and growing in personal holiness.

IAIN CAMPBELL

4.13.18 - 4.14.3

Calvin concludes his discussion on vows by noting a misinterpretation of 1 Timothy 5:12 regarding widows who remarry, and whom Paul accuses of 'having abandoned their former faith'. These marriages, in Calvin's view, are preventing the widows from fulfilling their promise of commitment to Christ. Paul's reasoning in this text is no argument for perpetual celibacy; nor is it a justification for asking young girls to enter a convent and take vows of lifelong virginity, since the passage in question deals with widows of mature and senior age.

Lest his scruples over rash and illegitimate vows should leave people concluding that it would be better to undertake no vows at all, Calvin clarifies that his argument has only been that 'all works that do not flow from a pure fountain and are not directed to a lawful end, are repudiated by God' (4.13.20).

Calvin now turns to deal with the sacraments. In some ways, this issue lay at the heart of the spiritual movement of reformation in which Calvin was caught up. He defines a sacrament as 'an outward sign by which the Lord seals on our consciences the promises of his good will toward us … and we in turn attest our piety toward him' (4.14.1).

The Church Fathers often used the Latin word *sacramentum* to translate the Greek word for 'mystery'. Hence, 'Great indeed, we confess, is the *sacramentum* of godliness: [God] was manifested in the flesh' (1 Tim. 3:16). In this passage, the hidden purpose is made manifest by an external sign: God's way of salvation is revealed externally, for example, in the incarnation.

There is an important principle here: 'a sacrament is never without a preceding promise but is joined to it as a sort of appendix, with the purpose of confirming and sealing the promise itself' (4.14.3). The promise is self-attesting, and stands in need of no sign, but the fact that God has given one is a mark of his mercy and favour. To use Calvin's language, 'our merciful Lord, according to his infinite kindness, so tempers himself to our capacity that … he condescends to lead us to himself even by these earthly elements' (4.14.3).

Calvin's principle of accommodation is an important one, and is worth pondering. Every act of revelation on God's part is an act of accommodation. How else could the finite ponder the infinite?

IAIN CAMPBELL

4.14.4 - 4.14.8

Following his rule that Word and sign belong together, Calvin insists: 'The sacrament requires preaching to begat faith' (4.14.4). Far from the Romanist allowance of a word-based formula, 'a mere noise' that was 'mumbled' by a priest, Calvin insists that faith in the preached Word, filled with meaning and begetting faith, causes the sacrament to function as a true sign pointing to Christ (4.14.4).

Sacraments are not only signs; they also serve as seals. Seals attached to government documents or other public acts are 'nothing taken by themselves', but serve to draw our faith to the promise in the public act. And so, the sacraments serve to assure and confirm to our hearts that the promise God holds out in the sacraments is true, trustworthy, and directed for us (4.14.5).

But there is another image that Calvin uses to talk about the sacraments: a mirror. Now 'mirror' language is important for Calvin — creation serves as a mirror to see God's glory (1.5.1); the Word serves as a mirror (3.2.6, 29); so does Christ (3.??.1). Here Calvin says, 'We might call [the sacraments] mirrors in which we may contemplate the riches of God's grace, which he lavishes upon us. For by them he manifests himself to us ... as far as our dullness is given to perceive, and attests his good will and love toward us more expressly than by word' (4.14.6).

And yet, the sacraments only serve as signs, seals and mirrors to those who receive them by faith: 'It is therefore certain that the Lord offers us mercy and the pledge of his grace both in his Sacred Word and in his sacraments. But it is understood only by those who take Word and sacraments with sure faith, just as Christ is offered and held forth by the Father to all unto salvation, yet not all acknowledge and receive him' (4.14.7).

Whether in baptism or the Supper, only those who receive the signified promise by faith will receive its benefit. In other words, it is not the bare reception of the sacrament but faith that enables one to receive it as a sign, seal and mirror of God's grace in Jesus Christ.

SEAN LUCAS

4.14.9 - 4.14.13

We ought not to think that we can stir up the faith required to receive the sacraments in a worthy fashion. Rather, God grants us his Spirit to accompany his Word and sacrament to move our hearts to cling to Christ. 'The sacraments properly fulfil their office only when the Spirit, that inward teacher, comes to them, by whose power alone hearts are penetrated and affections moved and our souls opened for the sacraments to enter in' (4.14.9).

If the Spirit does not act, then neither the Word nor the sacraments accomplish anything. Calvin draws from the human analogy of persuasion, where engendering faith in the authority of the one speaking is crucial.

Calvin's lesson is worth quoting at length:

> The Spirit does this same sort of work in us. For, that the Word may not beat your ears in vain, and that the sacraments may not strike your eyes in vain, the Spirit shows us that in them it is God speaking to us, softening the stubbornness of our heart, and composing it to that obedience which it owes the Word of the Lord. Finally, the Spirit transmits those outward words and sacraments from our ears to our souls (4.14.10).

Therefore, the sacraments only have value as instruments that God uses to draw our hearts to him. After all, 'God uses means and instruments which he himself sees to be expedient, that all things may serve his glory, since he is Lord and Judge of all' (4.14.12). If this is true, our confidence should not rest in the sacraments; rather, it should rest in God's glory displayed in and through them as he chooses to use them to confirm and assure our hearts.

SEAN LUCAS

4.14.14 – 4.14.19

While the sacraments are wonderful gifts of God to us, we must acknowledge that they are not required for salvation. Nor are they even required for assurance of salvation:

> Assurance of salvation does not depend upon participation in the sacrament, as if justification consisted in it. For we know that justification is lodged in Christ alone, and that is communicated to us no less by the preaching of the Gospel than by the seal of the sacrament, and without the latter can stand unimpaired (4.14.14).

The sacraments find their significance only as they point us to Christ. 'Christ is the matter or (if you prefer) the substance of all the sacraments,' Calvin says, 'for in him they have all their firmness, and they do not promise anything apart from him' (4.14.16). We are only helped by the sacraments if they 'foster, confirm, and increase the true knowledge of Christ in ourselves ... to possess him more fully and enjoy his riches' (*ibid.*). This knowledge of Christ is confirmed as we receive the sacraments by faith in God's promises.

The sacraments also serve as covenantal pledges of faithful recipients. There is a sense in which the mutuality between God and his people in the covenant is affirmed in baptism and the Supper. Calvin says these signs serve as 'marks of profession, by which we openly swear allegiance to God, binding ourselves in fealty [loyalty] to him' (4.14.19); or, as he puts it a bit later, 'God leagues himself with us and we pledge ourselves to purity and holiness of life, since there is interposed here a mutual agreement between God and ourselves' (4.14.19).

SEAN LUCAS

Calvin argues that saints in the Old Testament also had sacraments that 'looked to the same purpose to which ours now tend: to direct and almost lead men by the head to Christ' (4.14.20). In particular, circumcision, baptisms and sacrifices in the Old Testament all served as signs and seals of God's promises by which his people looked forward in faith to the promised Messiah (4.14.21).

But New Testament sacraments surpass the previous ones even as they hold out the same Christ to us. 'As for our sacraments,' Calvin writes, 'the more fully Christ has been revealed to men, the more clearly do the sacraments present him to us from the time when he was truly revealed by the Father as he had been promised. For baptism attests to us that we have been cleansed and washed; the Eucharistic Supper, that we have been redeemed' (4.14.22).

There is a fundamental continuity and discontinuity, therefore, between the Old and New Testament sacraments. In terms of continuity, the substance of the promises endures through both eras: 'whatever is shown us today in the sacraments, the Jews of old received in their own — that is, Christ with his spiritual riches' (4.14.23).

The discontinuity between the two Testaments comes not with the substance, but with the signs themselves. Drawing on Colossians 2:12, Calvin holds that 'baptism is today for Christians what circumcision was for the ancients' (4.14.24). Likewise, the Old Testament sacrificial system and especially the Passover found their fulfilment in Christ, and are replaced by the Supper, which declares the Lord's finished death until he comes.

Any who would return to the old forms under Moses miss how fitting it was 'that they should be abrogated by [Christ's] coming, just as shadows vanish in the clear light of the sun' (4.14.25).

SEAN LUCAS

4.15.1 - 4.15.8

Having discussed the nature of the sacraments generally, Calvin moves to unpack the sacrament of baptism. He defines baptism as 'the sign of the initiation by which we are received into the society of the church, in order that, engrafted in Christ, we may be reckoned among God's children' (4.15.1).

As a result, baptism is given first to serve our faith before God, and then to serve as our confession before men. Baptism is not merely a means by which 'we confess our religion before men, as soldiers bear the insignia of their commander as a mark of their profession' (as our Baptist friends believe). Rather, it actually is God's testimony to us — confirming for us that his promises to cleanse those who trust in him are trustworthy and sure (4.15.1).

But baptism does not effect what it promises without and apart from faith in the Word of God. This is not a magical ritual nor does the water of baptism have power in and of itself. Rather, as we pass through the waters of baptism, we have our eyes drawn from the water to Christ that we might 'fasten our minds upon Christ alone' (4.15.2).

What baptism signs and seals for us — cleansing from sin, assurance of pardon, the reality of repentance, mortification and renewal in Christ, union with Christ — is not just for our past sins. Rather, we can return to our baptism again and again in trust that its testimony is true for our entire lives: '...we must realize that at whatever time we are baptized, we are once for all washed and purchased for our whole life. Therefore, as often as we fall away, we ought to recall the memory of our baptism and fortify our mind with it, that we may always be sure and confident of the forgiveness of sins' (4.15.3; see also 4.15.4).

SEAN LUCAS

4.15.9 - 4.15.16

One suspects that Calvin's candour in his treatment of baptism makes us uneasy. Today, we fear the connection between the 'sign' and the 'thing signified' that we tend to be more cautious than the Reformers (or Paul!) in asserting inferences by way of synecdoche (that part-for-the-whole figure of speech again!). Calvin on the other hand, whilst clear that water has no innate regenerative or sanctifying power, moves freely from the sign (baptism) to that which it signifies (in this section, mortification of sin) without feeling the need to reassert that what baptism signifies is only effective in those who believe.

Calvin's baptismal theology gives the occasion to discuss certain distinct patterns of Christian living in the world. Baptism does not open the door to licence; Calvin views baptism as covenantal and therefore conditional upon faith. By reminding us of Paul's use of the ordeal of water-judgement in the exodus at the Red Sea in 1 Corinthians 10, Calvin ensures that we recall the effects of baptism on those who failed to believe — they were drowned. The sign became effectual in those who believed, and moreover, while baptism was a sign of death to the unbeliever, it was a sign of life and obedience to those in whom the Spirit dwelt.

Since baptism is a sign (to faith) of justification, the same antinomian temptation applies: since we have been baptized, can we then sin at leisure? No, of course not! For Calvin, the baptized life is a constant war against sin. Taking the latter half of Romans 7 as depicting the experience of the believer, Calvin says, 'He therefore says that he has a perpetual conflict with the vestiges of his flesh, and that he is held bound in miserable bondage, so that he cannot consecrate himself wholly to obedience to the divine law [Rom. 7:18-23]. Hence, he is compelled to exclaim with groaning: "Wretched man that I am! Who will deliver me from this body subject to death?" [Rom. 7:24]' (4.15.12). The answer, of course, is in the next verse.

DEREK THOMAS

4.15.17 - 4.15.22

Various problems concerning baptism are now dealt with: those baptized (infants) often wait many years before repentance is seen. Does this invalidate the baptism? No, 'This promise was offered to us in baptism; therefore, let us embrace it by faith' (4.15.17). Is there not an example of re-baptism in the case of the Ephesians in Acts 19:2-7 who knew only the baptism of John? No, conscious to give no ground on re-baptism (perhaps with Anabaptists in his sights), Calvin argues that John's disciples in Ephesus were not re-baptized with water but received, in addition to John's baptism, the laying on of hands and the reception of the Holy Spirit that followed. The baptism is synonymous with the expression, 'laid his hands upon them' (v. 6).

What of the addition of rituals to the simple formula of baptism as described in the New Testament? These he variously describes as 'alien hodgepodge', 'grosser mockeries', 'theatrical pomp' and 'outlandish pollutions' (4.15.19). What about 'emergency baptisms' (an infant who may expire before a minister can be found)? To administer (lay) baptism in such circumstances is to suggest that without it, all are lost. This would be a worse condition than 'under the law' (4.15.20); for at least in the Old Testament it was held that the promise was sufficient *before* the eighth day and the ritual of circumcision (Gen. 17:7).

And may women baptize in any circumstance (the example of Zipporah is sometimes upheld)? Calvin's answer? No.

DEREK THOMAS

4.16.1 - 4.16.6

Calvin's polemic in favour of infant baptism is built on the following platform:

1. A spiritual relationship between circumcision and baptism: both are covenantal signs and seals to faith of forgiveness of sin; the power of the signs consist in the underlying promise of God rather than any *ex opere operato* ('from the work performed') understanding of the efficacy of the sacraments.

2. Both promise (in covenant and to faith) God's fatherly favour, the forgiveness of sins and eternal life — all of which come to pass through regeneration. However different they are externally, inwardly both sacraments point to the same reality: 'it appears incontrovertible that baptism has taken the place of circumcision to fulfil the same office among us' (4.16.4).

3. In both administrations, covenant signs and seals include infants.

4. There is, therefore, an organic unity across the Testaments between the promise made with Abraham and covenant baptism. 'The covenant is common, and the reason for confirming it is common. Only the manner of confirmation is different — what was circumcision for them was replaced for us by baptism' (4.16.6).

Calvin's argument for paedobaptism, therefore, is made on theological grounds — the unity of the covenant of grace as operative under both Old and New Covenant eras.

DEREK THOMAS

4.16.7 - 4.16.13

'What does this have to do with baptism?' is the frequent response to citing Jesus' blessing the little children (Matt. 19:13-15), apparently as much in Calvin's day as today. Calvin's response? 'If it is right for children to be brought to Christ, why not also to be received into baptism, the symbol of our communion and fellowship with Christ? If the Kingdom of Heaven belongs to them, why is the sign denied which, so to speak, opens to them a door into the church, that, adopted into it, they may be enrolled among the heirs of the Kingdom of Heaven?' (4.16.7). These were babies, not half-grown children, he insists, and of such is the kingdom comprised.

And who 'in his senses' (4.16.8) can deny that children were not included in the household baptisms in Acts? In truth, any attack on the fitness of infants receiving baptism as the sign and seal of the covenant is equally an attack upon Old Testament circumcision. The latter was more than a physical sign of earthly, physical enjoyment in Canaan; its primary import was union and communion with Jesus Christ, and its equation with baptism in Colossians 2:11-12 proves as much. In both Testaments, those who receive the covenant sign are called 'children of Abraham'.

Baptism floods the hearts of parents with gratitude as the sacrament manifests God's love. And the baptized children receive some benefit, too: 'being engrafted into the body of the church, they are somewhat more commended to the other members. Then, when they have grown up, they are greatly spurred to an earnest zeal for worshipping God, by whom they were received as children through a solemn symbol of adoption before they were old enough to recognize him as Father' (4.16.9).

DEREK THOMAS

4.16.14 - 4.16.19

Not through yet, Calvin considers another objection to infant baptism: infants are incapable of understanding the gospel and therefore cannot be regenerated; hence, they should not be baptized. If, Calvin argues, they are not in Christ, they must be in Adam (there is no middle ground). This means that all infants who die (perhaps the majority in the sixteenth century) are consigned to damnation.

But the premise needs to be challenged: because we cannot 'see' regeneration does not mean it has not taken place. We dare not limit it to those who have understanding. John the Baptist was regenerated in his infancy, after all. True, in the ordinary economy of salvation, faith comes by hearing and hearing by the Word of God (Rom. 10:17), but we cannot say that God cannot grant faith and repentance to whom he desires. A child may not possess as much faith as an adult, but it may be true and saving faith nevertheless.

Calvin has by no means finished with his case for paedobaptism, but we have already seen that the arguments he deals with are very much the same arguments that arise today. Whether credobaptist or paedobaptist (and Calvin's strength of language is perhaps typical of the sixteenth century when the credobaptist argument was viewed with deep suspicion of orthodoxy), one must concede to the Reformer's theological and exegetical skill in theological debate.

DEREK THOMAS

4.16.20 – 4.16.24

For some, Calvin seems to be at his most feisty when he writes on the sacraments. Against those who complain that infant baptism is a travesty of the gospel, he stoutly insists: 'these darts are aimed more at God than at us' (4.16.20)! But a little reflection reveals he is also at his most thoughtful in these pages, and his analysis of sacramental signs can strengthen credobaptists as well as paedobaptists.

If repentance and faith are in view in baptism, how can infant baptism be biblical? Calvin responds that the same was true of circumcision (hence references to Jer. 4:4; 9:25; Deut. 10:16; 30:6), yet infants were circumcized.

How then can either sign be applicable to infants who have neither repented nor believed? Calvin's central emphasis here is simple, but vital: *Baptism, like circumcision, is first and foremost a sign of the gospel and its promise, not of our response to the gospel.* It points first of all to the work of Christ for us, not to the work of the Spirit in us. It calls for our response. It is not primarily a sign of that response. So, like the proclamation of the gospel (of which it is a sign), baptism summons us to (rather than signifies) repentance and faith.

In fact all believers are called to grow into an understanding and 'improvement' of their baptism. This is as true for those baptized as believers as for those baptized as infants. Consequently, whether baptism follows faith or precedes faith, its meaning remains the same. Its *efficacy* in our lives is related to (lifelong!) faith and repentance. But its *meaning* is always the same — Christ crucified and risen, outside of whom there is no salvation.

To see baptism as a sign of my repentance and faith, then, is to turn it on its head. It diminishes, if not evacuates, the sign of its real power in our lives — which is to point us to Christ and to the blessings which are ours in him, and thus to draw forth faith. Grasp this whole-Bible principle, holds Calvin, and all the New Testament's teaching on baptism beautifully coheres.

SINCLAIR FERGUSON

Calvin was, and remains, a theologian of the ages. Of course his theology comes to us clothed in the garments of the sixteenth century. But some things never change — including many of the arguments, for and against, in relation to the baptism of infants. This he passionately believed to be a biblical doctrine.

Calvin meets many of the arguments against infant baptism head on. Typically, he deals with them by underlining ways in which they depend on a misreading of Scripture. Thus, faced with the insistence that regeneration is required for baptism, he questions the use of Scripture that lies behind such thinking. Rebuffed by arguments that the order of biblical language ('teach, baptize') presupposes instruction prior to baptism, he points out that of course this is the order when adults are hearing and responding to the gospel for the first time. It would be a logical fallacy to think that the corollary of 'adults should hear, believe and be baptized' is 'infants must not be baptized'! One would no more deduce that infants must not be fed because Paul states that those who refuse to work should not eat (2 Thess. 3:10).

But there is one argument that credobaptist proponents, then and now, have often used as a kind of *reductio ad absurdum*: if you baptize infants, you ought also to give them the Lord's Supper.

But Calvin sees a serious flaw here. For while both baptism and the Supper point to Christ, they each point to different aspects of union with him. Baptism points to a once-and-for-all initiation into Christ. It is done to us, not done by us. We do not baptize ourselves, we are baptized. The Supper, however, is not a sacrament of initiation but of communion. That is why we are active and engaged at the Lord's Table. For it is essential to be able to: (1) discern the Lord's body; (2) examine oneself; (3) proclaim the Lord's death; and (4) celebrate the Supper 'in remembrance' of Christ.

Just why Calvin is so passionate about this — when, after all, baptism is never more than a sign — will become clear in the next reading.

SINCLAIR FERGUSON

4.16.31 - 4.16.32

One of the perplexities we modern Christians encounter in admiring magisterial Reformers like Calvin is the severity of their attitude to, and treatment of, Anabaptists. In Calvin's case, this may seem all the more mysterious since he married the widow of a former Anabaptist!

Our problem is partly due to the unspoken assumption that credobaptism involves personal faith and a commitment to evangelical fundamentals. Sadly it has become clear that there is no necessary connection between the two. If a credobaptist can point the finger at the baptized babies who now have no connection with the church, the paedobaptist can note churches of fourteen thousand members baptized on profession of faith with a weekly attendance of only eight thousand. The sign is not the reality it signifies.

Perhaps this makes it possible for us to understand Calvin a little better. For him 'Anabaptist' was not a synonym for 'Evangelical'. After all, the best-known Anabaptist with whom he had long-term, though unhappy, personal dealings was Michael Servetus. Horrific though it may sound to a credobaptist, Servetus held to 'believer's baptism'. His attempted demolition of orthodox Christianity — none too subtly titled *Christianismi restitutio* — included an attack on infant baptism.

Calvin responds in the *Institutio* with twenty theological 'karate chops'. The culprit is a flawed hermeneutic — '[Servetus] always falls back into the same false reasoning for he preposterously applies to infants what was said concerning adults alone' (4.16.31).

It is in this context that Calvin reveals the reason for his passion in the whole controversy. Baptism is intended to give the Lord's people the assurance of sight (in the visible sign) as well as of sound (in the audible word of promise). *Ignore the sign of the promise and little by little the promise itself will be obscured.*

For Calvin, the obscuring of any, and every, divine promise is attributable ultimately to one being: Satan. So the little Frenchman will muster all the weapons he can to vindicate the promise of our God and Father that, even after our death, he will be to our children everything he has been to us — all within the context of faith. The sign is no more than a sign, but it is never a bare sign (*signum nudum*) — not so long as the one who gives it is the covenant-making and covenant-keeping God!

SINCLAIR FERGUSON

4.17.1 - 4.17.5

Calvin now turns to the theme of the Lord's Supper. His concern is twofold: (1) to provide a simple explanation of the Supper; and (2) to resolve difficulties related to it. What he does in 4.17.1 is worthy of imitation, namely, to provide a simple but rich exposition of the meaning of Communion so the Lord's people grasp what it means.

The Supper is the Father's provision of nourishment in Christ for his children (Calvin's use of *adoptio* — adoptive sonship — is particularly striking here, and underscores again how important this is in his theology — as it was in his life). The Father means to give assurance to his children. In essence, the Supper is a gospel drama:

1. Christ is set before us as the One who was crucified for us;
2. Christ is offered to us as food to be received by us;
3. Christ is received by us so that we feel him to be working in us.

Calvin's poetic eloquence here should be allowed to stand on its own:

> This is the wonderful exchange which, out of his measureless
>   benevolence,
>   *he has made with us;*
> That, becoming Son of man with us,
>   *he has made us sons of God with him;*
> That, by his descent to earth,
>   *he has prepared an ascent to heaven for us;*
> That, by taking on our mortality,
>   *he has conferred our immortality upon us;*
> That, accepting our weakness,
>   *he has strengthened us by his power;*
> That, receiving our poverty into himself,
>   *he has transferred his wealth to us;*
> That, taking the weight of our iniquity upon himself (which
>   oppressed us)
>   *he has clothed us with his righteousness* (4.17.2).

So, urges Calvin, let us make neither too little of the signs by severing them from the living Christ, nor too much so that we obscure him.

SINCLAIR FERGUSON

4.17.6 - 4.17.11

Calvin's great concern is that Christians should 'rightly use the Lord's Supper' (4.17.6). He is, first and last, a pastoral theologian. In seeking to serve the church he wants to be sensitive to two things: (1) the mystery of the Lord's Supper; and (2) the nature of communion with Christ.

With respect to (1), he encourages those who can to go beyond him. With respect to (2), a number of Reformed writers have felt that he has already gone too far! Statements such as those in 4.17.9 are typical: 'Whoever has partaken of his flesh and blood may ... enjoy participation in life...'; and, 'The flesh of Christ is like a rich and inexhaustible fountain that pours into us the life springing forth from the Godhead into itself.' In context, Calvin's logic here is:

1. The Father gave life to the incarnate Son so that he might give us life.
2. This life is in the incarnate Son; it is not a something extraneous.
3. In order to enjoy this life we must be united to the incarnate Son
4. This union with the incarnate Son is realized through the Holy Spirit.

In other words, our salvation and eternal life are resourced in Christ, incarnate, crucified, buried, raised, exalted, ascended, reigning and returning. Our experience of salvation comes only from Spiritual union and communion with his still-incarnated Person. There is no other source of salvation and life than this incarnate Person. What is unique about the Supper, therefore, is not so much the mysterious nature of the communion between Christ and the believer, but the focus in that communion on the bodily Christ specifically as crucified and now risen.

For Calvin, therefore, the communion of the Table is not a communion with the Spirit, but a communion with Christ in and through the Spirit. But there is no other Christ with whom we can have communion than the embodied Son of God.

Sometimes Calvin's view is described as 'spiritual'. Indeed, it is Spiritual (through the Spirit). But it is so because it is Christological. The Spirit glorifies the incarnate Son in our eyes. In this way, in our Table communion with the Lord Jesus Christ, we 'feel his power in partaking of all his benefits' (4.17.11).

SINCLAIR FERGUSON

Calvin's doctrine of the Supper, often (too often!) referred to (incorrectly) as one of 'real presence', is one of communion with Christ crucified and resurrected. Its focus on the bodily nature of this communion (there is no other Christ with whom we may commune other than the [bodily, enfleshed] risen Christ) begs the question as to the association of the sign (bread, wine) with the body (flesh, blood) of Christ.

First, what of the Roman doctrine of transubstantiation? Calvin affirms that Christ's body is in heaven and will remain there until the Second Coming. Its physical nature makes ubiquity impossible (a category mistake). True, Rome calls for subtleties 'worthy of Aquinas' (as we sometimes say): distinguishing 'form' and 'substance' — the bread may look and taste like bread, but its substance masks the flesh of Christ. Ordinary folk, oblivious to these 'deceitful subtleties' (4.17.13), assume bread for God.

Of transubstantiation, Calvin says: (1) it is a doctrine 'devised not so long ago' (4.17.14) and not alluded to in the Church Fathers; (2) should we not equally assign a similar change to baptismal water (something which devotees of transubstantiation do not do); (3) it is a failure to appreciate the way signs operate to faith. Alluding to Paul's use of water in 1 Corinthians 10:4, the water 'gushing from the rock in the desert [Exod. 17:6] was for the fathers a token and sign of the same thing as wine represents for us in the Supper' but it was water that 'beasts of burden and cattle' also drank (4.17.15). The water retained its substance despite its different uses.

All this is to teach us that our salvation and continued communion with Christ is with Christ incarnate, enfleshed, crucified, resurrected, exalted, ascended, reigning, returning — who, at this time, remains in heaven. Through the sacrament and by the Spirit, 'it is God's plan ... to lift us to himself' (*ibid.*) — hence, Calvin's use of the *sursum chorda* ['Lift up your hearts'] in the liturgy of the Supper.

DEREK THOMAS

4.17.16 - 4.17.20

Transubstantiation and (Lutheran) consubstantiation equally infer the ubiquity of Christ's physical body, a matter which Calvin now begins to address. The notion that Christ's physical body (in Bethlehem's manger, on the cross, resurrected and walking along the Galilean shore) is in every place at the same time implies that what was (is) seen is a phantasm. With a double-edged sword, Calvin suggests this is to 'raise Marcion from hell' (4.17.17) — since the second-century thinker had advocated such a view and was condemned as a heretic in Roman Catholic tradition — and, engaging in some subtleties of his own, Calvin asks what the implication might be of wine and bread (separated on a table) if Christ's body is attached to both. Absurd? Yes.

Summarily dismissing these ideas, Calvin now reaches eloquence itself. In the Supper, we must equally ascribe to him those properties which belong to both his divine and human natures. Thus, Calvin comes to address what 'Is' means in the formula, 'This is my body ... This is my blood.' Unless we abandon all sense, these words must be understood as employing a figure (metonymy) of speech — the one (covenantally) representing the other. Their effectiveness is to faith: 'a covenant ... would not benefit us unless there were joined to it that secret communication by which we are joined to Christ' (4.17.20). To the one who has faith, the bread and wine — by the Spirit's secret (hidden, mysterious) power — draw us to commune with the enfleshed Christ in heaven.

And Calvin has only just begun his own distinctive explanation of the Supper.

DEREK THOMAS

What does 'is' mean in 'This is my body'? Metonymy, Calvin answers, in the same way that Scripture represents one thing by another in such expressions as 'circumcision is a covenant' (see Gen. 17:13), the 'lamb is the Passover' (see Exod. 12:11), etc.

Calvin's detractors lose all sense (of grammar and much else) in insisting on a special import to the verb 'is', as though when Paul says, 'so it is with Christ' in 1 Corinthians 12:12 having spoken of the church, Christ is to be equated with the church's members. This is to fail to see the literary nature of Scripture, bearing the marks of human (as well as divine) authorship. Thus we find in the Bible acrostics, alliteration, analogy, anthropomorphism, assonance, cadence, chiasm, consonance, dialogue, hyperbole, irony, metaphor, metre, onomatopoeia, paradox, parallelism, repetition, rhyme, satire, simile and more.

So why should we stumble over the meaning of 'is' as metonymy? What hermeneutical hurdle have we jumped over? If this smacks of elevating human reason above divine mystery (as Calvin's detractors alleged), suggesting that to fail to believe in transubstantiation is in some way to deny God his power, Calvin answers that it is not a matter of what God can do but what God has done. Our flesh is not ubiquitous (existing everywhere at the same time), and to suggest that Christ's flesh is, removes him from being our elder brother. And if that is so, our salvation is lost.

Had the Christian church followed Calvin's obvious path much damage would have been spared! Still, we may tread ahead with him; for we might say that in reading Calvin's *Institutes*, Calvin is with us — in our minds and hearts, instructing us, feeding us, rebuking us, encouraging us.

DEREK THOMAS

4.17.25 - 4.17.28

Calvin identifies in the polemics of transubstantiation a fatal hermeneutical flaw: interpreting the text to fit the theory rather than allowing the theory to be governed (in this case, abandoned) by the text. When you add to this a suspicion about Scripture's perspicuity (the *Westminster Confession of Faith* a century later would insist: 'all things that are necessary to be known, believed, and observed, for salvation, are so clearly propounded, and opened in some place of Scripture or other, that not only the learned, but the unlearned, in a due use of ordinary means, may attain unto a sufficient understanding of them' [*WCF* 1:7]) and you have a recipe for what Calvin calls a 'monster' (4.17.25).

As we have seen, central to Calvin's view of the Supper, and not always sufficiently appreciated, is an insistence that Christ's body is in heaven — and therefore talk of Calvin's doctrine of the 'real presence of Christ in the Supper' (an expression he did not and would not have used), even by sympathizers of Calvin, misses the point. Transubstantiation, with its view of the ubiquity of flesh (present everywhere in space and particularly in the consecrated sacrament), is an absurdity.

DEREK THOMAS

4.17.29 - 4.17.32

Calvin continues his distaste for transubstantiation, attacking the notion that Christ's ascended body is ubiquitous and invisible ('by a special mode of dispensation' [4.17.29]). His arguments run as follows:

1. There is no scriptural support for either notion ('they cannot show a syllable from the Scriptures' [*ibid.*]).
2. Servetus (and we all know what happened to him) held to the view that Christ's body was 'invisible' — 'swallowed up by his divinity' (*ibid.*).
3. The resurrected Christ himself urged his disciples to touch him (Luke 24:39).
4. Since our bodies are to be made like Christ's body (Phil. 3:20-21), our bodies, too, would be invisible and ubiquitous — is there anyone dull enough to believe this?
5. And some, like Eutychians (and Servetus), have erred by compounding the two natures (human and divine) — a heresy condemned by the ecumenical councils of the church. 'But from Scripture we plainly infer that the one person of Christ so consists of two natures that each nevertheless retains unimpaired its own distinctive character' (4.17.30).

Once again, Calvin insists that our communion with the body and blood of Christ in the Supper is in heaven — something made possible by 'the secret working of the Spirit' (4.17.31).

DEREK THOMAS

4.17.33 - 4.17.34

Calvin cannot stop extolling the virtues of the spiritual presence of Christ in the sacrament of Communion over and against the errors of the physical presence of Christ within the sacraments (the view of transubstantiation). One of the dangers that Calvin sees is the idea of the 'automatic' sacrament: because it is Christ's body and blood, the mere taking of it means one receives the grace. Under this view, to use Calvin's words, 'even the impious and wicked', those 'estranged' from God, receive grace while they partake (4.17.33). By contrast, such eating is, in Paul's words, that which brings condemnation not redemption.

Those people who eat unworthily, Calvin continues, do so because they do not have the Spirit by faith; and without the Spirit, they do not partake of grace. As Calvin says in an earlier paragraph, 'The secret [mysterious] power of the Spirit is the bond of our union with Christ' (4.17.33).

Here is the genius of Calvin. Even in the midst of his polemics, he is gently shepherding us to see brilliant truths. Here is something for which to be thankful and to keep in mind the next time you partake of the Lord's Supper:

> Christ himself is the matter of the Supper; and the effects flow from the fact that by the sacrifice of his death we are cleansed of sins, by his blood we are washed, and by his resurrection we are raised to the hope of heavenly life (4.17.33).

STEPHEN NICHOLS

4.17.35 - 4.17.39

Calvin continues his discussion of the errant Roman Catholic view of the sacrament of the Lord's Supper by railing upon two of his frequent topics: superstition and idolatry. These two, for Calvin, go together like ham and eggs. These practices, in this particular instance, the piled-on traditions of adoring the 'consecrated host', are repugnant to Calvin because they are extra-biblical (actually, he makes the case that they are anti-biblical) and injurious to the Christian life.

How quickly the church can lose its way; how quickly we can lose our way. Some things, in other words, are worth getting polemical about (see 4.17.35-37).

But Calvin isn't all about nay-saying. He ends with a positive call, stressing how the Lord's Supper is a palpable, 'forceful' means to 'inspire us both to purity and holiness of life, and to love, peace, and concord' (4.17.38). The Lord's Supper is ultimately about unity because through it we are symbolizing and experiencing union with Christ — not as individuals, but as his body, as one body. Then he adds one more crucial point: 'The sacrament cannot stand apart from the Word' (4.17.39), since the Word expresses the promise displayed in the sacrament.

I come away with two fundamental principles for practising theology:

1. Always focus on unity, but never focus on unity at the cost of doctrinal fidelity.
2. Always focus on the Word. To paraphrase Calvin: 'Theologizing — both in theory and in practice — cannot stand apart from the Word.'

STEPHEN NICHOLS

4.17.40 - 4.17.45

One of the other debated issues in the Lord's Supper, in addition to the nature of Christ's presence, is that of 'fencing the table'. Who may participate? What does it mean to eat and drink unworthily (1 Cor. 11:27)? Who is worthy? Who is unworthy?

Calvin takes up these questions in 4.17.40-42. He also deals with the question of how the Supper is to be administered in terms of the liturgy of the Communion service (4.17.43). Finally, he tackles the question of frequency (4.17.44). All of these questions are worthy of book-length treatments in and of themselves. Calvin offered a few on the subject. If you read up on the life of Jonathan Edwards you will see he had some thoughts on these issues, too. But here in these several chapters, Calvin offers some balanced, thoughtful, and (for this may his name be blessed) concise discussion. Just read it; you'll be glad you did.

Then comes 4.17.45. Amidst all of these debatable issues of the Lord's Supper — how ironic it is that the practice that signifies the unity of the body of Christ has been the source of so much disunity through the centuries of the church's life! — Calvin tells us above all to participate, to eat and to drink of the body and the blood of Christ. Participate, he will add, 'frequently' (4.17.44-45).

I think American evangelicalism on the whole has lost sight of the necessity and luxury of this practice of the Lord's Supper. May it not be true of us, of me.

STEPHEN NICHOLS

4.17.46 - 4.18.1

Scottish Highland Presbyterians need to hold their breath for a second while Calvin refers to an annual Lord's Supper ritual as 'a veritable invention of the devil' (4.17.46). Calvin then adds something which he has been cited for ever since, that the Supper should be 'spread at least once a week' — a desire he never experienced. Nor could he have; the Supper required a strict discipline procedure in Geneva involving the consistory (the church council) — a task impossible to accomplish on a weekly basis.

Those who entertain weekly Communion today (in the name of Calvin) almost certainly abandon the discipline associated with the Supper to ensure against unworthy eating and drinking. Today's church views examination as an entirely personal obligation.

Not content to view annual Communion alone as demonic, Calvin views as 'from the same shop' (4.17.47) the practice of withholding the cup from God's people, adding a five-fold argument for 'Communion in both kinds' (the giving of wine *and* bread).

Again, Calvin's use of both Scripture and early church tradition comes to the surface: undermining Roman Catholic veneration of apostolic succession and the barring from the cup by arguing their unhistorical precedence. Masterful!

DEREK THOMAS

4.18.2 - 4.18.7

Now we turn to the Mass. At the heart of Calvin's theological method in assessing the value of the Mass is the cross of Christ. The Mass signifies an ongoing ritual of sacrifice, undermining the 'once-for-all' meaning of Calvary. By its constant repetition, it declares all prior 'sacrifices' — including Calvary — insufficient to forgive sins ('the cross of Christ is overthrown as soon as the altar is set up' [4.18.3]). It denigrates Christ and makes his life and work of less value. By participating in the re-sacrifice ritual, we abandon 'free grace' and declare that we are forgiven by something that we do. Again, there rises from the heart of man the reflex of self-justification.

Calvin's Reformed theological method is clearly observable in this piece of polemical theology. Its language and style may appear blunt — even coarse — by today's sanitary evaluation of theological exchange; but Calvin is exercised (emotionally) because in the Mass he sees a dishonouring of Jesus. And where that is viewed, he cannot be silent. Nor should we.

DEREK THOMAS

4.18.8 - 4.18.13

With regard to private Communion (or Masses), Calvin is against them. True, he is against the Mass in any shape or form; but *mutatis mutandis* he is against private celebrations of the Lord's Supper for the same reason: the Supper is meant to define the communion of the body, not its separation and individuality.

As for alleged defences of the Mass on historical grounds, Calvin is subject to the antics of historical revisionists as much as we are in our time. Citing detached, non-contextualized sentences from the Church Fathers is a game anybody can play, but the Mass is (largely) an invention of the medieval period and cannot be supported entirely from antiquity. For the Reformation (Calvin's argument, you may recall, in his prefatory remarks in the *Institutes* to the French King) is not (as Roman Catholics asserted) something 'new', but rather, ancient and historic.

Calvin is at his redemptive-historical best here as he explains Old Testament anticipations of the singular sacrifice of Christ: before Calvary, Christ was represented by way of a blood-shedding ritual on an altar; after Calvary, he is represented by a blood-less feast at a table. Unfortunately, some of the Church Fathers applied a broadened interpretation to the word 'sacrifice' in the New Testament, concluding what the gospel disallows — a denial of the once-for-all nature of the sacrifice of Christ at Calvary.

Gospel, justification and grace are at issue in the re-sacrificing of Christ in the Mass as commonly understood — which amounts to a damning indictment of the ritual.

DEREK THOMAS

4.18.14 - 4.18.20

Calvin had studied Plato — no friend to Christianity — and is amused how accurately he depicted (in *The Republic*) the antics of medieval priests in celebrating the Mass, preying on the innocent and uneducated by fooling them into believing nonsense through magical 'hocus pocus' conjuring tricks with bread and wine.

Against such a tragedy, what is to be the posture of the clear-eyed recipient at the Supper? In gospel-shaped dynamics, the Lord's Supper falls into the category of indicative-imperative: the Supper is a way of saying 'thank you', an act of gratitude for grace already received (4.18.16). It is not to be viewed as a performance of duty that obliges God to act differently toward our sins — an aspect of the cycle of self-justification that is pandemic in the natural (religious) man.

The sacraments of the new covenant, baptism and the Supper, operate according to their sanctioned design. Both were established for the church by Christ. One, an initiatory sign and seal; the other, a confirming, discipling memorial of thanksgiving; both of which point to Jesus Christ alone as the way of salvation, and 'the cleanness of God's mysteries is but polluted when man adds anything of his own' (4.18.20).

DEREK THOMAS

4.19.1 - 4.19.6

Calvin has yet more to say on sacraments invented by men. Using the formula that sacraments are 'visible signs of an invisible grace', Calvin notes that there is no limit to the inventions that can be claimed to pass this test. So he reverts again to the argument of recent novelty, arguing that the seven sacraments of medieval Catholicism were unknown in the early church. History shows them to be a recent invention (addition) of man and they fail for that reason.

Sola Scriptura must be the basis on which sacraments are judged, since 'the decision to establish a sacrament rests with God alone' (4.19.2). How many sacraments did Jesus give to the church? Two and only two: baptism and the Lord's Supper.

Interestingly, Calvin argues a cessationist line against those who point to the apostolic practice of 'laying on of hands' to defend the sacramental status of confirmation, another ritual of initiation to the Roman church where the Spirit was said to be bestowed. While he approved of the laying on of hands as merely 'a form of blessing' (4.19.4), Calvin contends that its apostolic function — to confer the Holy Spirit — was an expediency of the infant church so long as the apostles remained. Once they died, 'those miraculous powers and manifest workings ... ceased' (4.19.6).

DEREK THOMAS

4.19.7 - 4.19.13

Confirmation, a sacrament in Roman Catholic theology, was an offence to Calvin because it sapped the meaning of baptism. In scholastic terms, baptism only washed away original sin and those sins committed before baptism. Confirmation was, in the eyes of many, as a sacrament of continuing grace.

Calvin, on the other hand, viewed baptism as a sign and seal of forgiveness and reconciliation for the entirety of one's life, making confirmation unnecessary. Besides which, Calvin contends the New Testament church knew nothing of it and, on this ground alone, confirmation is an intrusion, an invention of man and essentially idolatrous (Calvin calls it 'this misborn wraith' [4.19.13]).

Instead of priestly anointing with oil, baptized children ought to confirm their faith by testifying to the church of the grace of God in their lives. Furthermore, to cultivate a testimony that is biblical and based upon solid foundations, Calvin urges the practice of catechizing. Calvin was so committed to this training that he produced a catechism upon his return to Geneva in 1541, which underwent two major revisions (1545 and 1560). Calvin's aim in writing the catechism of 1545 was to set a basic outline of doctrine that could serve as a pattern for what parents should teach their covenant children. It began:

Master: What is the chief end of human life?
Scholar: To know God by whom men were created.

DEREK THOMAS

4.19.14 - 4.19.19

Calvin continues his critique of Catholicism by contrasting the Roman rite of penance with the biblical definition of a 'sacrament'. He begins with a clear and careful distinction between public repentance, as it was practised in the early church, and the private absolution offered through the so-called sacrament of penance.

Public repentance traditionally included an assurance of pardon and the offering of peace. Calvin believes that such an act of assurance was spiritually wholesome and thus he wanted to see it restored to the church. He was also open to the possibility that this could include a 'laying on of hands' (4.19.14), a practice he regarded as a matter of indifference when properly conceived, and thus permissible.

What Calvin opposes, however, is regarding penance as a sacrament — that is to say, 'an outward ceremony instituted by the Lord to confirm our faith' (4.19.15). Following Augustine, he maintains that penance cannot be a sacrament because it does not include an outward and visible element that represents an inward and spiritual reality. There is nothing in penance to correspond to the water of baptism, for example, or to the bread and wine of the Lord's Supper.

If there is a sacrament that is properly connected to repentance, Calvin argues, that sacrament is not penance but baptism. Here Calvin quotes John the Baptist, who referred to 'a baptism of repentance for the forgiveness of sins' (Mark 1:4).

When Calvin turns, at last, to 'extreme unction' (which is yet another purported sacrament of the Roman Catholic Church), with its alleged powers to ease bodily ailments, he strongly asserts that the spiritual gift of healing has ceased. The miraculous power of the apostles to heal the body was only a temporary gift that quickly disappeared. God has decreed its disappearance so as 'to make the new preaching of the gospel marvellous for ever' (4.19.18).

PHILIP RYKEN

4.19.20 - 4.19.25

Calvin continues his case against false sacraments of the Roman Catholic Church, wrapping up his rejection of its sacrament of extreme unction with two criticisms. First, the alleged proof text for the practice (James 5:14) does not pertain to the church today but only to the apostolic age with its now-ceased gift of healing; besides, what the Roman priests do in extreme unction bears little resemblance to what James actually commanded.

Calvin's rebuke points up a frequent problem in Protestant and Evangelical circles as well: a flimsy appeal to a misread proof text that does not apply. Calvin's summary statement could describe any number of evangelical groups today, not least the 'emergent' churches and their highly creative practices: 'Lo, how beautifully they profit when they have been allowed freely to abuse James's testimony according to their own whim!' (4.19.21).

Next, Calvin turns to the false sacrament of 'holy orders' (i.e., ecclesiastical offices) which he subjects to a devastating critique. This is in practice actually seven different sacraments (doorkeepers, readers, exorcists, acolytes, subdeacons, deacons and priests) since each order has its own rite with its own meaning. The bizarre interpretations of Scripture that govern Catholic sacramentology continue, as each of these orders is claimed to have been fulfilled by Christ. For instance, they argue that Christ established the sacramental office of doorkeeper when he cleansed the temple. Calvin answers the Roman teaching with 'laughter' (4.19.23); but I am afraid that he would respond similarly to the many ecclesiastical innovations of the evangelical movement today.

Rather than structuring our churches and ministries according to our own wisdom, we would do much better to devote ourselves only to the full scope of the Bible's teaching. The biblical pattern of elders and deacons has never proved itself a failure, yet is seldom really tried by evangelical churches.

Let ministers and elders remember that we represent Christ in our offices. We are, therefore, required to practise his teaching and resist the temptation to invent our own.

RICHARD PHILLIPS

4.19.26 - 4.19.32

In this section, Calvin focuses on the Roman Catholic sacrament of orders, first attacking the rite of consecration known as 'tonsure', whereby newly admitted clergy shave the crowns of their heads. Attempts to substantiate this practice by appeals to Priscilla and Aquila misread Scripture, he says; and Paul vowed and shaved his head (*cf.* Acts 21:23-24) out of love for the Jerusalem Jews who still clung to Moses' ceremonial laws, not to perpetuate a law of piety.

The historical origins of the tonsure as recorded in 4.19.27 read like a story of teenage angst: first, the clergy shaved their heads to avoid any hint of 'effeminate ornament' (*ibid.*); then, when this style became common, they let their hair grow long — only to reshave it when 'long hair became the fashion again' (*ibid.*)! As superstition and novelty increased, the church accrued its 'minor' sacramental orders, assigning to each its own tokens of 'secret power' (*ibid.*): keys for the doorkeepers, formulas for the exorcists, tapers and cruets for the acolytes. Calvin rejects them all, since genuine sacraments carry a promise as a holy validation, made by neither angels nor men, but God alone.

The consecration practices of the 'major' orders of priest and deacon fare no better by Calvin. The priest's assignment to perform altar sacrifice, bless God's gifts, and expiate supplicants finds not even an 'iota of the Word of God' (4.19.28) for support. By fancying themselves 'sacrificers' rather than stewards of the gospel, they tear Christ from heaven and counterfeit his ministry 'like apes' (4.19.29). Likewise, Rome's deacons are ordained as though they were worthy of the prerogatives of an apostle, but in reality they are called only 'to burn incense, to dust images, to sweep churches, to catch mice, and to chase away dogs' (4.20.32). All the oils, sacrifices, sprinklings and incense, in Calvin's view, do not represent true religion, but a patchwork of Christianity, Judaism and paganism.

The medieval practices Calvin rejects were all extreme expressions of the sin of self-importance. There is a word here for all of us. Anyone in the church (perhaps pastors especially) can fall prey to the desire to be recognized as important, to have influence, to feel as though the church would crumble to the ground were it not for them. The paradox, however, is that it is people who know they would be undone without the bride of Christ who make her the most beautiful.

CARLTON WYNNE

4.19.33 - 4.19.37

Marriage has been instituted by God, but it is not a sacrament. 'For it is required that a sacrament be not only a work of God but an outward ceremony appointed by God to confirm a promise' (4.19.34). The fact that marriage illustrates Christ's relationship to the church does not make it a sacrament either; in fact, many are the things that illustrate it, but they are not sacraments.

True, Paul calls marriage a 'mystery' (Eph. 5:32) that refers us to Christ and his church. Says Calvin, 'Truly, indeed, this is a great mystery, that Christ allowed a rib to be removed from himself to form us; that is, when he was strong, he willed to be weak, in order that we might be strengthened by his strength; so that we ourselves should no longer live, but he should live in us' (4.19.35).

The problem is, however, that the Greek word for 'mystery' in this passage has been translated into the Latin as *sacramentum*, which led to a sacramental view of marriage. Calvin levels an oblique attack by asking some obvious questions. If marriage is a sacrament, why debar priests from it? Why are the clergy, charged with overseeing the sacraments of the church, forbidden to participate in this one?

Calvin contends that the church's declaration of marriage as a sacrament has introduced a 'den of abominations' (4.19.37) as she consolidated her control over related social and civil matters. The church now intrudes into issues of a personal and individual nature in ways that transgress the biblical parameters within which marriage is to be celebrated and enjoyed.

The issue of the proper boundaries of the church's authority in a society leads Calvin into the final chapter of the *Institutes*, on civil government. 'Whoever knows how to distinguish between body and soul, between this present fleeting life and that future eternal life, will without difficulty know that Christ's spiritual Kingdom and the civil jurisdiction are things completely distinct' (4.20.1).

IAIN CAMPBELL

4.20.1 - 4.20.7

Calvin begins Chapter 20 by establishing his understanding of 'a twofold government' to which human beings are subject: an 'inward' government, in which God rules over the individual human soul for eternal life; and an 'outward' government, in which God establishes civil justice and outward morality through human mediators (4.20.1). For him, these two governments are not antithetical. In fact, civil government has several purposes: (1) to cherish and protect religious worship; (2) to defend sound doctrine and the church's position; (3) to adjust our life to the society of men; (4) to enforce civil righteousness; (5) to reconcile us to one another; and (6) to promote general peace and tranquillity (4.20.2; *cf.* a similar list in 4.20.3). This demonstrates that the twofold government functions under one divine rule. Civil government, in Calvin's words, 'provides that a public manifestation of religion may exist among Christians and that humanity be maintained among men' (4.20.3).

In order to provide a clear method for discussing what the Bible teaches about civil government, Calvin follows Cicero's ancient three-fold division: magistrates, laws and people. He spends the rest of this section and the following three (sections 4-7) discussing the role of the magistrate. The magistrate, says Calvin, serves by God's mandate, rules with God's authority, and acts as God's vicegerent. Therefore, civil rulers should remain faithful as 'vicars of God' (4.20.6); and in response, those ruled by governments should hold that they are 'ordained of God' (4.20.7).

This means that all government leaders, not just those whom we like, are God's agents to provide for peace that the gospel might go forth and that humanity might be maintained. How should we now live and pray (1 Tim. 2:1-2)?

SEAN LUCAS

4.20.8 - 4.20.11

Calvin here shows two things: his concern about the dangers of tyrannical government; and his apparently relaxed attitude regarding forms of political government.

On the latter, you may say that he derives the possible forms from the ancient world, but, as a matter of logic, there are only three: rule by a king, by a few, or by all. Calvin rejects rule by everyone, since 'it is easiest of all to fall from popular rule to sedition' (4.20.8). (Note that in these remarks about government, and those that follow, he is concerned to avoid any suggestion of sympathy with the communal excesses of the left wing of the Reformation.)

About government, provided that it is not 'popular', he is somewhat contextual in his approach. Different cultures find themselves with different forms of government, and there is nothing wrong with that. Yet he reasons in favour of an aristocracy, and some of what he says seems at places to foreshadow the more formal arrangement of 'checks and balances' that is characteristic of eighteenth-century government in the United States, Great Britain, and elsewhere. 'Therefore, men's fault or failing causes it to be safer and more bearable for a number to exercise government, so that they may help one another, teach and admonish one another; and, if one asserts himself unfairly, there may be a number of censors and masters to restrain his wilfulness' (*ibid.*).

It would be wrong to think that Calvin's references to 'freedom' herald that of modern democratic society. For there are clear limits to freedom of expression and of worship (4.20.10).

PAUL HELM

4.20.12 - 4.20.18

Calvin borrows from Augustine the idea of a 'just' war. Everything is to be tried in order to preserve the peace before war is declared, though waging war obviously means that reparations must be made, if necessary. A consideration of such reparations naturally leads Calvin to the question of taxation. Rulers are not to be extravagant and the people ought not to be tax dodgers. Nothing much has changed, has it?

From the magistracy Calvin turns his attention to laws. Basically, 'there are some who deny that a commonwealth is duly framed which neglects the political system of Moses, and is ruled by the common laws of nations' (4.20.14). Do not be fooled by the double negative here: Calvin is telling us that he is not a theonomist, isn't he? He accepts the traditional three-fold distinction of Mosaic law (moral, ceremonial and judicial), but argues only for the perpetuity of the first, the moral law. Further, he thinks that the variety of systems of laws across nations should be respected, provided that these laws reflect common norms, as they usually do: the norms of the natural law and especially 'equity' (4.20.16). The discretion we are permitted is to cover only the mode of punishment for infringements; at least Calvin gives no other example of tolerable differences.

Once again, we note that Calvin is not a modern social pluralist. Nevertheless, his attitude did much to 'internationalize' Calvin's arm of the Reformation. As regards the civil law, the Christian may use litigation, but not out of vengeance, defending only what is his by right. Still, 'an upright litigant is rare' (4.20.18).

PAUL HELM

4.20.19 - 4.20.26

No doubt having the Anabaptists again in mind, and having already defended the right to litigate, Calvin proceeds to defend the entire judicial process. He discourages using the law for the taking of revenge, but upholds the use of due process, by which God works 'through the ministry of man for our good' (4.20.19). (It is interesting that Calvin seems primarily to have in mind not Geneva, which by this time in his career he believed was governed along right lines, but countries where the law may remain hostile to evangelical Christianity.)

The use of the law is not incompatible with Christ's injunctions in Matthew 5 to turn the other cheek, Calvin says, since seeking legal help may not be incompatible with personal friendliness to one's adversaries (this seems a hard saying, does it not?). He thinks that he has Paul (1 Cor. 6:5-8) on his side. But he has a word for the litigiousness of his own time: 'Christians ought indeed so to conduct themselves that they always prefer to yield their own right rather than go into a court, from which they can scarcely get away without a heart stirred and kindled to hatred of their brother' (4.20.21) (this seems more realistic!).

But what about obeying the law when the rulers are wicked? Calvin's basic principle is that the magistrate is God's minister, and so disobedience to him is disobedience to God (4.20.23). This obedience is not to be less when the ruler is 'a most wicked tyrant' (4.20.26), who might be playing the role of God's scourge.

PAUL HELM

4.20.27 - 4.20.32

Calvin's sensitivity to the different circumstances in which people live leads him to adapt his thoughts accordingly, or at least to be somewhat ambivalent in his attitude to the magistrate. Citing the case of Nebuchadnezzar (Jer. 27), he notes that Scripture requires obedience to bad kings, and even to pray for the well-being of the country of exile (Jer. 29:7). No doubt Calvin has his own city of exile, Geneva, in mind. But should not rulers, who also have responsibilities, be kept on track? Yes, but not by ourselves; by Almighty God.

This leads to discussion of the vexed question of civil disobedience. Calvin is strongly in favour of civil compliance, no doubt with such revolts as the Peasants Wars and Munster in the back of his mind. But yet ... the Lord sometimes raises up avengers: 'Let the princes hear and be afraid' (4.20.31). What of those of his readers who are not princes but 'private individuals' (*ibid.*)? To them no command 'has been given except to obey and suffer' (*ibid.*).

There are two further checks upon a wicked ruler, however. First, magistrates of the people, senates and parliaments may be appointed by God to restrain kingly misrule. 'I am so far from forbidding them to withstand, in accordance with their duty, the fierce licentiousness of kings, that, if they wink at kings who violently fall upon and assault the lowly common folk ... they dishonestly betray the freedom of the people, of which they know that they have been appointed protectors by God's ordinance' (*ibid.*). Second, however wicked the prince to whom obedience is due, we are not to obey men rather than God. If rulers command anything against the King of Kings, 'let it go unesteemed' (4.20.32). Let the ordinary folk beware of false modesty when honouring the magistrate. Their courage in the Lord must not grow faint.

On this rather ominous note Calvin brings his great work, the *Institutes*, to a close.

God be praised.

PAUL HELM

A wide range of Christian books is available from EP Books. If you would like a free catalogue please write to us or contact us by e-mail. Alternatively, you can view the whole catalogue online at our web site:

www.epbooks.org

EP BOOKS
Faverdale North, Darlington, DL3 0PH, England

e-mail: sales@epbooks.org

133, Hanover Street, Carlisle, PA 17013, USA

www.epbooks.us

e-mail: usasales@epbooks.org